*Congress Makes a Law*

STEPHEN KEMP BAILEY

# Congress Makes a Law

## THE STORY BEHIND THE
## EMPLOYMENT ACT OF 1946

GREENWOOD PRESS, PUBLISHERS
WESTPORT, CONNECTICUT

**Library of Congress Cataloging in Publication Data**

Bailey, Stephen Kemp.
  Congress makes a law.

  Reprint of the ed. published by the Columbia University Press, New York.
  Bibliography: p.
  Includes index.
  1.  United States. Laws, statutes, etc. Employment
act of 1946. 2. United States--Full employment policies. I. Title.
KF6055.A313A163  1980    344.73'0102632    80-12550
ISBN 0-313-22407-2 (lib. bdg.)

Reprinted in 1980 by Greenwood Press,
a division of Congressional Information Service, Inc.
51 Riverside Avenue, Westport, Connecticut 06880

Printed in the United States of America

10 9 8 7 6 5 4 3 2 1

# TO MY PARENTS

WHO, IN THE PROCESS OF RAISING A LARGE FAMILY
PROVIDED CONVINCING EVIDENCE THAT
THE WELFARE AND SECURITY OF THE GROUP
ARE NOT INCOMPATIBLE WITH THE FREEDOM AND INITIATIVE
OF THE INDIVIDUAL

# *Preface*

> When we shall have examined all its
> parts without sentiment, and gauged all
> its functions by the standards of practi-
> cal common sense, we shall have estab-
> lished anew our right to the claim of
> political sagacity.
> —Woodrow Wilson, *Congressional Gov-*
> *ernment* (13th ed., Boston, 1898), p. 333.*

ON JANUARY 22, 1945, three months before V-E Day and seven months before an atomic bomb ended a war and initiated an era, there was introduced on the floor of the United States Senate a bill numbered S.380. A year later, on February 20, 1946, President Harry S. Truman signed Public Law 304 of the 79th Congress.

Behind these dull facts there lies a dramatic story of the birth, growth, and metamorphosis of a public policy. For most Americans, the drama of Congressional policy-making is played behind closed curtains. It is much as though the citizenry were seated in a huge auditorium, allowed printed programs, but kept in almost total ignorance of what was happening on the stage. To the handful of citizens who have watched the show from the wings, this separation of players from audience is a dual tragedy: a tragedy for the players who might profit from audience reaction, a tragedy for the members of the audience who miss both entertainment and vitally needed education.

* All quotations at the chapter openings are taken from this remarkable and still pertinent book which was first published in 1885.

The story of S.380 is the story of the so-called "Full Employment Bill." The narrative has no real beginning and no clear ending. The period from the introduction of the bill to the President's signature sets formal but completely artificial limits to the policy-making process. Popular and official concern about the dangers of widespread unemployment in America began long before January, 1945. That concern still exists three years after the passage of the Employment Act of 1946.

The importance of the thirteen-month period which circum-scribed the formal legislative action on S.380 rests in the fact that it spotlights the peculiar place of the national legislature in the continuum of policy formulation. Particular plans for the solution of our economic problems may issue full blown and crystal clear from the minds of college professors, lobbyists, or public officials. But under our American system of government, these plans must usually pass through a legislative gantlet before they become an official part of our national policy. And few plans emerge from the legislative gantlet unscathed. This obvious fact and its implications seem to have been ignored or discounted by many social planners, especially by economists.

What can happen to an idea between the time it is conceived and the time it is the law of the land is of no little significance to the future of our democracy. The question posed by Finletter, *Can Representative Government Do the Job,*[1] means in substance: Can representative government formulate and effectuate such social policies as will meet the needs and secure the uncoerced support of its citizens? In a world of dramatic political alternatives, American democracy must succeed in meeting the complex physical and spiritual demands of its people or it must die.

We often tend to be sanguine about our governmental institu-tions, failing to recognize that the past pliability of our constitu-tional system has been the result, as well as the cause, of a fluid and expanding social and economic environment. Within the past generation rigidities have developed in that environment which have forced many serious students of our society to recognize that the luxury of inefficient and irresponsible government may no longer be tenable. Alternatives are rapidly narrowing in our inter-national and domestic life. The day of policy planning by hap-

[1] Thomas K. Finletter (New York, 1945).

hazard pressures and personal and political whim is fast running out, for the basic assumption underlying such irresponsible policy-making has been that our society was resilient enough to stand it. What if a needed policy were warped out of shape by the nature of our political processes? No great and lasting harm was done. There was always time to start again, explore new paths, skip around in a labyrinth of blind alleys. But what if we guess wrong today? The power and problems of government have become so enormous that false moves or excessive temporizing may result in physical destruction or economic disaster.

Although the following narrative is an attempt to present a reasonably objective picture of the formulation of a public policy in the Congress, the analysis is conditioned by certain underlying assumptions which I hold concerning desirable standards of performance in our national legislature. These standards may be reduced to three general propositions: first, that Congress should act responsibly—that is, that it should act in such a way that the voting public may be able to hold individual members and the separate parties reasonably accountable for their actions; second, that Congress should act democratically, that is, that it should formulate policy through a process of majority rule while allowing for the free expression of minority opinions rather than vice versa; and third, that it should act in the public interest rather than in the interest solely of local or narrowly vested group pressures.

A word needs to be said about this last proposition. The concept of the public interest is one of the most elusive in the vocabulary of democratic politics. It is a distressing fact that the most meaningful words in the lexicon of government are those least capable of clear definition. Liberty, justice, freedom, equality, democracy, the public interest—these are the symbols of democratic government, but like all symbols they are too rich in connotation and too charged with emotion to permit of neat verbal circumscription.

There are rough rules of thumb, however, which can be applied even to the vaguest and richest of word symbols. It is obvious that the public has no right in a democracy to expect unanimity about the "public interest" character of any particular legislative proposal. The disagreement of honest minds about what is best for the country is the priceless condition of democracy. What the public does have a right to expect, however, is that a national legislator will attempt honestly to abide by the campaign promises of his party and, within that general framework, to analyze a pending national policy in the light of the broadest and highest ethical norms of which he is capable. The difficulty of formulating meaningful ethical norms in the hurly-burly political world of appetites, pressures, rationalizations, and compromises is one of the implicit themes of this volume.

The chapters which follow are an attempt to make a vector analysis of legislative policy-making. Pendleton Herring has defined the policy-making process as the interaction of ideas, institutions, interests, and individuals. In the narrowest sense this book is an attempt to describe how these four I's interacted in a particular historical context in relation to a particular economic issue. In a much broader and more fundamental sense, however, this is a study of the types of forces which impinge upon, or work through, the American Congress as it attempts to formulate major public policies in the middle of the twentieth century. It is, of course, obvious that the history of every bill is unique. But just as certain inferences can be drawn about the human race from introspection and from a limited observation of the behavior of a few men, so perhaps certain inferences can be made about Congressional policy-making from the study of one bill. At least these inferences can be stated as hypotheses for further verification.

A word about sources. The bibliography gives sufficient indication of written sources. Some of the most significant material in the study however came from interviews. Live sources are not necessarily more reliable than written ones. But unless live sources are used in a study of Congressional policy-making, a meaningful analysis is virtually impossible. In the legislative process, what is committed to writing represents only the seventh of the iceberg above water. Although four hundred interviews have not exposed all of the submerged data about S.380, they do perhaps give some indication of the types of forces at work in the legislative process. Many of these interviews took place far from the nation's capital.[2]

[2] Field research included brief visits to the States or Congressional Districts, and home towns of the twelve members of the Conference Committee: Senator Alben Barkley, Kentucky (Paducah); Senator Clayton Douglass Buck, Delaware (Wilmington); Senator Abe Murdock, Utah (Beaver); Senator George Radcliffe, Maryland (Baltimore); Senator Robert Taft, Ohio (Cincinnati); Senator Glen Taylor, Idaho (Pocatello); Senator Charles Tobey, New Hampshire (Temple); Representative George

One of the major working hypotheses established at the beginning of this study was that Members of Congress accept or reject ideas about national policies in part at least on the basis of their personal histories and the effective economic, social, and political pressures in their home constituencies.

It is only fair that I be frank about my own biases. Although I have made a consistent attempt to present facts and draw conclusions objectively, there is always the possibility that my "inarticulate major premises" have interfered. My sympathies are "a little left of center," which means in terms of S.380 that my emotional bias was toward the sponsors rather than the opponents of the original bill. In making this study, however, I have tried, in so far as is humanly possible, to divorce head from heart.

This leads me to a final prefatory remark. In an attempt to make this study readable I have frequently been forced to use words which to the careful semanticist may seem lacking in precise definition. I refer on numerous occasions to "liberals" and "conservatives" without being able to circumscribe those terms.[3] Except when I attempt to present the definitions of others, I make no effort to define "full employment," assuming in the words of Ira Mosher, former president of the National Association of Manufacturers, "that the phrase has no hidden implications and merely summarizes the legitimate and attainable economic aspirations of a free people."[4] I can only trust that the bulk of my exposition is sufficiently unambiguous to preclude the possibility of widespread misinterpretation.

---

Bender, Congressman-at-Large, Ohio (Cleveland); Representative John Cochran, Thirteenth District, Missouri (St. Louis); Representative Clare Hoffman, Fourth District, Michigan (Allegan); Representative Carter Manasco, Seventh District, Alabama (Jasper); and Representative William Whittington, Third District, Mississippi (Greenwood).

[3] When discussing attitudes toward the Full Employment Bill itself, I use the word "liberal" to denote those who wanted the bill passed in something close to its original form; the word "conservative" to denote those who wanted the bill killed or substantially modified. In more general contexts, I use the terms to distinguish roughly between those who tend to believe that a further extension of government power for the purpose of social control would not necessarily be a threat to democracy and the "American Way of Life," and those who tend to believe that such an extension would be a threat. A clear-cut distinction between the two groups, however, is impossible, and there are many people who would disagree with my particular classifications. Representative Will Whittington, whom I would call a "conservative" classifies himself as a "conservative liberal."

[4] Hearings before the House Committee on Expenditures in the Executive Departments, on H.R.2202, 79th Cong., 1st Sess. (Sept. 25–Nov. 7, 1945), p. 547.

I cannot begin to list my total indebtedness. Scores of people have given me information with the understanding that their names would not be used. Many librarians and clerks have given me invaluable anonymous assistance.

There are, however, a few acknowledgments which I must make out of special gratitude: to Professor Joseph E. Smith, now of Youngstown College, who more than fourteen years ago at Hiram College gave me my initial interest in political economy; to Lord Beveridge, G. D. H. Cole, Harold Wilson, and Sir John Maud, who tutored me at University College, Oxford, in the interrelationships of government and economic life, and who turned my attention specifically to the problems of full employment in a free society; to Pendleton Herring, who started me out on my study of the Full Employment Bill and whose encouragement in the early stages of my research was a constant inspiration; to the Social Science Research Council, the Research Committee of Wesleyan University, and the United States Veterans Administration without whose financial aid this study would have been impossible; to Professor Merle Fainsod of Harvard University, for whose patient and expert supervision of my research and writing I am particularly grateful; to my Wesleyan colleagues, E. E. Schattschneider, Sigmund Neumann, Victor Jones, A. Burr Overstreet, and Lyle Fitch, who have furnished frequent advice and encouragement; to Mrs. Edwina Dimes and Mrs. Esther Carling, who transcribed my cuneiform into a legible manuscript; and finally, to my wife who has contributed much and suffered long.

As is customary, I absolve everyone except myself from responsibility for the errors which unfortunately must exist in the following pages.

S. K. B.

*Middletown, Connecticut*
*March 1, 1949*

# Contents

*Congress Makes a Law*

# *The Political*
# *and Economic Background*

Legislation unquestionably generates legislation. Every statute may be said to have
a long lineage of statutes behind it.—
Wilson, *Congressional Government,* p. 297

THE FULL EMPLOYMENT BILL of 1945 was the product of a long
history. Any comprehensive attempt to describe the bill's family
tree would lead the genealogist back through devious and dismal
paths of history to the earliest human cries against economic insecurity. In the broadest perspective of time, the modern concern
about full employment is but the latest version of man's age-old
petition, "Give us this day our daily bread." If attention is now
addressed to Washington or London or Moscow rather than to
heaven, it is only because man has changed his mind about the relative competence of God and government in dealing with pressing
economic issues.

### BUSINESS PROMOTION AND HUMAN LAISSEZ FAIRE

A genealogical search would not be materially simplified even if
limited to American archives. Who is to say when the federal
government first concerned itself with questions of business prosperity? The fiction that the political economy of America from its
beginnings in 1789 to the end of the nineteenth century was one of
*laissez faire* is a stubborn myth. As Walter Lippmann has pointed

out, "While the theorists were talking about laissez faire, men were buying and selling legal titles to property, were chartering corporations, were making and enforcing contracts, were suing for damages. In these transactions, by means of which the work of society was carried on, the state was implicated at every vital point." [1] The measure of full employment achieved in the expanding economy of the nineteenth century was the direct result of a partnership between private and governmental forces. Nor did the federal government confine itself to the establishment and enforcement of contractual sanctions. Business promotion was a central concern of our early governments, just as business security was a signal factor in the drafting of our Constitution.

It may be argued that the promotion of business and commercial enterprise by the federal government is not in the direct ancestral lineage of the Full Employment Bill of 1945; that the Full Employment Bill as originally introduced was aimed specifically at work security, not at business promotion. While this criticism is in part justified, it is not without interest to note the opening declaration of policy of S.380: "It is the policy of the United States to foster free competitive enterprise. . . ." In American history, business prosperity and high-level employment have been closely intertwined.

If we turn to federal concern with the problem of widespread unemployment as such, we need go back less than a generation. It is true of course that the federal government made occasional studies of the "panics" of the nineteenth century [2] and put forth a few feeble attempts to revive economic activity through such measures as the repurchase of government bonds (in the panic of 1873), or the repeal of the Silver Purchase Act (in the panic of 1893).[3] But almost no attention was paid to the human problems of insecurity, hunger, debt, and disease which followed in the path of business decline, and scant attention was given to possible measures for influencing the course of the business cycle. The

[1] *The Good Society* (London, 1937), p. 187.

[2] See, for example, the *First Annual Report of the Commissioner of Labor* (Washington, 1886), especially pp. 292–293; and the "Investigation by a Select Committee of the House of Representatives Relative to the Causes of the General Depression in Labor and Business . . . ," House Misc. Doc. No. 29, 45th Cong., 3d Sess. (Washington, 1879).

[3] Louis M. Hacker and Benjamin B Kendrick. *The United States since 1865* (New York, 1932), pp. 55. 88–89.

human problems were left to local and usually private charities; the course of the trade cycle was left to God and economic "laws." During the panic of 1837, the magazine *New Era* commented, "Men who would feel happy to toil . . . cannot now obtain the privilege of doing so. This is really an awful fact in a free and equal country like this." [4] But the President of the United States could only reply,

If therefore I refrain from suggesting to Congress any specific plan for regulating the exchanges of the country, relieving mercantile embarrassments, or interfering with the ordinary operations of foreign and domestic commerce, it is from a conviction that such measures are not within the constitutional province of the General Government, and that their adoption would not promote the real and permanent welfare of those they might be designed to aid. [5]

Although a large number of private citizens and burdened economic groups pressed forward during the nineteenth century with new conceptions of federal obligation which reflected the relentless logic of political democracy,[6] the official attitude of the federal government continued into the twentieth century to minimize the responsibility of government for taking direct action to mitigate the effects of economic depression or for taking positive measures toward controlling the business cycle.

It is not, in fact, an exaggeration to say that the great depression of the 1930s was the first occasion in our nation's history when the federal government took active and positive steps to alleviate widespread economic suffering, and undertook to use its offices to harness destructive economic forces and to establish institutional mechanisms for protecting the individual against economic disaster. The

[4] Arthur M. Schlesinger, Jr., *The Age of Jackson* (Boston, 1945), p. 221. There is a tendency for modern Americans to believe that the depressions of the nineteenth century were relatively mild affairs. For a heartrending picture of the human suffering brought on by the panic of 1837, see R. C. McGrane, *The Panic of 1837* (Chicago, 1924), p. 131.

[5] Charles A. and Mary R. Beard, *America in Midpassage* (New York, 1939), p. 89.

[6] In 1878, for instance, when a select committee was appointed in the House of Representatives to make an investigation of "the Causes of the General Depression in Labor and Business," testimony was received from scores of citizens recommending, among other things, such federally induced remedies as minimum wage legislation, a commodity dollar, graduated income tax, eight-hour law, public works, depositors insurance, regulation of rents by law, reciprocal trade, federal credit, regulation of the volume of currency, public housing, regulation of wages according to the cost of living, abolition of monopolies, limitation of profits resulting from the exploitation of patents, regulation of interest rates, and "destructive" taxing of corporations. House Misc. Doc. No. 29, 45th Cong., 3d Sess. (Washington, 1879), pp. 656–664.

Unemployment Conference of 1921, the first federally sponsored meeting of its type, was of course an important symbolic landmark in the history of governmental interest in the unemployment problem; the bills to relieve unemployment through a system of timed public works that were introduced during the twenties by Senator Kenyon, Senator Jones, Senator George Wharton Pepper, Senator Wagner, and others were important progenitors of later federal policies; Congressional concern with the agricultural depression of the twenties was a harbinger of new concepts about the legitimate place of the federal government in the economy; the central banking activities of the Federal Reserve System during the boom period, although ineffective in precluding the depression, were not without significance in the development of national economic policy. But until the crash of 1929, the general attitude toward unemployment was expressed in the words of two Republican Presidents. In 1921, Harding had stated, "There has been vast unemployment before and there will be again. There will be depression and inflation just as surely as the tides ebb and flow. I would have little enthusiasm for any proposed remedy which seeks either palliation or tonic from the Public Treasury." [7] President Hoover in his acceptance speech of 1928 pronounced the triumphant words,

We in America are nearer to the final triumph over poverty than ever before in the history of any land. . . . We have not reached the goal, but given a chance to go forward with the policies of the last eight years, we shall soon with the help of God be in sight of the day when poverty will be banished from this nation.[8]

The kindest commentary is that God refused to cooperate.

THE IMPACT OF THE GREAT DEPRESSION

The economic disaster which started with the stock market crash of October, 1929, had a revolutionary impact on the minds of the American people. As year followed year and conditions of unemployment and insecurity became steadily worse, the great majority of Americans came to realize that something profound and terrifying had occurred. Insecurity and fear were ubiquitous. Louise V. Armstrong, writing of Chicago in 1932, notes, "One vivid, gruesome moment of those dark days we shall never forget. We saw a crowd

[7] *Report of the President's Conference* (Washington, 1921), p. 27.
[8] Quoted in F. L. Allen, *Only Yesterday* (Pelican Book Edition, 1938), II, 419.

of some fifty men fighting over a barrel of garbage which had been set outside the back door of a restaurant. American citizens fighting for scraps of food like animals." [9]

The same could have been written of New York or Boston or Los Angeles or New Orleans. Farmers, whose conditions had been depressed since the early twenties, blockaded roads, overturned milk trucks, and sponsored "shot-gun auctions" on farms which had been taken over by foreclosure. Unemployed veterans formed a bonus army and marched on Washington.

Out of despair came a desperate groping for answers and action. As Frederick Lewis Allen reports,

Magazine editors were being inundated with manuscripts explaining how the Depression could be ended—manuscripts proposing huge bond issues for public works, recommending inflation, recommending all sorts of other expedients, rational or ridiculous: "hot money" which would decline in value if unspent; the Douglas credit plan, other complex improvements in the banking and credit systems; schemes for the general reduction of debts; "work-sharing" schemes for shorter hours of labor to soak up unemployment; proposals for the seizure and operation of industries by the government. Communism was notably gaining strength, both among the unemployed workers and—more rapidly—among the urban intellectuals.[10]

Common to all this groping and intellectual and moral ferment was the awareness that whatever the theoretical causes or cures of depressions, the federal government was the only institution with sufficient power to do anything substantial—and at a practical level —about the economic collapse. The experience of the great depression forced the federal government to extend its functions and responsibilities. This change in public attitude about the legitimate sphere of federal activity in economic affairs, and the public's broadening conception of economic rights, were necessary prerequisites to, as well as products of, the New Deal of Franklin D. Roosevelt. Without this change there would have been no Full Employment Bill of 1945.

### THE "DISMAL" THIRTIES

The relief and recovery programs of the thirties were remarkable in their scope and their vitality; remarkable also in their improvised

[9] Quoted in F. L. Allen, *Since Yesterday* (New York, 1940), p. 64.

[10] *Since Yesterday* (New York, Harper & Bros., 1940), p. 89. Reprinted by permission of the publishers.

and chaotic character. When it is remembered that the federal government was entering on uncharted seas, the improvisation and chaos is not surprising. As Frances Perkins has said in commenting upon the modest scale of the first New Deal public works program,

It is well for those who would be critical . . . to realize the uncertainty of everyone who had responsibility and knowledge of economic factors. This was an entirely new pattern. It was, indeed, a small project in managed economy. It was an attempt to change the direction of economic trends, which were little understood and about which there were no experimental data.[11]

While in no way discounting the significance of the federal program of the thirties, it must be remembered that in spite of the experimentation which began during the Hoover administration with such measures as the Federal Employment Stabilization Act,[12] the R.F.C., and the H.O.L.C., and continued under the New Deal with a vast congeries of federally sponsored economic policies, the enigma of unemployment was not solved at the end of that sorry decade. Eight to nine million jobless remained in 1939. It was the war which "cured" the unemployment problem.

As we shall see, the experience and the thinking of the thirties both at home and abroad provided the river of ideas which found their way into the Full Employment Bill. As we have already noted, S.380 would have been impossible without the changes in public expectations which the depression effected. But in terms of social dynamics, probably the most important cause of the Full Employment Bill was the wartime memory of the public and of officials, alike, that the problem of unemployment had really never been solved in the days of peace. The fact that it had been solved by war

11 Frances Perkins, *The Roosevelt I Knew* (New York, The Viking Press, Inc., 1946), pp. 276–277. Reprinted by permission of the publishers.

12 The Federal Employment Stabilization Act was probably the most significant legislative precedent underlying the Full Employment Bill of 1945. It was "an Act to provide for the advance planning and regulated construction of public works, for the stabilization of industry, and for aiding in the prevention of unemployment during periods of business depression." An Employment Stabilization Board was established, "composed of the Secretaries of Treasury, Commerce, Labor, and Agriculture. . . . The functions of the Board were (1) to advise the President about the trend of business activity in the Nation, and (2) to make progress reports." For a description of the work and fate of the Board see U.S. Senate, "History of the Employment Stabilization Act of 1931," *Report to the Committee on Banking and Currency*, Senate Committee Print No. 3, 79th Cong., 1st Sess., July 30, 1945.

only stimulated people to ask the question well posed by Lord Beveridge, "Unemployment has been practically abolished twice in the lives of most of us—in the last war and in this war. Why does war solve the problem of unemployment which is so unsolvable in peace?" [13]

WARTIME FEARS ABOUT THE POSTWAR WORLD

Some indication of the sharpness of wartime memories about the depression of the thirties and of the wartime fears about the postwar world is reflected in a poll taken by *Fortune* early in the fall of 1944. In answer to the question, "Do you think the Federal Government should provide jobs for everyone able and willing to work, but who cannot get a job in private employment?" 67.7 percent said it should.[14]

Perhaps an even more striking indication was the volume of postwar planning which mushroomed during the war years. On the question of how to maintain full employment in the postwar years, thousands of government officials, businessmen, labor leaders, farmers, journalists, planners, economists, and other interested citizens thought, wrote, and spoke. When the Legislative Reference Service of the Library of Congress prepared an annotated bibliography of the major books and articles on full employment which had been written between 1943 and 1945, the report came to fifty-six tightly packed pages.[15] When the Pabst Brewing Company announced a prize-essay contest on the subject of postwar employment, nearly 36,000 manuscripts were submitted.[16] By mid-1943, the staff of the Senate Post-War Economic Policy and Planning Committee was able to list comprehensive planning programs being undertaken in the Department of Commerce, the Department of Agriculture, the War Production Board, the Public Roads Administration, the Maritime Commission, the Defense Plant Corporation, the Bureau of the Budget, the Rural Electrification Administration, the National Housing Agency, the Treasury Department, and the State

[13] William H. Beveridge, *The Pillars of Security* (New York, 1943), p. 51.
[14] Washington *Evening Star*, Oct. 30, 1944.
[15] U.S. Senate, "Bibliography on Full Employment," *Report to the Committee on Banking and Currency*, Senate Committee Print No. 2 (Washington, 1945).
[16] For a useful analysis of these essays see Lyle Fitch and Horace Taylor, *Planning for Jobs* (Philadelphia, 1946).

Department. And this list, by the Senate Committee's own admission, barely scratched the surface.[17] In 1944, the Twentieth Century Fund's organizational directory of *Postwar Planning in the United States* listed thirty-three federal agencies.

Rival or at least diverse concepts emerged. By and large, the business community believed as it had for generations that long-term full employment could be achieved by business initiative if only the government would follow policies aimed at promoting business confidence.[18] Just what *would* promote confidence, however, was a subject of intramural debate. Some businessmen and economists on the Committee for Economic Development and members of the Brookings Institution viewed the national government as a potential ally of a rejuvenated and socially conscious business community which would lead the way to national economic stability through local planning and a low-price, high-wage industrial policy. Other business spokesmen like some from the N.A.M., the Chamber of Commerce, and the Committee for Constitutional Government placed their emphasis on "less government interference," "more government economy"—generally, upon a reduction of the number and scope of government economic activities.

Labor leaders in general saw a need for federal measures to protect the interests of labor as a basic condition of a full employment economy. They placed heavy emphasis upon such issues as higher minimum wages, a liberalized unemployment compensation program, fair employment practices, and the advance planning of public works. They also placed heavy emphasis upon cooperative planning on the part of government, business, agriculture, and labor.[19]

Out of the minds of the thousands of government and private

17 U.S. Senate, "Postwar Economic Policy and Planning," *Report of Hon. Joseph C. O'Mahoney to the Special Committee on Postwar Economic Policy and Planning,* Senate Document No. 106, 78th Cong., 1st Sess. (Washington, 1943), pp. 35–55.

18 See, for example, National Association of Manufacturers: *Can We Avoid a Post-Armament Depression* (New York, 1941); *Jobs, Freedom, Opportunity* (New York, 1943); *Second Report of the Postwar Problems Committee of the N.A.M.* (New York, 1943). See also the *Post-War Readjustments Bulletins* of the U.S. Chamber of Commerce, 1943–1944.

19 See, especially, American Federation of Labor, "After the Emergency—What Then?" reprinted from the *American Federationist* of March, 1941; A.F.L., *Post-war Program* (Washington, April 12, 1944); C.I.O. Political Action Committee, "Full Employment," *Proceedings of the Conference on Full Employment,* New York City, Jan. 15, 1944; Philip Murray, *Re-employment,* C.I.O. Dept. of Research and Education, Publication No. 116, 1944.

planners came suggestions and solutions which fell somewhere between the two polls of traditional *laissez faire* and comprehensive
government controls over important parts of the economic system.

It should not be forgotten that America was not alone in its widespread wartime concern about the future—a concern based upon
the hard realities of the past. The depression had been a world-wide
phenomenon. Common fears, experiences, and theories spread from
country to country and from continent to continent with the speed
of the wireless and the airplane. It is not coincidence that by the
end of World War II a score of countries, and the United Nations,
had written into their constitutions and statute books clauses about
full employment and/or the "right to work." [20] The climate of
opinion which promoted the Full Employment Bill in America
was in fact world-wide.

### ADMINISTRATIVE DEVELOPMENTS

Political institutions as well as economic ideas changed during
the thirties and early forties. In the United States the needs of the
depression and the war, and the variety of responses thereto,
brought pressures for administrative changes. Two administrative
developments are of particular relevance to this study: first, the
attempts to strengthen the Presidency in order to enable the President to coordinate policy more effectively; second, the attempts to
institutionalize and centralize long-range planning.

Under the first category must be listed such developments as the
National Emergency Council established by Roosevelt in 1933 to
aid him in coordinating the work of emergency agencies; the Reorganization Act of 1939 which established the concept of the Executive Office of the President, and included under it administrative
assistants and an Office of Government Reports to help the Chief
Executive keep abreast of his manifold responsibilities; the Office
for Emergency Management, which, as a legal framework, allowed
the majority of war agencies to be managed as part of the President's
Executive Office; the Office of War Mobilization and Reconversion,
and its predecessor which acted as a war and reconversion coordinating body for the President; and finally, and most important, the
Bureau of the Budget, which became, under the Reorganization

[20] Brazil, Cuba, Estonia, Germany, Liechtenstein, Lithuania, Nicaragua, Paraguay,
U.S.S.R., and Uruguay. England, Canada, and Australia had all produced "White
Papers" on full employment by the end of the war.

Act of 1939 and by the skill, ambition, and foresight of its wartime director Harold Smith, the most powerful staff unit in the Executive Office.

Under the category of long range planning the National Resources Planning Board and its predecessors were of overriding significance. The specific relevance of NRPB to this story is discussed below, but it is important in terms of the general background of the Full Employment Bill to emphasize that the idea of central planning as a part of a strengthened Executive Office of the President had been a product of the administrative thinking and experience of the preceding fifteen years.

# CHAPTER TWO

# Economic Ideas and Political Brokers

> Legislation is not a thing to be known
> beforehand. . . . It is an aggregate, not
> a simple, production. It is impossible to
> tell how many persons' opinions and in-
> fluences have entered into its composi-
> tion.—Wilson, *Congressional Govern-*
> *ment*, p. 320.

IF THE great depression and the war set the stage for the legislative
drama of the Full Employment Bill, they did not write the script.
Necessity is the mother of invention but it is not the invention.
In the realm of public policy the theories of experts and a variety
of institutional and personal channels through which such theories
gain political currency are necessary links between a social need
and a resultant legislative proposal.

The Full Employment Bill, as introduced, attempted to do four
things: first, to establish once and for all the principle of the
"right to work" and the federal government's obligation to assure employment opportunities for all those "able to work and
seeking work"; second, to place responsibility on the President for
seeing to it that the economy was purposively analyzed at regular
intervals, and that the Congress was informed of economic trends
and of the President's program to meet the challenge of those
trends; third, in case the economic barometer read "stormy," to
commit the federal government to undertake a series of measures
to forestall serious economic difficulty—the measure of last resort

being a program of federal spending and investment which was
to be the final guarantor of full employment; and finally, to establish a mechanism in Congress which would facilitate legislative
analysis and action, and fix legislative responsibility for the carrying out of a full employment policy.

The Full Employment Bill, then, was composed of (1) a statement of économic right and federal obligation, (2) an economic
program, and (3) governmental mechanisms for the effectuation of
that program. The intellectual origins of these three segments
of the proposed legislation are, in one sense, lost in the labyrinthian
past. Historical causation is infinitely complex and elusive. In a
study of this type we can deal with proximate influences only.

The proximate influences behind the concepts of economic right
and federal obligation, and behind the suggested governmental
mechanisms will not be analyzed separately for reasons which will
become clear as the story unfolds. Special attention must be given
at this point, however, to the economic assumptions underlying
the Full Employment Bill.

### THE CONTRIBUTION OF KEYNES

There are few who would question the contribution of John
Maynard Keynes to the theoretical underpinnings of the Full Employment Bill. Care should be taken, however, in assigning his
proper historical role. Keynes was not the inspired prophet of a
new mystical theology. He was the great verbalizer and rationalizer
of a theoretical attitude which was being forced, by the cold facts
of the depression experience, upon a number of European and
American Economists. In the discussion which follows it should
be appreciated that the name of Keynes is being used as a symbol
for an intellectual movement. This movement is personalized for
reasons of stylistic simplicity. Any other approach would necessi-
tate an impossibly complicated delineation of economic theory and
policy from Malthus through men like Veblen and J. A. Hobson
to the articles, reviews, books, and experiences which "pre-
Keynesed" Keynes during the twenties and thirties.

It is true of course that there was more to the economic substance
of S.380 than the contributions of one particular intellectual movement. The Full Employment Bill doffed its hat to a whole series
of economic policies and activities dealing with "banking and cur-

rency, monopoly and competition, wages and working conditions, foreign trade and investment, agriculture, taxation, social security, the development of natural resources, and such other matters as may directly or indirectly affect the level of non-federal investment and expenditure." That these are mentioned is a tribute to the halting, experimental, and often contradictory policies of the federal government during the decade of the thirties, and to the various often unrelated economic ideas which stimulated these policies.

It is also true that a vast amount of indigenous conceptual thinking of a statistical nature led up to the bill's references to the "Gross National Product" [1] and the "National Budget." [2]

But the bill's terminal reliance upon a program of federal investment and expenditure cannot be understood without an appreciation of the theoretical contributions of the late Lord Keynes and the movement of which he was a symbol.

*Keynes General Theory of Employment, Interest, and Money.—* Keynes's *General Theory*,[3] one of the great watersheds in the history of economic thought, was an attack upon the basic concept of "classical" and "neo-classical" economic thought that the free market capitalistic economy was a self-adjusting mechanism which tended to produce a condition of full employment and a maximum utilization of economic resources. Unemployment, to the classicist, was due to rigidities and imperfections in a system which sub-

[1] The work of the National Bureau of Economic Research and particularly of Simon Kuznets is of historical importance. For a discussion of some of these statistical concepts see U.S. Dept. of Commerce, *Income in the United States, 1929–35* (Washington, 1936), pp. 1–20; Simon Kuznets, *National Income and Capital Formation, 1919–35* (New York, National Bureau of Economic Research, 1937), pp. 1–7; and National Bureau of Economic Research, *Studies in Income and Wealth* (New York, 1939), Vol. I. See also, Simon Kuznets, *National Income and Its Composition, 1919–1938*, National Bureau of Economic Research (New York, 1941).

[2] The concept of a national budget in the sense in which it is used in S.380 was developed particularly by the Fiscal Division of the Bureau of the Budget in the early 1940s (see below, and see Grover W. Ensley, "A Budget for the Nation," *Social Research*, X, No. 3 [September, 1943], 280–300). During the '30s, however, the National Resources Planning Board and its predecessors had done a lot of spade work in this conceptual field. Beardsley Ruml was a particularly important catalyst. The books of Charles Beard and G. H. E. Smith on foreign policy, especially *The Idea of National Interest* (1934) and *The Open Door at Home* (1935) move in the direction of a national budget concept. See also Stuart Chase, *Goals for America* (New York, Twentieth Century Fund, 1942).

[3] John Maynard Keynes, *The General Theory of Employment, Interest and Money* (London, 1936).

sumed perfect competition, perfect mobility of labor and capital, and perfect knowledge on the part of decision-makers. Saving was a major economic virtue, since all savings tended to be invested in the development of new capital goods, which in turn brought employment and increased productivity. The possibility of un-utilized savings was discounted since it was believed that, given a tendency in that direction, the interest rate would fall, and a low rate of interest would stimulate further investment. It would also encourage consumer spending, which would in turn stimulate business expansion. Conversely, if savings tended to fall in relation to the demand for investment capital, the rate of interest would rise, coaxing a greater proportion of income into savings. It was a neat theory, but to many it seemed hardly adequate to meet the demonstrated facts of life in the Britain of the twenties and thirties, and the America of the thirties, where, theory or no theory, a vast amount of involuntary unemployment existed and the economic system showed few signs of moving automatically toward the full utilization of resources.

One of the most adequate short analyses of Keynesian theory has been made by Sir William Beveridge (now Lord Beveridge) in his book *Full Employment in a Free Society.*[4]

The gist of the new approach to the problem of employment . . . can be put shortly. Employment depends on spending, which is of two kinds —for consumption and for investment; what people spend on consumption gives employment. What they save, i.e. do not spend on consumption, gives employment only if it is invested, which means not the buying of bonds or shares, but expenditure in adding to capital equipment, such as factories, machinery, or ships, or in increasing stocks of raw material. There is not in the unplanned market economy anything that automatically keeps the total spending of both kinds at the point of full employment, that is to say, high enough to employ all the available labour. Adequate total demand for labour in an unplanned market economy cannot be taken for granted.

According to the Keynesian analysis, the possibility of prolonged mass unemployment lies in the fact that decisions to save and decisions to invest are made by different sets of people at different times and for different reasons and thus may get out of step. The amount which any community will try to save is governed, not primarily by the outlets for saving, i.e. the opportunities for investment, but by the total income of

4 (New York, W. W. Norton, Inc., 1945), pp. 93–95. Reprinted by permission of the publishers.

the community and its distribution; broadly speaking, if incomes are evenly distributed, less will be saved out of the total than if they are unevenly distributed. The amount which any community will seek to invest is governed, not primarily by the amount of savings available for investment, but by expectation of profits. Savings and investment do not start with any initial tendency to march in step and there is no automatic painless way of keeping them in step or bringing them together if they fall out. The rate of interest, which was supposed to serve this purpose, of regulating automatically the processes of saving and investment, fails to do so. If savings are tending to outrun investment, the rate of interest will fall only after a severe decline in the national income. . . .

The argument, it will be seen, is not that the savings of a community in total can outrun the investment. In the sense in which these terms are used in the Keynesian analysis the total savings that a community is, in fact, able to make, can never exceed the total invested; if a number of individuals in the community together try to save more than is being invested, the income of other members of the community will be correspondingly reduced; their losses in poverty and unemployment, their spending of former savings or running into debt will cancel out some of the savings of others and will thus reduce the total savings of the community to that which can be spent in investment. . . .

The Keynesian analysis attacks directly and destroys one of the economic harmonies betwen savings and investment through the rate of interest, which according to the older theory were assumed to keep the free capitalist system in prosperous equilibrium, with the demand for labour painlessly adjusted to the supply of labour. It destroys incidentally another of these harmonies also—the assumption made by Professor Pigou in 1913 that wage rates could be so adjusted as to abolish unemployment completely, and the inference that in any given situation employment could be increased directly by a general reduction of money wages.

In the shortest possible compass, the Keynesian analysis added up to a reminder that if people stop consuming and stop investing, national income, which according to the Keynesian formula is the sum of consumption and investment, is bound to fall; that the only way to increase national income is by means of increasing either consumption expenditures or investment expenditures or both, and finally, that there are governmental means of doing this in case private enterprise by itself cannot or will not do it.

*The Impact of Keynes on American Thinking.*—Keynes's *General Theory* was published in 1936 and gained currency in America just as the recession of 1937 was in the process of undermining the government's belief that the economy would permanently recover on the basis of a few intravenous injections of purchasing power. To many American economists in and out of the government, Keynes's analysis provided a theoretical summation of the reasons for the failure of the American economy to recover from the depression. Suddenly everything was clear: an economic plateau had been reached in the United States far below the level of full employment; there was no automatic mechanism within the system which would tend to produce the maximum utilization of resources; full employment could not be reached, consequently, unless the government undertook positive measures on a continuing basis.

With this analysis in mind, American economists and other policy planners began to reevaluate the New Deal program and to search for the underlying causes of the economic stagnation. The redistribution of income through steeply graduated income taxes, inheritance taxes, and undistributed profits taxes, came to be recognized, not simply as a matter of social justice, but as a positive economic good—since, as Keynes had pointed out, high income groups save proportionately more (and consequently spend proportionately less) of their income than low income groups. The 1937 recession came to be explained on the basis, not that government spending had failed, but that it had not been tried on sufficient scale. Budget balancing as a goal came to be discredited, and a vast literature began to grow around the idea that public borrowing for the purpose of increasing investment and consumption would so raise the national income that the increasing debt burden could be carried with relative ease. Monopolistic elements in the industrial structure came to be viewed in the light of the impact of monopoly upon the rate of saving. As one economist has put it, "a regime of monopoly means high profits which tend to be hoarded; a regime of competition means lower profits which tend to be employed." [5]

All the New Deal attempts to raise purchasing power, promote public works, and foster the development of natural resources came to be endorsed, not just as necessary depression expedients, but as part of an inclusive long-term program of government in-

[5] Moses Abramovitz, "Savings and Investment: Profits vs. Prosperity?" *The American Economic Review*, Part II (Supplement), June, 1942, p. 88.

vestment, expenditure, and control, based upon the Keynesian analysis.[6]

In defense of the reason that private enterprise could not take care of idle savings on its own and thereby obviate the necessity of all this government activity, the American Keynesians built up what has come to be called the "maturity" thesis. One lucid statement reads as follows:

We reach the conclusion that the expansion of the nineteenth and early twentieth centuries was based on building for the future, which carried with it an adequate demand for consumable goods and services in the present. Building for the future was good business in an expanding economic universe with a rapidly growing population. When the limits of expansion had been reached, when the rate of population growth slowed down, building for the future became an increasingly hazardous adventure. Its volume contracted and with it the ability to buy in the present. Expansion fed upon itself in the past; contraction feeds upon itself in the present. These are the basic changes which underlie the reversal of trend from 1929 to the present.[7]

*The Opposition.*—The analysis of the American Keynesians met with stout opposition from businessmen and from non-Keynesian economists. And of course there developed hot intramural fights within the Keynesian fraternity itself. The business community in general called the "maturity" thesis ridiculous, classifying it as old and discredited hogwash,[8] and claiming that the economic stagnation about which the Keynesians talked, was purely and simply the result of unsettling and hostile New Deal policies. A let-up on "soak the rich" taxes, a decrease in federal

[6] In this connection the work of the Fiscal and Monetary Advisory Board appointed by President Roosevelt on November 18, 1938, should be noted. The Board consisted of the Secretary of the Treasury, chairman; Marriner Eccles of the Federal Reserve Board; Acting Budget Director, D. W. Bell; and Frederick A. Delano, chairman of the Advisory Committee of the National Resources Committee. With the staff help of Washington economists like Lauchlin Currie and Leon Henderson, the Board was instrumental in the drafting of the abortive Spend-Lend Bill of 1939, probably the first legislative proposal firmly grounded in Keynes's *General Theory*. The impact of Keynes on the New Deal is briefly discussed in Henry Morgenthau, Jr., "The Morgenthau Diaries," *Colliers*, October 4, 1947, p. 21. For a recent and comprehensive analysis of the contributions of Keynes to economic theory and public policy see Seymour Harris, ed., *The New Economics* (New York, 1947).

[7] Seven Harvard and Tufts Economists, *An Economic Program for American Democracy* (New York, Vanguard Press, 1938), p. 22. Reprinted by permission of the publishers.

[8] See George Terborgh, *The Bogey of Economic Maturity* (Chicago, 1945), Chap. V.

expenditures, a reduction in the national debt, a curtailing of the "irresponsible" power of organized labor and other measures favorable to business confidence, would, they claimed, open the road to business expansion, full employment, and general prosperity.

The depression experience, and Mr. Keynes, set off a long debate which has by no means ended. The impact of Keynesian thinking on federal policies was only slightly, even if clearly, noticeable prior to the war, but its influence on the postwar employment planning which developed during the war, was, as we shall see, enormous. Although the major exponent and modifier of Keynesian theory as applied to American problems was Professor Alvin Hansen of Harvard, hundreds of economists and government policy planners had come by the end of the thirties to accept the Keynesian analysis as the new orthodoxy. Like most disciples, they sometimes misunderstood and frequently reinterpreted the master, but they paid him homage even in their defections. In spite of, and perhaps, on occasion, because of, the general hostility of the business world to the analyses and projected programs of American Keynesians, the influence of the latter continued to grow.

### KEYNES TO S.380: CONNECTING LINKS

Between Keynes and the Full Employment Bill were intellectual middlemen whose job it is to weld theory and policy. Special mention must be made of four organizations in this connection, two private and two public: the National Planning Association, the National Farmers Union, the Fiscal Division of the Budget Bureau, and the National Resources Planning Board.

*The National Planning Association.*—This Association, which has its headquarters in Washington, D.C., was incorporated during the early days of the New Deal "for the purpose of bringing together responsible leaders of major economic groups, both within and without the government" [9] to study and recommend for consideration plans for coping with the future. Its main function has not been basic research, although original material often appears in its monographs. But N.P.A. has been one of the most important policy catalysts in Washington. Its board is made up of twenty-one representatives of business, agriculture, and labor and is meant

[9] U.S. Senate, "Postwar Economic Policy and Planning," p. 56.

to represent all phases of American economic life. "All phases" does not mean "all points of view," however, and the list of names on its board and committees is sufficient to indicate the Association's liberal leanings.

In general, N.P.A., while by no means ignoring the policy issues of the moment, attempts to anticipate the policy problems of tomorrow. Taking 1943 as a typical year, N.P.A. concentrated its attention on such issues as war contracts, surplus property, the use and disposition of government plants, the organization and structure of agriculture after the war, international relief problems, the influence of tax laws on war and postwar reserves for industry, savings, income, and investment, and the work of labor-management committees.

Under the executive direction of E. J. Coil, the N.P.A. has influenced national policy through its short, clearly written pamphlets and through Association-sponsored luncheons and discussion meetings, which are often attended by some of the most important policy figures in Washington. It is sufficient to note here that although the major N.P.A. study on the full employment issue [10] did not appear until early 1945, it had been in progress for over a year, and was the product of the cooperative effort of a number of important Washington technicians. As we shall see, participants like Louis Bean, Gerhard Colm, Mordecai Ezekiel, and Samuel Thompson loom large in the history of the Full Employmen Bill. So do names like Alvin Hansen, Beardsley Ruml, and James G. Patton of the Association's Board of Trustees.

Essentially the N.P.A. attitude toward the full employment problem was based upon Keynesian assumptions. It is not too much to say that its two main studies on full employment, *National Budgets for Full Employment,* and John Pierson's *Fiscal Policy for Full Employment* [11] represented the forefront of Keynesian thinking among prominent Washington economists.

*The National Farmers Union.*—Of the three major farm organizations in the United States, the National Grange, the American Farm Bureau Federation, and the National Farmers Union, only the Farmers Union worked on over-all postwar economic plan-

[10] National Planning Association, *National Budgets for Full Employment,* Planning Pamphlets Nos. 43 and 44 (Washington, 1945).
[11] Planning Pamphlet No. 45 (Washington, 1945).

ning, and even this organization's work—although crucial in terms of our story—was fragmentary. It was true of course that the Farm Bureau and the Grange, through their legislative representatives in Washington, conducted research and took positions on a number of important pending bills which were concerned directly or indirectly with postwar questions. It is also true that the Grange established a Post-war Agricultural Planning Committee and a Public Welfare and International Agricultural Committee, but neither of these issued any reports.

For that matter, the National Farmers Union had no continuing committee on postwar problems. Their postwar planning was done by their regular staff, Gardner Jackson, Robert Handschin, Paul Sifton, and Russell Smith, in the Union's Washington office. These four, who had come from a variety of New Deal and labor backgrounds, sparked a broadly based liberal program which was dramatized nationally by the Farmers Union president, James Patton. The general theme running through all the public statements of the Union, regardless of the particular reconversion or postwar issue under consideration, was that farmers could not disassociate themselves from the other economic interests of the nation; that what was good for consumers and workers was bound to be good for the farmers; and that the federal government had the major responsibility, with the cooperation of all important economic interests of the nation, for planning the abundant life.

In April, 1944, Patton was asked to testify on the Kilgore Reconversion Bill and other pending reconversion legislation being considered by the Senate. In its original form, the Kilgore bill (S.1823) was an ambitious and far-reaching measure.[12] A new Office of War Mobilization and Adjustment ("Adjustment" was later changed to "Reconversion") was to be established with executive responsibility for all reconversion activities. This office was to include a "Bureau of Programs" which would be responsible for "full employment and full production planning." Furthermore, the bill asked for a greatly extended unemployment compensation program, which it was hoped would serve the double function of insuring against disastrous economic instability as a result of reconversion and of giving advance notice to management that it would not be able to break the back of organized labor with the club of starvation. This it was

12 78th Cong., 1st Sess.; introduced March 29, 1944.

felt would lead to orderly wage adjustments through peaceful collective bargaining.

In his testimony before the Senate subcommittee, Patton made a strong statement to the effect that the Kilgore bill, like other reconversion legislation under consideration by the War Contracts Subcommittee of the Senate Committee on Military Affairs, was woefully inadequate. Even on the subject of the Bureau of Programs, Patton was caustic:

Mr. Chairman, this is the polite and accepted formula for delaying action—another study, another set of recommendations, more hearings, and perhaps, years from now, after our wartime machinery of production for abundance has been broken, dispersed, and destroyed, after we have fumbled the transition from war to peace production, after a possible post-war boom has fallen into a disastrous tail spin, a minor bureau of an emergency office having no definite tenure of life may make recommendations, which, were they to be considered and acted upon now, would save us incalculable human and material losses in the years ahead. Here in this brief paragraph are lumped our most important national problems of the century. Their analysis and solution cannot safely be postponed. It is to these problems that we should address ourselves now, not later.[13]

Patton summed up his position with the words: "I propose . . . the positive goal of the permanent planning of the economy for full employment."

Russell Smith, legislative representative of the Farmers Union, was in the hospital in April, 1944, following a severe automobile accident. A former newspaper man and a former public servant in the Bureau of Agricultural Economics and the Board of Economic Warfare, Smith was familiar with the thinking of Keynes and Hansen and the various schools of American Keynesians in Washington. On the basis of the Patton statement before the War Contracts Subcommittee, and his own appraisal of the inadequacy of the Kilgore bill, Smith jotted down notes for a broad employment program in which the federal government would underwrite the total national investment necessary to insure full employment. When he left the hospital in June, he discussed this outline with a few friends, including Louis Bean of the Budget Bureau. Bean suggested on the basis of National Bureau studies that the yearly proportion of in-

13 National Farmers Union, "Statement Prepared for the Senate Military Affairs Committee Hearing," press release, April 14, 1944.

vestment to the gross national product had averaged in the past about one to five. He recommended, therefore, that if Smith were aiming at a $200 billion gross national product he should shoot at a $40 billion total national investment. Bean further suggested that Smith work out a full written statement of his plan which might be discussed with an informal group of government economists.

With this encouragement, Smith drafted a statement which was presented, as planned, at one of Bean's weekly "bull-sessions." Present at the lunch were Mordecai Ezekiel of the Bureau of Agricultural Economics, Geoffrey Shepard of the C.E.D. and the Commerce Department, Gerhard Colm of the Fiscal Division of the Budget Bureau, and others. These economists were prolific with criticisms, but they were unanimously behind Smith's goal of arousing public discussion.

Smith rewrote his draft, incorporating some of the suggestions of the luncheon group, and then talked with Alvin Hansen. Hansen disagreed with the $40 billion investment figure (he felt it was too high), but he had no basic fault to find with Smith's approach. This was of course to be expected, since Smith's draft was based to a large extent on the employment theories of Keynes and Hansen. After more thinking and writing, Smith discussed his draft with Patton and it was finally decided to submit the draft as an amendment to the Kilgore bill.

In outline, the so-called Patton amendment [14] provided that the Joint Committee on Internal Revenue Taxation, with the help of appropriate government agencies, should make annual studies of prospective total investment in the nation and determine to what extent that prospective investment would fall below $40 billion. When that deficiency figure was determined, the Committee through the President of the Senate and the Speaker of the House would notify the Reconstruction Finance Corporation of the amount of loans to be made available to private industry and state and local governments in order to reach the $40 billion total investment required to produce full employment. If such loans were not applied for or utilized in sufficient quantity to bring about full employment, Congress would then appropriate for public works and other federal projects the amount of money necessary to accomplish the stated end.

[14] See National Farmers Union press release for Monday A.M., Aug. 7, 1944.

We shall discuss the important ramifications of the Farmers Union amendment in the following chapter.

*The Fiscal Division of the Bureau of the Budget.*—The Budget Bureau, under the leadership of Harold Smith, began as early as 1939 to think of the budgetary process in the broader context of government fiscal policy and economic program formulation. In 1939, a Fiscal Division was established in the Bureau to examine "questions of fiscal policy and [to give] staff assistance in the formulation of the President's financial program." [15]

Under the intellectual guidance of J. Weldon Jones, Gerhard Colm, Arthur Smithies, and Grover Ensley, the Fiscal Division during the war years gradually evolved a conception of the "Nation's Budget" which found its way into the President's Budget Message of January 3, 1945.[16] The concept of the nation's budget was a logical off-spring of Roosevelt's statement in January, 1941, that "the Budget of the United States presents our national program. It is a preview of our work plan, a forecast of things to come. It charts the course of the nation." [17] What had been added by 1945 was an official recognition of the essentially Keynesian proposition that the federal budget should be used to contribute to the larger context of the total national economy. An analysis of the budget messages from 1940 to 1945 gives a clear indication that the annual budget was on its way to becoming an important instrument of national policy programming in the economic field. In one sense, the Full Employment Bill of 1945 was an effort to give statutory recognition and encouragement to an activity which had been pioneered by the Fiscal Division of the Budget Bureau. It was no accident that the closest cooperation developed between the Fiscal Division and the Congressional staff charged with the drafting and legislative handling of the Full Employment Bill.

*The National Resources Planning Board.*—This Board, which grew out of the National Planning Board of the Public Works Administration was originally created by President Roosevelt in 1934. According to George Galloway, it "was substantially the pro-

15 Fritz Morstein Marx, "The Bureau of the Budget: Its Evolution and Present Role," I, *American Political Science Review*, August, 1945, p. 684.
16 *The Budget of the U.S. Government for the Fiscal Year Ending June 30, 1946* (Washington, 1945), pp. xxiv–xxvii.
17 *The Budget of the U.S. Government for the Fiscal Year Ending June 30, 1942* (Washington, 1941), p. xiv.

jection of the Advisory Council, proposed by President Hoover's Committee on Recent Social Trends." [18] During the thirties, the Board "made fundamental studies and contributions to intelligent national policy in relation to land use, water use, mineral and energy use; by broad programming of public works; scientific studies of population trends, of the social effects of inventions, of research as an actual resource; of regions and cities; reports upon the structure of our national economy, of consumer expenditures and consumer income." [19]

Under the Reorganization Act of 1939, the N.R.P.B. was placed in the newly created Executive Office of the President and became the central long-range planning agency for the Executive branch. The Board used the services of experts in the various government departments as well as recognized authorities in various professions, in the preparation of its reports. It remained relatively cloistered from the rough and tumble of Congressional politics—perhaps too cloistered for its own eventual good, but it was both a reflection of and a contributor to the liberal social thinking of President Roosevelt.

During the late thirties the Planning Board was one of the great centers of Keynesian thinking. In the deliberations and recommendations of its Industrial Committee, in its quarterly reports to the President on employment trends (pursuant to the Federal Employment Stablilization Act of 1931), and in it growing concern with inventories of the total economy, it was a major catalyst and reagent in the field of progressive economic thought.

On March 10, 1943, President Roosevelt transmitted to Congress two massive reports prepared by the N.R.P.B. dealing with postwar policy.[20] The first, 400,000 words long, was called *Security, Work, and Relief Policies;* the second, which was considerably shorter, was on national resources development. We are here concerned with the former.

[18] George B. Galloway and associates, *Planning for America* (New York, 1941), p. 493.

[19] *Ibid.*

[20] These studies were prepared in response to a directive sent by President Roosevelt to the N.R.P.B. on November 12, 1940, instructing that agency "to collect, analyse, and collate all constructive plans for significant public and private action in the post-defense period insofar as these have to do with the natural and human resources of the nation." *After Defense—What?,* N.R.P.B. Pamphlet on Post-Defense Planning (Washington, 1941), p. 9.

*Security, Work, and Relief Policies* was an elaborate program
which rested on what the Board called a "New Bill of Rights":

1. Right to work, usefully and creatively through the productive
   years.
2. The right to fair pay, adequate to command the necessities and
   amenities of life in exchange for work, ideas, thrift, and other
   socially valuable service.
3. The right to adequate food, clothing, shelter, and medical care.
4. The right to security, with freedom from fear of old age, want, de-
   pendency, sickness, unemployment and accident.
5. The right to live in a system of free enterprise, free from compulsory labor, irresponsible private power, arbitrary public authority,
   and unregulated monopolies.
6. The right to come and go, to speak and to be silent, free from the
   spying of secret police.
7. The right to equality before the law, with equal access to justice in
   fact.
8. The right to education, for work, for citizenship, and for personal
   growth and happiness.
9. The right to rest, recreation and adventure, the opportunity to
   enjoy and take part in an advancing civilization.[21]

In order to achieve these goals in the postwar years, the Board
suggested a broad social security program, a national health and
education program, a permanent policy of large-scale public works,
comparatively heavy taxation (emphasizing individual incomes and
inheritances), and effective measures against monopoly. The program was fundamentally Keynesian in its economic assumptions,[22]
and represented, perhaps better than any other single document
of the war years, the cutting edge of progressive postwar thinking
in the federal government. It was a powerful impetus to those
forces which two years later combined to make possible the introduction of the Full Employment Bill. For its prophetic ideas, however,
the N.R.P.B. was killed by Congressional action in an appropriations bill three months after its postwar report had been issued.[23]

What we have seen so far is sufficient to indicate that the background of the Full Employment Bill was composed of a national,
even world-wide, economic experience; of popular wartime fears

21 New York *Times,* March 11, 1943, p. 12.
22 See "Charter for America," *The New Republic,* Part II, April 19, 1943, p. 523.
23 57 Stat. 170, June 26, 1943.

about the postwar world; and of the impact of particular economic ideas, especially those of Lord Keynes, upon certain public and private planners in this country. Most of this picture has been snapped at a considerable height and has revealed only the broadest contours. We must now dive close to the ground and photograph the United States Congress at work on postwar problems during the late war years. In these close-ups, we will find the legislative origins of the Full Employment Bill of 1945.

THE LEGISLATIVE BRANCH AND THE STRUGGLE OVER
RECONVERSION POLICY

There was more than coincidence in the fact that the first Congressional postwar planning committee was established in the Senate two days after the publication of the National Resources Planning Board report. It is true that Senator George of Georgia had introduced a resolution to create such a committee a month earlier,[24] but the appearance of the N.R.P.B. report seemed to galvanize the Senate into action. On March 12, that body without a word of debate created a Special Committee on Postwar Economic Policy and Planning under the chairmanship of Senator George. The George Committee, and its "opposite number," the Colmer Committee, established by the House early in 1944,[25] were chaired by men who had little sympathy for the type of program outlined by the National Resources Planning Board. The consequence was that many of the committees' postwar recommendations, which appeared in various annual and special reports, reflected the policy platforms of conservative interests.

These special committees were not to usurp the regular legislative functions of the various standing committees, but were to "investigate and report to Congress upon all matters relating to postwar economic policy and problems . . . to the end that Congress may be . . . in a position to formulate solutions with respect to them."[26] In spite of the fact that these committees were concerned indirectly with a tremendous amount of legislation dealing with reconversion and other postwar problems, their official state-

<hr/>

[24] S.102, 78th Cong., 1st Sess.        [25] H.R.408, 78th Cong., 2d Sess.
[26] U.S. House of Representatives, "Postwar Economic Policy and Planning," *Eleventh Report of the House Special Committee on Postwar Economic Policy and Planning,* H. Report No. 2729, 79th Cong., 2d Sess. (Washington, 1946), p. 1.

ments were often couched in such vacuous language, and so many other forces were at work in the development of postwar programs, that it is difficult to say how far their influence actually extended.

The work of the postwar planning committees cannot be understood without reference to the problems facing Congress as a whole in 1943 and 1944. Group pressures being what they are in our national life, it is not surprising that Congress should have found itself by the middle years of the war being urged to consider those problems which reflected the haunting reconversion worries of diverse economic interests. Business was particularly concerned about the termination of war contracts and the disposal of surplus property; labor, about transitional unemployment and postwar earnings. By late 1943, two things were becoming increasingly clear to certain members of Congress.[27] One was that specific legislation would be needed to handle these problems; the other was that some special federal mechanism, or mechanisms, would have to be established to administer reconversion policy.

This latter belief had more behind it than a ready appreciation that laws do not administer themselves. Mobilizing the resources of the nation for war had been an awkward and a halting process, and an early failure to provide for administrative coordination of war controls had resulted in waste, duplication, delay, and mismanagement. Furthermore, since the instrumentalities of mobilization could not be separated from the instrumentalities needed for demobilization, it became obvious to a number of legislators that intelligent planning for reconversion was dependent to a large extent upon a more effective administrative pattern for waging war. As the Tolan Committee on Defense Migration put it as far back as 1941, "It is the belief of this committee . . . that many of the most important decisions regarding the postwar world are being settled daily by those in charge of our organization to wage this war." [28] Consequently, it was with postwar as well as wartime prob-

27 Some legislators were concerned much earlier than this, notably Senators Kilgore, Murray, Pepper, and Truman, and Congressman Tolan. It is also interesting to note that Senator Wagner introduced a Joint Resolution to Establish a Post-Emergency Economic Advisory Committee as early as Jan. 9, 1941 (S. J. Res. 16, 77th Cong., 1st Sess.).
28 U.S. House of Representatives, *Final Report of the Select Committee Investigating National Defense Migration,* House Report No. 3, 77th Cong., 1st Sess. (Washington, 1941), p. 17.

lems in mind that the Kilgore-Pepper-Tolan bill to establish an Office of War Mobilization was introduced late in 1942 and was reintroduced with a larger sponsorship early in 1943.

On May 28, 1943, partly in response to Congressional pressure, President Roosevelt established an Office of War Mobilization by Executive Order. To those in Congress who were worrying about reconversion problems, the issue then became one of trying to define what relationship, if any, should exist between projected reconversion policies and the activities of the newly created Office of War Mobilization. The Office itself was sufficiently concerned about this problem to establish on November 6, 1943, a new unit, headed by Bernard Baruch, to "deal with war and postwar adjustment problems and to develop unified programs and policies to be pursued by the various agencies of government concerned." [29]

At the Congressional end, an almost unbelievably confusing struggle developed in the Senate for control of postwar legislation. Senators Kilgore, Murray, and George and their respective staffs spent most of late 1943 and early 1944 jockeying for position in the race to dominate reconversion policy. The three-cornered struggle was due partly to differences in philosophy, partly to Senatorial and staff jealousies. In the simplest language, here is the story of the struggle over reconversion legislation as it developed chronologically from September, 1943, to August, 1944. The story is of vital importance to an understanding of the genesis of the Full Employment Bill.

CAST OF MAJOR CHARACTERS

Senator James E. Murray of Montana, Chairman of the War Contracts Subcommittee of the Senate Military Affairs Committee

Bertram M. Gross, Staff Director of the War Contracts Subcommittee

Senator Walter F. George of Georgia, Chairman of the Senate Committee on Postwar Economic Policy and Planning, and Chairman of the Senate Finance Committee

Scott Russell, Counsel for the Senate Committee on Postwar Economic Policy and Planning

Senator Harley M. Kilgore of West Virginia, Chairman of the War

[29] E. Jay Howenstine, Jr., *The Economics of Demobilization* (Washington, 1944), p. 59.

Mobilization Subcommittee of the Senate Military Affairs Committee

Herbert Schimmel, Chief of Investigations for the War Mobilization Subcommittee

*Scene 1.* In September, 1943, a War Contracts Subcommittee of the Military Affairs Committee was appointed to consider contract settlement legislation. While the subcommittee staff was at work in the fall and early winter of 1943–44 preparing basic material for an eventual bill draft, the George Postwar Planning Committee was holding hearings on the general problem of contract settlement. In order to keep track of what the George Committee was doing, and perhaps in order to insure the support of a conservative Congress, Senator Murray asked Senator George to become a co-sponsor of the then embryonic Contract Settlement Bill being worked up by the War Contracts Subcommittee staff. George agreed, and on February 11, 1944, a Murray-George omnibus Contract Settlement Bill was introduced on the floor of the Senate.[30] The bill provided for an Office of Contract Settlement under a director to be appointed by the President. The new office was apparently to be completely separate from the Office of War Mobilization.

*Scene 2.* In the meantime, starting in November, 1943, Senator Harley M. Kilgore had set his staff to work on an omnibus reconversion bill which would place special emphasis upon a planning and administrative mechanism in the federal government to oversee the orderly liquidation of the war economy, ease the "human side of reconversion," and plan for the future. Herbert Schimmel, chief of investigations for the War Mobilization Subcommittee, came up with a preliminary recommendation which by-passed the O.W.M. issue completely. What Schimmel suggested was a permanent three-pronged secretariat to the Presidential Cabinet, superseding the present Bureau of the Budget. One division would be devoted to over-all fiscal analyses; a second, to be called a Bureau of Programs, to the formulation of broad economic policy; and the third, to the coordination of that policy relative to departmental and Congressional action. It was obvious after short consideration, however, that a major governmental reorganization of this type would be politically impossible in the middle of a war. Schimmel then turned his

[30] S.1718, 78th Cong., 2d Sess.

efforts to drafting a bill enlarging the powers of the O.W.M. to include over-all responsibility for reconversion. The Kilgore bill was not introduced until March 29, 1944.[31]

*Scene 3.* On February 15, 1944, the Baruch-Hancock Report [32] was submitted to War Mobilization Director James F. Byrnes, and, simultaneously, was made public. The report pointed to the need for immediate planning for reconversion, and proposed an enlargement of the powers of the Office of War Mobilization (and the creation of new instrumentalities under it), to take care of such problems as contract termination, surplus property disposal, and the "human side of reconversion."

The writing and issuing of this report was marked by a growing animosity between Baruch and the two Senate Committees working on contract settlement legislation. Baruch did not like the Senate bill and resented the fact that it had been introduced four days before his report had been issued. Senator George and his staff, and to a lesser extent Senator Murray and his staff, resented what they felt to be Baruch's "prima donna" attitude, as well as the venerable gentleman's attempt to by-pass Congress in his recommendations for an enlarged O.W.M. to be created without Congressional sanction.

As a result of this friction with Baruch, Senator George's staff director, Scott Russell, in something of a white heat, drew up a bill to establish an Office of Demobilization, separate from the O.W.M., to include supervision over contract settlement and surplus property disposal. Senator Murray, after insisting on certain changes, became a co-sponsor in order to insure that this new bill would be referred to his War Contracts Subcommittee. The George-Murray Demobilization Bill was introduced on February 22, 1944,[33] just a week after the issuance of the Baruch-Hancock Report.

*Scene 4.* On March 29, 1944, the long-waited Kilgore bill was introduced, providing for an Office of War Mobilization and Adjustment, with a National Production-Employment Board composed of representatives of industry, labor, and agriculture, and with a Bureau of Programs to take care of long-range postwar planning. The bill also provided for the handling of surplus property,

31 S.1823, 78th Cong., 2d Sess.
32 Bernard Baruch and John M. Hancock, *Report on War and Post-War Adjustment Policies* (Washington, 1944).
33 S.1730, 78th Cong., 2d Sess.

and a scheme of "interim pay benefits" and an enlarged unemployment insurance program to meet the traditional needs of labor.
Contract settlement was not included in the bill, but Kilgore made
his strategy quite clear in this regard when he said in a short report
accompanying his bill: "We recognize that such a comprehensive
bill as this might well have included a title on Contract Termination. We feel, however, that the question has been well handled
by Senators Murray and George's bill S.1716, *which can very easily
be joined to this bill.*" [34] (Italics added.) Kilgore made certain that
his new bill was assigned to Senator Murray's War Contracts Subcommittee, in the hope that Murray would see fit to join forces and
report out an omnibus bill to end all omnibus bills.

*Scene 5.* By April, 1944, Murray's War Contracts Subcommittee
had managed to get control of every important piece of proposed
legislation dealing with reconversion and postwar problems. The
question of what to do about these various suggestions, how to
harmonize them if they were harmonizable, how to keep them
separate if they were not, fell largely to Bertram Gross and Kurt
Borchardt of the subcommittee staff. Hearings were held on the
various bills in April, and it soon became quite apparent that the
Kilgore strategy was not going to work. Senator Murray and his
staff assistants had labored for eight months on the Contract Settlement Bill. This bill had been sweated out of endless conferences
with businessmen and government officials. By the late spring it
was about ready for final action, and Murray and his staff had no
desire to see eight months of hard work go down the drain with
an omnibus bill which they felt sure would be cut to shreds by a
conservative Congress.

There was something else. Murray, like James Patton of the
Farmers Union, had little faith in the Bureau of Programs approach
to the complex problems of long-term economic stability. He felt
it was a mistake to have the planning function two steps removed
from the President, and remembering the fate of the National Resources Planning Board, he had no faith that the planning function
would be separable from the projected Office of War Mobilization
and Adjustment when the latter was terminated.

When it became obvious that no omnibus legislation was going
to be permitted by Senator Murray, Senator Kilgore and his staff,

[34] *Congressional Record*, 78th Cong., 2d Sess., March 29, 1944, p. 3242.

and a large body of liberal lobbyists who had rallied around the Kilgore bill, became extremely bitter. They felt that Murray and his staff had betrayed the "cause," a charge which seemed to them easy to support at that time since Murray's name was linked to that of Senator George in connection with the Contract Settlement Bill.

*Scene 6.* This feud between Murray and Kilgore and their respective staffs led to a dual redrafting job. Bertram Gross for Senator Murray worked on a revision of the original George-Murray Demobilization Bill, attempting to devise a compromise between the original and a few of the "sounder" provisions of the Kilgore bill. This draft included many of the ideas which were finally written into law. In the meantime, however, the Kilgore staff worked up a revised bill of its own,[35] and by June 8, 1944, had succeeded in selling it to eight liberal Senators including Senator Truman, one of the three members of the War Contracts Subcommittee. This placed Senator Murray in a nasty spot of deciding between supporting conservative Senator Revercomb, the third and minority member of the subcommittee, or of joining Truman in sponsoring a revised Kilgore bill with which Murray was not in complete sympathy. He finally decided on the latter course, Gross's revised George-Murray bill was shelved, and the new Kilgore bill was redrafted as the Kilgore-Truman-Murray bill.[36]

*Scene 7.* The denouement occurred early in August, 1944. Senator George, desirous of blocking the liberal provisions of the revised Kilgore bill (particularly those sections dealing with a Bureau of Programs and extended unemployment compensation under federal control), introduced a brand-new bill on August 1, 1944,[37] dealing solely with a modest and state-controlled unemployment compensation plan to cover the transitional period. On August 3, the new George bill was reported favorably by Senator George's own Finance Committee and was placed on the calendar. On August 7, the Kilgore-Truman-Murray bill was reported out of the Senate Military Affairs Committee and placed on the calendar, but, of course, behind the George bill.

Between August 8 and August 11, the situation came to a climax: the George bill was called off the calendar for Senate action, the

[35] S.1893, 78th Cong., 2d Sess.; introduced May 4, 1944.
[36] S.2061, 78th Cong., 2d Sess.; introduced Aug. 7, 1944.
[37] S.2051, 78th Cong., 2d Sess.

Kilgore-Truman-Murray bill was offered as a primary amendment thereto, the George-Murray Demobilization Bill which had been rewritten by Gross was exhumed by Senator George, modified, and offered as a secondary amendment to his own bill, the secondary amendment was passed by a confused Senate, and an Office of War Mobilization and Reconversion Bill, stripped of the unemployment compensation and planning measures championed by the Kilgore staff, was sent to the House. With further modifications by the House, the bill was sent to the White House and became law in October, 1944.[38] Separate Contract Settlement and Surplus Property Acts [39] were passed during the summer and fall of that same year, but both were integrated into the O.W.M.R. Act as finally approved.

### THE SIGNIFICANCE OF THE STRUGGLE
### OVER RECONVERSION LEGISLATION

This tangled background to the establishment of the O.W.M.R. is important to our story for a number of reasons. In the first place, it dramatizes the Congressional concern about, and groping toward, an answer to the pending postwar uncertainties. This concern was a reflection of the worries of the American people in the late war years. The fact that the George rather than the Kilgore version of the O.W.M.R. bill was finally passed, meant that a void was left in legislative policy dealing with comprehensive postwar planning for jobs. Had the Kilgore provisions for a Bureau of Programs been enacted into law, the probability is that the emergence of a separate Full Employment Bill would have been delayed or precluded.

In the second place, the struggle between Kilgore and George was symptomatic of a broad ideological split within Congress. The later Congressional debate over the Full Employment Bill was presaged by the struggle between conservative and liberal legislators over reconversion policy.

In the third place, a number of ideas which were written into the various drafts of the reconversion bills later found their way into the Full Employment Bill: the idea of a central planning agency; the idea of advisory councils made up of representatives of busi-

[38] 58 Stat. 785, Oct. 3, 1944.
[39] 58 Stat. 649, July 1, 1944, and 58 Stat. 765, Oct. 3, 1944, respectively.

ness, labor, and agriculture; the idea of a Joint Congressional Committee; and others.

And finally, the limited goals of reconversion planning, as we saw earlier, had led the National Farmers Union to suggest a new frame of reference for postwar thinking. The chairman and the staff of the War Contracts Subcommittee were in a receptive mood for this type of suggestion.

# CHAPTER THREE

# A Bill Is Born

Indeed, only a very slight examination of the measures which originate with the Committees is necessary to show that most of them are framed with a view to securing their easy passage. . . . The manifest object is to dress them to the liking of all factions.—Wilson, *Congressional Government*, pp. 100–101.

A MAJOR POLICY BILL does not burst like a mature Athena from the head of Zeus. The Full Employment Bill had a gestation period of at least six months, and as we have seen, its ancestry dates back a long way. If we are searching for the moment when the idea of a separate Full Employment Bill came into existence, we should probably have to choose that instant of time in August, 1944, when the Patton amendment to the Kilgore bill was first brought to the attention of Senator James E. Murray of Montana. Although Patton had submitted his amendment to a wide variety of Congressional leaders as well as to President Roosevelt and Vice-President Wallace, it was Senator Murray who assumed responsibility for having the proposal printed in the form of an amendment to the Kilgore bill and circulated for comment to various government agencies—although he made it clear that he did not intend to call for action upon it at that time. Granted the logic of events in the Senate fight over reconversion policy, it was obvious to Murray that the Patton amendment would have no chance of becoming part of the pending

O.W.M.R. legislation. His real interest was in the fact that the National Farmers Union proposal had placed the full employment issue on a new plane of permanent federal obligation, far transcending the limited reconversion concepts which had dominated the thinking of most of Congress for a year or more.

In this general awareness by Senator Murray and his War Contracts Subcommitte staff that limited reconversion legislation was not enough and that the Patton amendment had created a new frame of reference for thinking about postwar employment problems, the Full Employment Bill of 1945 had its real beginning.

Before proceeding to an analysis of the actual drafting of the bill, it is important to look briefly into the story of its major sponsor and into the issues of the 1944 Presidential election. The birth of a public policy is after all the result of the impact of seminal ideas on strategic persons at propitious times.

### SENATOR JAMES E. MURRAY OF MONTANA

Senator James E. Murray [1] is one of the great anomalies in the United States Senate. One of the wealthiest men in the Upper Chamber, he ranks as one of the most ardent champions of liberal social legislation in recent national history.

Murray was born in Canada in 1876. His father died when he was young, but insurance and a fabulous uncle kept the family in a reasonably secure financial condition. After graduating from St. Jerome's College in Ontario, Murray entered New York University as a special student in 1897, going on to the Law school a year later. In 1900 he took out citizenship papers, and the following year went to Butte, Montana, where his uncle James A. Murray had accumulated a fortune in mining and banking. During the next thirty years, Murray married, raised a family, quietly built up a law practice and a fortune in small enterprises and watched his city and his state become the battleground of giant interests whose financial stake in Montana soil and politics made Murray's fortune in comparison look like a piggy bank. The decentralized nature of Murray's hold-

[1] The following biographical sketch is based upon an interview with Senator Murray, July 9, 1946; also, upon Dorothy M. Thayer, "New Faces in the Senate," Washington *Post*, Nov. 23, 1934; an N.A.N.A. release from Butte, Montana, which appeared in the Washington *Star*, Nov. 27, 1934; "Murray of Montana," *The Nation*, Oct. 10, 1942, pp. 332-333; and Forest Davis, "Millionaire Moses," *The Saturday Evening Post*, Dec. 8, 1945, pp. 9 ff.

ings and the empire character of firms like Anaconda and Clark help to explain the fact that Murray has always identified himself with small business. In relation to the powers he fought in his home state, Murray always *has* been in small business.

Until 1930, when Murray was elected Democratic Chairman of Silver Bow County, his only experience in politics had been a two-year stint as a county prosecutor, in 1906–1908. The story is that he refused a second term because he disliked prosecution of capital offenses. In 1932, Murray helped line up state delegates for Roosevelt, and in 1934 in a complicated political tangle following the death in office of Senator Thomas J. Walsh, Murray was elected by a large majority to the United States Senate. His militant liberal record in the Senate did not begin until 1938 when the combination of the recession of 1937 and his intra-party fight with his Montana colleague, Senator Wheeler, seemed to galvanize him into action for the Roosevelt New Deal cause. In recent years, Murray has probably sponsored more far-reaching social legislation than any other Senator on Capitol Hill. Since 1943 he has sponsored major bills concerned with national health, social security, aid to education, aid to small business, minimum wages, Missouri Valley Authority, and full employment.

Murray's liberal philosophy, although delayed in its overt manifestations, is the product of a lifetime. When asked about such matters today, he recalls a variety of conditioning experiences: watching the change that overtook Butte, Montana, when Anaconda Copper made it into a company town—a change, he says, from "self-respect to serfdom"; seeing militia, before World War I, riding in ore cars back of his house on their way to break a strike in the mines (Murray had worked briefly in one of his uncle's mines years before, and had learned to appreciate the problems of the mine workers); losing heavily in the crash of 1929, and becoming acquainted with the financial power of what he still calls "Wall Street."

But other men have gone through similar experiences, and have not been drawn into an active fight for the little man. Congenitally or somewhere along the line Murray was endowed with an unusually sensitive social conscience which in the last few years has developed into an almost messianic fervor for social justice. His world is a world of light and darkness with the powers of evil symbolized by big business. During the recession of the late thirties,

Murray epitomized his own feelings about monopoly, industry, and finance in a radio address called "Economic Security and Justice":

> . . . the collapse of 1929 was due to a whole train of violations of economic rules, which industry and finance in a mad and greedy rush for profits had failed to adhere to. . . .
> The monopoly fixation of prices is shown to be a major cause of the present (1937) recession, as well as in the 1929 depression. . . .
> While the government was engaged in priming the pump with a national public works and work relief program involving the expenditure of billions of dollars, they [big business] were engaged in skimming the cream off the government spending. They ran up prices to increase profits. . . .
> Industry has been over-anxious for profit and simply prices itself out of business. It failed to cooperate in the national program of recovery and thereby contributed to its own distress and injury as well as bringing renewed misery to the country in the way of increased unemployment.[2]

His philosophy has not changed.

Murray's receptivity to the Farmers Union proposal in August, 1944, can be understood only in terms of three interrelated beliefs arising from his social philosophy: (1) that we need big government to cope with big business; (2) that federal legislation can go a long way toward correcting the evils of society; and (3) that the reconversion legislation with which he was forced to deal as chairman of the War Contracts Subcommittee did not go to the heart of the postwar problem.

In all these views, Murray was aided and abetted by large committee staffs which he had built up during the war to assist him with his legislative program. Off and on during 1944–45, he had approximately seventy-five staff assistants and secretaries working for him and his committees.[3] Most of these assistants had been borrowed on a temporary basis from executive agencies and departments, and, as we shall have reason to notice, a few of them became of central importance in the history of the Full Employment Bill.

[2] "Economic Security and Justice," radio address by Hon. James E. Murray of Montana, March 18, 1938 (reprint from the *Congressional Record*, 75th Cong., 3d Sess., April 7, 1938).

[3] Murray was chairman of the Special Senate Committee on Small Business, chairman of the War Contracts Subcommittee of the Senate Military Affairs Committee, and chairman of the Senate Education and Labor Committee. For a detailed (though incomplete) breakdown of his various staffs, see the *Congressional Record*, 79th Cong., 2d Sess., April 1, 1946, especially pp. 2928–2936.

It is important to recognize, however, that the basic policy decisions which led up to the writing and introduction of the Full Employment Bill were Murray's. Fundamentally, it was his spark of will which transformed an idea into a specific legislative proposal.

## THE ELECTION OF 1944

While the reactions of Executive agencies and departments to the National Farmers Union amendment were being prepared and returned to Senator Murray in September and October of 1944, the nation as a whole was undergoing the dizzying experience of a Presidential election. President Roosevelt had set the tone for a debate on domestic issues in his message to Congress the previous January. Following the lead of the National Resources Planning Board, Roosevelt proclaimed objectives for postwar America in a new Bill of Rights which began with "the right to a useful and remunerative job in the industries or shops or farms or mines of the nation." [4] Actually, the year before in his State of the Union Message Roosevelt had said, referring to veterans, "They will have the right to expect full employment—full employment for themselves and for all able-bodied men and women in America who want to work." [5] With these precedents, the Democratic National Convention in 1944 adopted a platform which began with the words: "The Democratic Party stands on its record in peace and in war. To speed victory, establish and maintain peace, *guarantee full employment* and provide prosperity. . . ." [6]

If the Democrats were looking for a clear-cut fight on the full employment issue, however, they were to be disappointed. The Republican Party platform was not as forthright as the Democratic in "guaranteeing" full employment, and it rejected "the theory of restoring prosperity through government spending and deficit financing"; but the cautious words, "we shall promote the fullest stable employment through private enterprise" [7] came close to implying an identity of goals between the two parties. As the campaign progressed during the summer and fall, the tweedle-dee tweedle-dum character of party stands on the postwar employment issue

[4] Quoted in U.S. Senate, "Building the Postwar Economy," *From the Year-End Report of the War Contracts Subcommittee to the Committee on Military Affairs*, Senate Subcommittee Print No. 12A, 78th Cong., 2d Sess. (Washington, 1945), p. 2.
[5] New York *Times*, Jan. 8, 1943, p. 12.      [6] *Ibid.*, July 21, 1944, p. 12.
[7] *Ibid.*, June 28, 1944, p. 14.

became even more obvious. No one of course could have been expected to endorse a program of postwar depression. The question boiled down to the nature of the government's obligation in the field of employment policy. Mr. Dewey in his Seattle and San Francisco speeches seemed to adopt an unequivocal position: [8]

We must have full employment. . . . The allout peacetime effort of your next administration will be to encourage business, both large and small, to create jobs and opportunity. We shall establish conditions which will make it not only possible but good business for management to join hands with the great free labor movement of this country in bringing about full employment at high wages. . . . Those who come home from the war—all our people—have earned a future with jobs for all.[9]

Government's first job in the peacetime years ahead will be to see that conditions exist which promote widespread job opportunities in private enterprise. . . . If at any time there are not sufficient jobs in private enterprise to go around, the government can and must create job opportunities, because there must be jobs for all in this country of ours . . . if there is one thing we are all agreed upon, it is that in the coming peacetime years we in this country must have jobs and opportunity for all. That is everybody's business. Therefore it is the business of government.[10]

Dewey's emphasis on the government's obligation to create necessary jobs forced the strategists of the Democratic Party to urge Roosevelt to deliver at least one important speech on domestic problems. It is true that Wallace had discussed the full employment issue in some of his campaign and precampaign addresses [11] and that the President had alluded to postwar employment in his famous Teamster's speech,[12] but until Dewey forced the issue, the Demo-

---

[8] In his acceptance speech at the Republican National Convention on June 28, 1944, Dewey had stated, "We Republicans are agreed that full employment shall be a first objective of national policy. And by full employment I mean a real chance for every man and woman to earn a decent living." New York *Times*, June 29, 1944, p. 10.

[9] New York *Times*, Sept. 19, 1944, p. 15.          [10] *Ibid.*, Sept. 22, 1944, p. 13.

[11] See particularly Wallace's Jackson Day and Lincoln Day addresses and his "Broadcast to the Little Businessmen of the Nation," reprinted in his *Democracy Reborn* (New York, 1944), pp. 253–268. See also his New York speech on September 21, 1944, New York *Times*, Sept. 22, 1944, p. 12.

[12] "And I know that they [the American people] can sustain a national income that will assure full production and full employment under our democratic system of private enterprise, with government encouragement and aid whenever and wherever that is necessary." New York *Times*, Sept. 24, 1944, p.26.

crats had attempted to place their major campaign emphasis upon Roosevelt as war leader.

On October 28, Roosevelt spoke in Chicago. The speech originally rough-drafted for him for that occasion was a relatively detailed outline of the federal government's responsibility for maintaining full employment after the war, and included specific programs of federal action. Roosevelt liked the draft, but felt that it was too controversial and too specific for a campaign address. The draft was scrapped with the exception of a few provocative lines:

> To assure the full realization of the right to a useful and remunerative employment, an adequate program must, and if I have anything to do about it, will, provide America with close to 60 million productive jobs. . . .
>
> I foresee an expansion of our peacetime productive capacity that will require new facilities, new plants, new equipment—capable of hiring millions of men. . . .
>
> If anyone feels that my faith in our ability to provide sixty million peacetime jobs is fantastic, let him remember that some people said the same thing about my demand in 1940 for fifty thousand airplanes.[13]

It is interesting to speculate what the public reaction would have been to the *original* draft of the Chicago speech. Four months later, in February, 1945, that discarded draft in the guise of original testimony was made available to the public through Henry Wallace, who was fighting for Senate confirmation of his nomination to the post of Secretary of Commerce. To this we shall have reason to return.

The election emphasis upon postwar jobs had the double effect of headlining the full employment issue and of convincing Senator Murray that the time was ripe for policy action in Congress. Even granting the extravagance of election promises, positive federal action in the field of postwar employment planning seemed to come as close to a bipartisan mandate as any issue in the 1944 campaign.

### AGENCY COMMENTS ON THE PATTON AMENDMENT

During September and October, 1944, comments on the Patton amendment dribbled in from the various government agencies. Most of the comments were favorable to the principle that some sort

---

[13] New York *Times*, Oct. 29, 1944, p. 34.

of federal action was needed, but various objections were raised to the Farmers Union "guaranteed investment" approach. The Secretary of Agriculture, for instance, felt that too much emphasis was placed on investment expenditures and too little on "expenditures for social services such as education, rural hospitals, and public health." He also felt that the $40 billion figure was too rigid, since "the amount of savings at full employment will differ with the price level, the total population, the tax structure in effect at the time, and possibly the changing habits of the population." He also questioned limiting loan-making to the Reconstruction Finance Corporation and mentioned the possibility of the Smaller War Plants Corporation making loans to small business.[14]

Mr. Hines of the Veterans Administration questioned the ability of the Joint Committee on Internal Revenue Taxation to predict prospective savings and felt that a sounder economy might be built upon voluntary investment of capital savings rather than upon forced taxation for the purpose of public undertakings.[15]

D. W. Bell, Acting Secretary of the Treasury, suggested that "there are so many factors upon which full employment depends that it is difficult to conclude that any single measure will be adequate." [16]

The eight other departments and agencies whose opinions were solicited by Senator Murray voiced these or similar doubts, but all of the comments from the Executive branch reflected a feeling of urgency for some kind of federal action in the field of postwar employment planning. The nature of the responses helped to convince Murray still further that action was needed, but it also reinforced his belief that the Farmers Union proposal was not necessarily the most satisfactory answer.

Immediately after the November election, Murray conferred with his War Contracts Subcommittee about the preparation of a Year-End Report. In these meetings, Murray asked Bertram Gross as subcommittee staff director to prepare a draft of a possible full employment bill which might be included initially as an appendix to the Subcommittee's Year-End Report and which later might be introduced as a new bill. It was agreed that the Patton amendment

14 National Farmers Union, "Reports of Executive Agencies on the Full Employment Proposal of the National Farmers Union," press release, Washington, Sept. 18, 1944, p. 1.
15 *Ibid.*, pp. 2–3.       16 *Ibid.*, p. 3.

would be used as a basis of discussion, but that a broader and politically more acceptable bill would be written. Time was short, for the Year-End Report had to be submitted by the middle of December—only a month away. Bertram Gross rolled up his sleeves and went to work.

### THE DRAFTING OF THE FULL EMPLOYMENT BILL

*The Drafters.*—Gross's first move was to call Russell Smith of the Farmers Union and tell him what was in the air. Through Smith and other contacts, Gross was able to organize an informal committee, the most faithful members of which were: Louis Bean, V. O. Key, and Gerhard Colm of the Budget Bureau; Emile Benoit-Smullyan, representing the views of John Pierson of the Bureau of Labor Statistics; Walter Salant of the O.P.A.; James Early, representing the views of Richard Gilbert of the O.P.A.; James Maddox of the Bureau of Agricultural Economics; Russell Smith of the National Farmers Union; and finally, Kurt Borchardt of the War Contracts Subcommittee staff.[17] With the exception of Smith and Borchardt, all these men were civil servants who were operating at the non-publicized, work-horse policy level of wartime administration. They all had a burning interest in postwar employment problems, and in terms of economic philosophy, they shared in the belief that the compensatory fiscal ideas stemming from the Keynes-Hansen analysis were basically sound.

On an average of twice a week from the middle of November to the middle of December, 1944, this group met with Gross on Capitol Hill and helped him mold a full employment bill. The drafting process was controlled by Gross. At the first meetings he explained the nature of the problem: the desire to draft a bill which would have the sweep of the Patton amendment but which would be more acceptable politically and would answer some of the criticisms which Murray had received from the Executive agencies and departments. In subsequent meetings, Gross submitted rough drafts and used the group as a sounding board. Out of the discussions came suggestions which were carefully weighed by Gross and often incorporated in later drafts. Between meetings Gross reworked his drafts with the aid of Charles Murphy of the Office of Legislative

---

[17] Other members of the committee included Daniel S. Gerig and Anne A. Scitovsky of the Social Security Board, and Collis Stacking of the War Manpower Commission.

Counsel. He also kept Senator Murray informed of developments, and solicited comments from people "around town" like Alvin Hansen and Leon Keyserling. Hansen's advice was sought for obvious reasons. Keyserling, who was at that time General Counsel of the National Housing Agency, had won second prize in the Pabst postwar employment essay contest. His essay had suggested certain relationships between the Executive branch and the Legislative branch of the federal government in the development of an economic program which Gross found suggestive.[18] Later on, in the summer of 1945, Keyserling became intimately associated with the redrafting of the Full Employment Bill, and throughout the full employment fight, he acted unofficially as an advisor to Senator Wagner and the Banking and Currency Committee staff.

*Stylistic Strategy.*—In preparing a bill on any controversial national issue there are certain governing rules of strategy. By far the most important is that a bill must be made to appeal to the widest possible group of potential supporters. This may seem axiomatic, but it is so axiomatic that it is often forgotten.

In this connection, the breadth of support a bill can claim in Congress is often in direct ratio to its viability as a symbol. It is for this reason that the early decision of Gross and the drafting committee to adopt as a draft title "The Full Employment Act of 1945" was of major significance. The term "full employment" was to cause the proponets of the bill numerous headaches and tactical defeats in the year ahead, but the early drafters found it hard to imagine public opinion, pressure opinion, and Congressional opinion mobilizing around a "Federal Employment and Production Bill" or a "High Level Employment and Stabilization Bill."

How conscious the drafters of the Full Employment Bill were of this problem of style can be judged also by glancing at the opening words of the Patton amendment and then at the beginning clause of the first printed draft of the new bill. The Patton amendment stated dryly,

18 Specifically, Keyserling emphasized that planning and the development of economic policies had to be a joint Executive-Legislative affair. He suggested a continuing "American Economic Committee" to be established along the general lines of the T.N.E.C. with representatives from the House, the Senate, and the Presidential Cabinet, and with additional representatives appointed from industry, agriculture, and labor. See Fitch and Taylor, *Planning for Jobs* (Philadelphia, 1946), pp. 430–443.

In order that there shall be full employment and full production through provision of means for private enterprisers to plan their capital outlays and through provision of means of productive investment of the savings of the people. . . .[19]

The new bill began,

The Congress hereby declares that every American able to work and willing to work has the right to a useful and remunerative job in the industries, or shops, or offices, or farms, or mines of the nation.[20]

These words of Roosevelt had a familiar, and to many, an inspiring ring.

*The Substantive Debate over "Spending."*—If the Patton amendment was cold, it was also rigid in its economic approach. Its concentration on federal investment and the arbitrary figure of $40 billion as the guaranteed annual level of investment were immediately challenged. Although the weight of opinion among the participating economists in the drafting committee was on the side of compensatory federal spending, there were minor differences as to whether the spending should be solely for investment and whether spending alone was a sufficient answer to the unemployment problem. Some argued that although the government could tinker with the economic system through changes in tax laws, discount rates, social security laws, anti-trust laws, and the rest, in the last analysis the only real guarantor of full employment was government spending; so why not call a spade a spade? Others agreed, but claimed that raising purchasing power directly by tax rebates or "food stamp" plans was far better than spending federal money on public works.[21] Still others felt that the entire tool kit of private industry and the government should be used to combat depressions and that spending should be considered only as a necessary last resort. Partly for political reasons, this last suggestion was adopted.

Some people close to the situation are still of the belief that every-

[19] National Farmers Union, press release, Aug. 7, 1944.

[20] U.S. Senate, "A Bill to Establish a National Policy and Program for Assuring Continuing Full Employment," Senate Committee on Military Affairs, Subcommittee Print No. 1, 78th Cong., 2d Sess., Dec. 18, 1944.

[21] The main protagonist for the position that the government's chief responsibility should be to underwrite private consumption was John Pierson of the Bureau of Labor Statistics, who made his position known to the drafters through Emile Benoit-Smullyan. Pierson was one of the pioneers in seeing the implications of Keynesian thinking for an integrated federal full employment policy. See particularly his book, *Full Employment* (New Haven, 1941). See Alvin Hansen, *Economic Policy and Full Employment* (New York, 1947), p. 197, for an attack on the "consumption" school.

thing in the original bill except the spending provisions was window dressing.[22] Both Senator Murray and Gross hotly dissent, however, claiming that the non-spending provisions of the bill and the emphasis on the initial responsibilities of private enterprise were sincere reflections of Murray's own thinking. It is difficult to analyze motivation in retrospect, but it is perhaps some indication of the importance which Murray and Gross originally placed on spending that the only anti-unemployment device which was spelled out in detail in the bill was a federal compensatory fiscal policy. All other government activities were alluded to in the "basket clause" referred to in Chapter II:

Such program may include, but need not be limited to a presentation of current and projected Federal policies and activities with reference to banking and currency, monopoly and competition, wages and working conditions, foreign trade and investment, agriculture, taxation, social security, the development of natural resources, and in such other topics as may directly or indirectly affect the level of non-Federal investment and other expenditures.[23]

It is perhaps of further significance that the following clause appeared in the printed draft: "There are hereby authorized to be appropriated such sums as may be necessary to eliminate any deficiency in the National Budget." [24] This authorization clause was dropped before the bill was introduced, but its place in the original draft is not without interest. There is no question that the drafters of the Full Employment Bill edged away from the bald spending plan of the Farmers Union proposal. But it seems equally obvious that they retained a healthy respect for the Patton amendment's underlying theory.

*Technical Jargon.*—In the technical sections of the early drafts of the Full Employment Bill, the heavy hand of the professional economist is readily observable. Under Title IV (the National Production and Employment Budget) of the December 18, 1944, print, sections may be picked almost at random to illustrate this point. For instance, Section (c) reads in part:

To the extent that such increased non-Federal investment and other expenditure as may be expected to result from actions taken under the program set forth in accordance with (b) of this section are insufficient

[22] This is certainly the position of Alvin Hansen (interview, Cambridge, Mass., February 25, 1946).
[23] S.380, 79th Cong., 1st Sess., Jan. 22, 1945, Sec. 3(b).
[24] Senate Committee on Military Affairs, Subcommittee Print No. 1.

to provide a full employment volume of the gross national product, the President shall include, in the Budget transmitted in accordance with section 201 of the Budget and Accounting Act of 1921, as amended, a general program of such Federal investment and other expenditure as will be sufficient to bring the aggregate volume of investment and other expenditure by private business, consumers, State and local government, and the Federal Government, up to the level required to assure a full employment volume of the gross national product.[25]

To the trained economist this type of language is readily intelligible, although professional differences of opinion have existed about the precise meaning of terms like "gross national product." To the skeptical politician, however, a passage of this sort might have seemed like intentional obfuscation, especially when compared with the dramatic, if ambiguous, language in the bill's opening declaration of policy. An interesting part of the bill's legislative history is the extent to which this technical jargon was simplified or abolished. The drafting economists were vaguely conscious of the political limitations of their technical language, for they appended to their draft a section on definitions. It is hard not to wonder, however, how lay readers must have reacted to the definition of gross national product as "the gross national production of goods and services, as calculated by the Department of Commerce." [26]

*Defining Full Employment.*—We have suggested earlier that the use of the term "full employment" in the title of the new bill was fundamentally a political device. We have also suggested that the use of the term caused almost as many headaches as it prevented. Certainly the central issue was the not-so-simple matter of definition. Like "gross national product," "full employment" as a technical economic term has been a point of friction among professional economists.

Sir William Beveridge, whose book *Full Employment in a Free Society* had appeared too late to have any direct effect on the drafting of the American bill, defined the phrase as meaning "always more vacant jobs than unemployed men . . . the jobs at fair wages, of such a kind, and so located that the unemployed men can reasonably be expected to take them." [27] The logic of Beveridge's definition, as the distinguished Englishman well knew, was possible

[25] *Ibid.*                    [26] *Ibid.*, Sec. 10.
[27] William H. Beveridge, *Full Employment in a Free Society* (New York, 1945), p. 18.

government control over the location of new industry, over the mobility of labor, over the use of investment funds, and perhaps over prices and wages.

The drafters of the Full Employment Bill never conceived of "full employment" as meaning that no unemployment would ever exist, or that there would always be, in Beveridge's phrase, "more vacant jobs than unemployed men." They believed that capitalism required a certain flexibility in its labor market and that full employment for the entire labor force at all times could be achieved only under a system of forced work. Both Germany and Russia during the thirties, and England (and, to a modified extent, America) during the war had virtually succeeded in abolishing unemployment by using the sanctions of government to freeze industrial labor in particular jobs. This as a peacetime arrangement would hardly have been acceptable to a majority of Americans.

But since the drafters agreed that "full employment" did not mean *full* employment, they were forced to try to work out a definition which would be politically acceptable and reasonably unambiguous. This turned out to be impossible. In the December 18, 1944, draft, "full employment" was defined as:

. . . a condition in which the number of persons able to work, lacking work, and seeking work, shall be no greater than the number of unfilled opportunities to work, at locally prevailing wages and working conditions for the type of work available, and not below minimum standards required by law, and in which the amount of frictional unemployment, including seasonal and technological unemployment, and other transitional and temporary unemployment is no greater than the minimum needed to preserve adequate flexibility in the economy.

Not only was this definition cumbersome, it glossed over a whole series of problems and disagreements. What sense would "full employment" make to an unemployed worker in New York when job opportunities existed only in Seattle? By what standards was the labor force to be judged? Who would decide when "frictional" unemployment had become large enough to be considered pathological? And what would be the criteria for judging "adequate flexibility in the economy"?

There are few political slogans which are amenable to unambiguous definition.

*Governmental Mechanisms: Economic Analysis and Planning Initiative.*—It will be remembered that the Patton amendment placed the major responsibility for analyzing economic conditions in an existing Joint Committee of Congress.[28] The drafters of the new bill were unanimous in agreement that the analysis of economic conditions and the planning initiative for a full employment program should be the responsibility of the President rather than of Congress. Furthermore, it was agreed that that part of the Executive Branch best equipped to help the President handle such duties was the Bureau of the Budget. In the first place it was a part of the Executive Office of the President and would therefore not be subject, the drafters felt, to departmental myopia. More important, perhaps, the Bureau seemed to be unusually well equipped to undertake these new responsibilities because of its past interest in the full employment problem, because of the very nature of the work of its staff in correlating budgetary data, and because of the fact that, through its Fiscal, Legislative Reference, and Administrative Management divisions, it was committed to a bird's-eye view of the total governmental program.

At the time, such an arrangement seemed appealing to the drafters for another reason. The Bureau of the Budget had been originally created by Congress. It was "respectable." The path of the Full Employment Bill might be eased, it was reasoned, by attaching it institutionally and semantically to the budgetary concept. To talk of a "National Production and Employment Budget" smacked of bookkeeping, accounting, conservative business procedures. At one point the drafters even toyed with the idea of counteracting the evil connotations of "Federal Investment and Expenditures" by adopting the felicitous expression "balancing the *National* Budget." [29]

Tied in with the concept of Executive planning was the idea of Executive discretion in adjusting the rate of federal expenditures "necessary for the purpose of assuring continuing full employment." Changing business conditions, the drafters felt, needed a type of flexible stabilization program which Congress was hardly equipped to handle. Provision was therefore made in the bill for

[28] The Joint Committee on Internal Revenue Taxation. See above, p. 24.
[29] This phrase is actually used in the *Year-End Report of the War Contracts Subcommittee*. See "Building the Postwar Economy," p. 6.

Presidential discretion in varying the rate of federal expenditures
to meet changing employment conditions.[30]

Many modifications were to be made in the sections of S.380 dealing with the responsibilities and institutional mechanisms of the
Executive branch. It is important, however, to note at this point
that the original draft of the bill was framed as an amendment to
the Budget and Accounting Act of 1921. This was to have an important impact on subsequent legislative strategy.

*Government Mechanisms: the Role of Congress.*—One of the
limitations on the effectiveness of the National Resources Planning
Board had been the fact that its reports were unilateral declarations of government goals. Congress had had no participating interest in the formulation of these goals and tended to resent the
cloistered nature of N.R.P.B.'s operations. Since the basic policy
decisions to implement a full employment program under the proposed bill would have to be taken by Congress, the drafters took
the view that Congressional participation in policy formulation
and review should be institutionalized.

The device proposed, a Joint Committee on the Budget which
would have the responsibility of making "a detailed study of the
information and estimates transmitted to Congress by the President" and of reporting to both Houses of Congress "its findings
and recommendations on the national budget," [31] was in part a
carry-over from early drafts of the George-Murray Reconversion
Bill. The preceding June, Bertram Gross had prepared a subcommittee print of the George-Murray bill which provided for a "Special Joint Committee on Post-war Adjustment" made up of four
members from each House.[32] Between this special committee and
an Office of War Mobilization and Postwar Adjustment in the
Executive Offices of the President a relationship was projected that
was quite similar in outline to the pattern suggested later in the
early drafts of the Full Employment Bill. In the latter case, however, one significant addition was made. In order to place clear responsibility on the Joint Committee, a suggestion was made that
the proposed committee should report out a joint resolution
"setting forth for the ensuing fiscal year a general policy on the total

[30] Senate Committee on Military Affairs, Subcommittee Print No. 1, Sec. 6.
[31] *Ibid.*, Sec. 4.
[32] Actually, these provisions in the O.W.M.R. Bill were passed by the Senate in
August, 1944, and knocked out later by the House.

volume of federal expenditures and other revenue, and the volume of borrowings or net debt retirement, for the purpose of serving as a guide to the individual committees of Congress dealing with such subjects." [33]

Some of the drafters saw both the Congressional Joint Committee on the Budget and the proposed extension of Budget Bureau responsibility in the field of economic planning and policy integration as instruments of potential reform which might ramify into the entire pattern of government operations, increasing efficiency and clarifying political responsibility and accountability.

Details concerning the exact membership and the specific functions of the Joint Committee changed frequently during the history of S.380, but the idea of the original drafters that such a committee should be established was never seriously questioned.

*Summary of the Drafting Process.*—By December 11, 1944, Bertram Gross felt justified in having a confidential subcommittee print of the new bill run off. In a month of enthusiastic discussion, members of the drafting committee had succeeded in compromising their minor differences to produce a draft which seemed to them to include the basic features of a workable Full Employment Bill. Feeling their way, they had dramatized policy goals, formulated an economic program, and outlined planning and operational mechanisms. They had drawn ideas from the complexities of economic theory and past governmental experience, and they had added that essential element of creative imagination without which new concepts are impossible. For good or for ill, they had given form to a policy proposal which could now be subjected to the rough gantlet of political and public debate.

THE YEAR-END REPORT OF THE WAR CONTRACTS SUBCOMMITTEE

On December 18, 1944, Senator Murray submitted to the Senate Committee on Military Affairs a *Year-End Report* entitled "Legislation for Reconversion and Full Employment." [34] This report was also "signed" by Senator Harry Truman, although Truman did not have a chance to read it before it was issued.[35]

[33] Senate Committee on Military Affairs, Subcommittee Print No. 1, Sec. 4(b)2.

[34] U.S. Senate, "Legislation for Reconversion and Full Employment," *Year-End Report of the War Contracts Subcommittee to the Committee on Military Affairs,* Senate Subcommittee Print No. 12, Dec. 18, 1944 (Washington, 1945).

[35] This is a common practice "among friends." Truman was out of town on this

The *Year-End Report* was a major landmark in the history of the Full Employment Bill. Not only did it include the first public printing of the proposed bill, it spelled out in detail why, in the mind of its sponsor, Senator Murray, such a bill was necessary. The report pointed to the "inadequacy of existing post-war legislation" and stated that "as measured against the background of our economic needs, the post-war laws that have been enacted add up to very little." It continued:

The balance sheet shows that the 78th Congress never came to grips with the problem of providing an economic substitute for war production. . . .

As yet, unfortunately, we do not have in America an adequate program to provide 60 million productive jobs. Nor will such a program develop out of thin air. The right to a job is not self-enforceable. It can be translated into reality only through the joint action of the people of our country—business, labor, agriculture, and all other groups—acting through the medium of their duly elected government. In short, the so-called right to a job is a meaningless figure of speech unless our government assumes responsibility for the expansion of our peacetime economy so that it will be capable of assuring full employment.[36]

The subcommittee report outlined what it conceived to be the federal government's responsibility in the field of postwar employment and appended the Full Employment Bill draft. In introducing the new bill, the report stated:

Your subcommittee has not had sufficient time to make a complete study of this new bill and there is not time to make such a study during the remainder of this session. However, the bill is transmitted herewith, without commitment, for the purpose of stimulating discussion. Your subcommittee believes that it raises challenging problems concerning the economic future of our country and that the central concept of balancing our National Budget by providing full employment merits the most careful analysis by the committee and the general public.[37]

The *Year-End Report* started a wave of newspaper comment. With the exception of *PM,* the *Chicago Sun,* and a few other consistently liberal journals, the press was generally hostile. Editorially, the *New York Times,*[38] the *Wall Street Journal,*[39] and the *Journal of Commerce*[40] condemned the bill as a deficit financing measure

occasion and his secretary authorized his signature. Truman, of course, had followed with close interest much of the earlier work of the War Contracts Subcommittee staff.
[36] *Year-End Report,* pp. 11–12. [37] *Ibid.,* p. 15.
[38] Dec. 23, 1944, p. 12. [39] Dec. 19, 1944. [40] Jan. 2, 1945.

and as leading toward the type of gradual collectivism which Mr. Hayek had challenged in his *Road to Serfdom*.[41] Since Hayek's book had come to be a type of conservative Bible by the end of 1944, Senator Murray took special pains to send letters of rebuttal to the leading conservative journals in which he quoted from Hayek about the legitimate sphere of government in economic life.[42] But the sharp reaction of the conservative press to the first public print of the Full Employment Bill was a harbinger of the general business hostility which was to face the bill all through its tortuous history.

The first official comment on the *Year-End Report* and proposed bill came in a speech by Henry Wallace before the American Statistical Association on December 22, 1944. Murray had submitted a page proof of the first confidential subcommittee print to Wallace as early as December 9, and Louis Bean was instrumental in getting Wallace to choose "Full Employment" as the topic for his address. Actually, Bean and Gross helped draft Wallace's speech. As might be expected, the speech was a ringing endorsement of the bill.

### THE STRATEGY OF CO-SPONSORSHIP

As soon as the first session of the 79th Congress opened, Senator Murray set to work to line up co-sponsors for his bill. His immediate choice of Senator Robert Wagner of New York and Senator Elbert Thomas of Utah is readily understandable. Both Senators had long and distinguished liberal records in and out of Congress. Their names would attract strong liberal support, and their enthusiasm for the bill would mean their willingness to contribute substantial time and effort to the legislative fight. The fact that they also happened to be chairmen of powerful Senate committees was an additional strategic consideration. Gross wanted to make sure that the Kilgore staff would not introduce a substitute full employment bill. By Murray's lining up Wagner and Thomas, Murray and Gross took out insurance against competition. The only committees to which the Kilgore staff might have referred a substitute bill with any hope of friendly consideration were the committees chaired by Murray, Wagner, and Thomas.

Murray's attempt to solicit the support of Senator O'Mahoney of Wyoming presents a slightly more complicated motivation. It is

[41] Friedrich A. Hayek (Chicago, 1944), *passim*.
[42] See, for instance, the New York *Times*, Jan. 6, 1945, p. 10.

dangerous to speculate about motives, but it seems fairly obvious that Murray's interest in O'Mahoney stemmed in part from a belief that the latter's support would give the bill a certain amount of "respectability." It was clear that the bill could not hope for success if its support came only from traditionally liberal and labor groups. O'Mahoney had the double advantage of being known among his colleagues as an independent, middle-of-the-road Democrat, and of having a reputation, following his chairmanship of the T.N.E.C., of knowing more economics than anyone else on Capitol Hill.

Murray approached O'Mahoney through Dewey Anderson. Anderson, who was about to become staff director of Murray's Small Business Committee, had previously served as Executive Secretary of the T.N.E.C. where he had worked closely with O'Mahoney. Anderson, at Murray's request, saw O'Mahoney and tried to sell him on the idea of co-sponsoring the bill. The Senator's initial reaction was strongly negative. It was not until Anderson and Murray had promised O'Mahoney virtually a free hand in rewriting certain sections of the bill, and had convinced him of the tentative nature of the extant draft, that the Wyoming Senator was willing to cooperate.

If it is true that Murray's interest in O'Mahoney was dominated by considerations of long-term political strategy, the Senator from Montana could hardly have made a better choice. As we shall see, in O'Mahoney's testimony before the Banking and Currency Committee and in his speech in the Senate during the floor debate, he probably did more than any other Senator to arouse support for S.380 in the Upper House.

### DRAFT REVISIONS

Lord Macaulay once said in referring to currency reforms in the reign of William III, "It would be interesting to see how the pure gold of scientific truth found by the two philosophers was mingled by the two statesmen with just that quantity of alloy which was necessary for the working." [43] Between January 8 and January 22, 1945, the Full Employment Bill went through seven revised drafts which represented the meeting of minds of the "philosophers" and the "statesmen."

[43] Quoted in E. H. Hankin, *The Mental Limitations of the Expert* (India: Butterworth & Co., Ltd., 1921), p. 27.

Gross, representing the original drafters, met with the bill's sponsors in a series of meetings for the purpose of improving the bill's substance and style. In each new draft, the impact of the political mind is clearly noticeable. It would be unnecessarily tedious to trace every change reflected in each of the revised drafts, but a comparison of the December 18 print with the bill as introduced on January 22 provides a wealth of examples of the impact of the political mind on policy formulation. Consider the following (emphasis supplied):

| *Subcommittee Print No. 1*<br>*December 18, 1944* | *The Bill as Introduced*<br>*January 22, 1945* |
| --- | --- |
| Sec. 2(a) [Opening declaration of policy] "Every American able to work and *willing to work* has the right to a useful and remunerative job in the industries or shops or offices or farms or mines of the nation." | Sec. 2(a) [Opening declaration of policy] "It is the policy of the United States to foster free competitive enterprise . . ." ("Right to work" relegated to second place and changed to: "All Americans able to work and *seeking work* have the right to . . .") |
| Sec. 2(b) "It is the *responsibility* of the Government to *guarantee* that right by assuring continuing *full employment*. | Sec. 2(b) ". . . it is the *policy* of the United States to *assure* the existence at all times of *sufficient employment opportunities* . . ." |
| | Sec. 2 (c) ". . . In order to carry out the policies set forth in subsections (a) and (b) of this section, and in order to (1) promote the general welfare of the nation, (2) foster and protect the American home and the American family as the foundation of the American way of life, (3) raise the standard of living of the American people, (4) provide adequate employment opportunities for returning veterans, (5) contribute to the full utilization of our natural resources, (6) develop trade and commerce among the several states and with foreign nations, (7) preserve and strengthen competitive private enterprise, (8) strengthen the national defense and security, and (9) contribute to the establishment and maintenance of lasting peace among nations, it is essential that continuing full employment be maintained in the United States." |

Sec. 3 "The Budget and Accounting Act of 1921, as amended, is hereby amended . . ."

[No reference to Budget and Accounting Act. This omission represented the fear of the sponsors that too close a tie-in with the Budget Bureau might arouse the jealousies of the Departments—especially Treasury.]

[Referring to what should be included in the National Production and Employment Budget] (subsection I):
"The estimated number of jobs needed during the ensuing fiscal year or years to assure continuing full employment, and the estimated dollar volume of the gross national product, at the expected level of prices, required to provide such number of jobs."

[Referring to what should be included in the National Production and Employment Budget] (subsection I):
"The estimated size of labor force, including the self-employed in industry and agriculture."

The National Production and Employment Budget
Sec. 3(c) [Referring to federal investment program]:
"Such program shall be designed to contribute to the national wealth or well-being, and may include, but need not be limited to specific programs for assistance to business enterprises, particularly small business enterprises, for useful public works as tend to promote increased investment and other expenditure by private enterprises; for useful public services as tend to raise the level of health and education; for slum clearance and urban rehabilitation; for conservation and development of natural resources; and for rural electrification. . . ."

The National Production and Employment Budget
Sec. 3(c) [Referring to federal investment program]:
"Such program shall be designed to contribute to the national wealth and well-being, and to stimulate additional non-Federal investment and expenditure."

Sec. 3(d) If survey of conditions warrant it, "the President shall set forth in such budget a general program for preventing *inflationary* dislocations. . . ."

Sec. 5 "There are hereby authorized to be appropriated such sums as may be necessary to eliminate any deficiency in the National Budget."

Sec. 8(d) ". . . the carrying out of, or any appropriations for, any program set forth in the National Budget [is not authorized] unless such program shall have been authorized by provision of law other than this act."

Sec. 10 Definitions of "Full Employment," "gross national product," and
"Federal investment and other expenditure."

[No definitions appended, although in
Sec. 2(b) an attempt is made to define
the labor force as] ". . . all Americans
who have finished their schooling and
who do not have full-time housekeeping responsibilities . . ."

This comparison is by no means exhaustive, but it does perhaps
indicate the extent and nature of draft revision at the hands of the
bill's sponsors. They were obviously concerned with broadening
the appeal of the bill and deleting those sections of the early draft
which might have stimulated violent opposition. This process annoyed some of the members of the original drafting committee who
felt that the bill was being hopelessly emasculated. The sponsors
knew, however, that when the chips were down they could count
on liberal support. The problem was how to gain necessary middle-
of-the-road and conservative support in and out of Congress. The
problem, in all fairness, was also how to bring the original draft
more closely in line with the considered opinions of its sponsors.

### THE INTRODUCTION OF THE FULL EMPLOYMENT BILL

On the afternoon of January 22, 1945, Senator James E. Murray
of Montana arose from his mahogany desk in the Senate chamber
and addressed his colleagues on behalf of himself, "the Senator from
New York, the Senator from Utah, [and] the Senator from Wyoming." [44] He introduced the Full Employment Bill, S.380, and
asked that it be printed in the body of the *Congressional Record*
along with a series of explanatory questions and answers. The latter
were to S.380 what the *Federalist Papers* were to the Constitution—
attempts to spell out the meaning of various sections and to allay
fears about the implication of the total program. There were twenty-
three questions asked and answered, ranging from such general issues as "Does the bill provide for a planned economy?" to "What is
the purpose of the joint resolution on the Budget?" Perhaps a typical example is number seven:

*Question:* Does the bill provide for deficit financing?
*Answer:* The bill provides a positive way for bringing about the
greatest possible activity on the part of business. This in turn would
make it possible to reduce government expenditures to a minimum.

[44] *Congressional Record,* 79th Cong., 1st Sess., Jan. 22, 1945, p. 377.

Therefore except in the most dire emergencies, the Government would
not have to step into the breach with a spending program.

Furthermore, Government spending does not necessarily mean "deficit financing." It is entirely possible for a Government-expenditure
program to be financed by money raised through taxes, rather than
through borrowing.[45]

This was hardly an unequivocal answer to the question, but in
politics there are often good and sufficient reasons for equivocation.

Senator Murray followed these insertions in the *Record* with a
five thousand word speech. He outlined past governmental action
in response to economic needs of the people, and indicated the
necessity of making our free enterprise system work. Carefully he
explained some of the major provisions of the bill and reaffirmed
the need for immediate action in the field of employment legislation. Both political parties, he pointed out, had supported the principle of full employment in the 1944 campaign. In a conciliatory,
humble, and politically shrewd conclusion, Senator Murray stressed
the need for constructive debate:

Of course some Members of Congress may disagree with the sponsors of
this bill. That is how it should be in a Democracy. Sound legislation can
be developed only by clarifying the differences between conflicting
schools of thought. The sponsors of this bill therefore welcome criticisms. We welcome debate on alternative methods of assuring post-war
full employment.[46]

The Senator from Montana was doubtless sincere, but one
wonders if he really sensed at this early date the basic cleavage in
American economic and political thought which the Full Employment Bill was to highlight in the ensuing months.

[45] *Congressional Record*, 79th Cong., 1st Sess., Jan. 22, 1945, p. 379.
[46] *Ibid.*, p. 383.

# The Staff in Room 15A

Once begin the dance of legislation, and you must struggle through its mazes as best you can to its breathless end,—if any end there be.—Wilson, *Congressional Government*, p. 297.

DURING the extensive hearings on the reorganization of Congress in 1945 much was said about the need for adequate staff assistance to Congressional committees and individual members. The growing complexity of government as a result of the economic and political changes of the past sixty years has made it impossible for the lay Congressional mind to deal adequately with the myriad technical problems of modern public law. T. Swann Harding has pointed out that

It is up to congressional committees and then to the Congress as a whole to grasp and decide upon the justice of appropriations for such projects as: The use of endocrines to increase egg production; the role of Johne's disease; coccidiosis and worm parasites in cattle production; the production of riboflavin from milk byproducts; spot treatment with soil fumigants for the control of root-knotnematode on melons; the use of mass releases of *Macrocentrus ancylivorus* to control oriental fruit moth injury; and the conversion of lactose into methyl acrylate to be polymerized with butadiene for the production of synthetic rubber.[1]

---

[1] T. Swann Harding, "The Marriage of Science to Government," *American Journal of Pharmacy*, Oct. 1944, reprinted in U.S. Congress, *Symposium on Congress by Members of Congress and Others*, Joint Committee Print, 79th Cong., 1st Sess. (Washington, 1945), p. 94.

To expect each member of Congress to be an expert in atomic science, international finance, labor relations, agricultural economics, public utilities, engineering, health, tariffs, monopolies, race relations, foreign affairs, social security, and the hundreds of other problems which make up the yearly legislative calendars, is of course to expect the impossible. When it is remembered that as high as 80 percent of the average member's time is spent on non-legislative work,[2] the question arises whether any Congressman can ever vote intelligently on anything. Even when a member attempts to specialize in some limited field of public law, he is literally swamped with tendentious and undigested information. As Roland Young has put it, "Congress is saturated with facts: briefs, petitions, testimony, witnesses, letters, pamphlets, reports, speeches—yet it does not have the time, the inclination, or the means to assimilate this barrage of material which is continually thrown at it." [3] When there is added to this confusion the burden of routine services which every member of Congress feels he must undertake for his constituents, it is perfectly obvious that Congress as a whole is woefully overburdened.

### GROWTH OF CONGRESSIONAL STAFF

Congress has had clerical and staff assistance of one sort or another for a long time. The first official appropriations for committee clerk service date back at least to the middle of the last century.[4] Most of the important standing committees had regular full-time staffs by the year 1900.[5] Clerk service for individual members who were not chairmen of committees was authorized from year to year during the latter half of the nineteenth century—although the amount of money allowed for such purpose was meagre.[6] The situation, as Lindsay Rogers has pointed out, changed rapidly in the first four decades of the twentieth century:

The annual clerk hire allowance for each Representative has been increased progressively since 1907 as follows: On July 1, 1907, from $1,200

[2] U.S. Senate, *Report of the Joint Committee on the Organization of Congress,* Senate Report No. 1011, 79th Cong., 2d Sess. (Washington, 1946), p. 15.

[3] Roland Young, *This Is Congress* (New York, 1943), p. 101.

[4] See Lindsay Rogers, "The Staffing of Congress," *Political Science Quarterly,* March, 1941 (reprinted in *Symposium on Congress,* especially p. 240, fn. 3).

[5] *Ibid.*

[6] Public Resolution 21, 52d Cong., 2d Sess., March 3, 1893, provided $1,200 for each member of the House for clerk hire.

to $1,500; July 1, 1917, from $1,500 to $2,000; July 1, 1919, from $2,000 to $3,200; July 1, 1924, from $3,200 to $4,000; July 1, 1929, from $4,000 to $5,000; and July 1, 1940, from $5,000 to $6,500.[7]

A similar increase has occurred in the Senate.

In the Legislative Appropriations Act for the fiscal year ending June 30, 1947, Congress provided nearly $7,000,000 for clerk hire to committees and individual legislators.[8]

Nothing could indicate more dramatically the mounting burden of Congressional work than this growth in the size of the staff— and even the official statistics do not tell the entire story. For years Congress has used and borrowed the staffs of Executive agencies. It is difficult to say how long this practice has been going on, but Senator Wherry in his testimony before the LaFollette committee states, "Almost every Senate committee has at some time had the services of experts and clerical assistants loaned them by Government departments. Some of these individuals often serve with Senate committees for months at a time. The practice of borrowing Government personnel is a long-standing one." [9] The war accelerated this tendency and by December, 1944, in the Senate alone there were approximately 100 persons on loan from 25 government agencies serving 14 standing and special committees.[10]

### STAFF FUNCTIONS

The overwhelming majority of clerks and other staff assistants in Congress have devoted their attention to routine matters. Committee clerks have been preoccupied with records, schedules of witnesses, clerical detail, and general housekeeping functions. Clerks assigned to individual members have performed perfunctory services for constituents, sorted mail, and handled day-to-day office routine. It is true, as we shall see, that some clerks, both at the member and committee level, have been given greater responsibilities in terms of substantive legislative activity; but the great majority have

7 "The Staffing of Congress," p. 239, fn. 2.

8 Public Law 479, 79th Cong., 2d Sess. The Legislative Reorganization Act of 1946 provided for a substantial increase in staff assistance to standing committees in both Houses. See Public Law 601, 79th Cong., 2d Sess., Sec. 202.

9 U.S. Congress, *Hearings before the Joint Committee on the Organization of Congress,* 79th Cong., 1st Sess., March 13 to June 29, 1945 (Washington, 1946), p. 168.

10 *Ibid.* This practice has been severely regulated by Sec. 202(f) of the Legislative Reorganization Act of 1946. For an attempt to stop this practice altogether, see S.R.77. 79th Cong., 1st Sess

been limited to what Edmund Burke called "mean and petty business." Lindsay Rogers, writing in 1941, estimated that only 200 of
the 3,200 clerks in Congress had tasks connected with the preparation and enactment of legislation.[11]

The war had an important effect upon staff activities in Congress.
Special and select committees established to investigate various
aspects of the war program relied heavily on borrowed and usually
temporary staff personnel. The quality of the men selected for this
work was of a calibre almost unknown previously on Capitol Hill
—except perhaps in the Joint Committee on Internal Revenue
Taxation, and in a few special committees like the LaFollette Civil
Liberties Committee and the T.N.E.C. Robert Lamb and Palmer
Weber for the Tolan Committee on Defense Migration; Hugh
Fulton for the Truman Committee on National Defense; George
Galloway for the LaFollette–Monroney Committee on the Organi-
zation of Congress; Dewey Anderson for the Senate Small Business
Committee; Joe McMurray for the Senate Labor and Education
Committee; Herbert Schimmel for the Kilgore Subcommittee on
War Mobilization; Bertram Gross and Kurt Borchardt for the War
Contracts Subcommittee, to name but a few, represented a new
emphasis on staff expertness in policy matters. At the beginning,
most of these men limited their activities to research, analysis, and
report writing. But as the war years progressed, some of them—
perhaps inevitably—became more and more engrossed in the
legislative implications of their research and the various strategic
factors in the legislative process. The increasing importance of
these staff assistants in the whole field of policy formulation is one
of the most significant developments in Congress in recent years
and deserves careful study and analysis. It is for this reason that we
now turn in some detail to the activities of Bertram Gross and the
other staff personnel who worked almost uninterruptedly during
1945 on the Full Employment Bill.

### THE FULL EMPLOYMENT STAFF

Room 15A is a dingy office on the subway floor of the Senate Office
Building. For over a year, prior to the introduction of the Full Em-
ployment Bill, it was the staff headquarters for the War Contracts
Subcommittee. We have seen in the preceding chapter how the

11 "The Staffing of Congress," p. 244.

activities of the War Contracts Subcommittee under the chairmanship of Senator Murray led directly to the drafting of S.380. We
have also seen the importance in this context of the staff functions
of Bertram Gross. Once the bill was introduced, it was only natural
that Gross should have been asked to continue work on full employment legislation, and when S.380 was referred to the Banking and
Currency Committee, Gross was transferred to that committee as
a special assistant to the chairman. Technically, Gross became responsible only to Senator Wagner who was chairman of the Banking
and Currency Committee, but at Senator Wagner's suggestion Gross
also continued to serve Murray and in one sense all other members
of Congress who were fighting for the passage of the Full Employment Bill. For fourteen months, Room 15A, as Gross's office, was
the nerve center of full employment activity on Capitol Hill.

The description which follows of the activities and accomplish-
ments of the staff gives little appreciation of the atmosphere which
pervaded Room 15A during the fourteen-month fight for S.380.
Telephones and typewriters competed for attention; a variety of
people wandered in and out for information or to converse with
the staff—lobbyists, newspapermen, interested citizens, clerks,
secretaries, Western Union messengers, pages, well-wishers, and job
seekers. Tables and shelves were piled high with reprints and documents and mimeographed material. Desks were cluttered with mail
and memoranda and carbons and big envelopes. Dominating the
scene from behind a screen at the rear of the room was Bertram
Gross.

Gross, who looks like a studious football player, turned out a
vast amount of work. He had spurts of interest in office organization, but his creative mind worked too fast to allow for much patience with administrative detail. From a telephone conversation he
turned to a memo; from a memo to a speech; from a speech to an
article; from an article to a series of letters; from letters to thought
about strategy; from strategy to a conversation with a visitor. And
few of these separate activities were carried through without inter-
ruption. Halfway through an article something he had written
would start a tangential train of thought and off he would go, dic-
tating a special memorandum or calling someone on the telephone.
He picked up loose ends by working late or taking unfinished material home.

Above all he was the spark plug of enthusiasm which fired the staff with a passionate zeal for the cause of full employment. The productivity of the staff—for good or ill—was the result of that zeal.

Gross's staff experience began in 1942, when he became Chief of Research and Hearings for the Senate Small Business Committee. This led him into a series of studies of the operations of the Smaller War Plants Corporation and of the procurement policies of the Army and Navy, which in turn led him, in the early months of 1943, into staff work for Senators Maloney and Taft on the Civilian Supply Bill of that year. His staff work for Taft helped to get the Civilian Supply Bill through the Senate, and although the bill never became law, the threat of legislation brought about a reorganization of the civilian supply functions of the War Production Board.

Gross's contacts with Senator Maloney had interesting repercussions. It was Gross who worked with Maloney in the preparation of the concurrent resolution which established a Joint Committee on the Organization of Congress.

We have already noted Gross's work on the War Contracts Subcommittee which he joined late in 1943. He had an important influence on the legislative history of the Contract Termination Bill, the Surplus Property Bill, and the Office of War Mobilization and Reconversion Bill. In August, 1946, six months after the Employment Act was passed, Gross was appointed assistant to Edwin G. Nourse, chairman of the President's Council of Economic Advisers.

For the first eight weeks after the introduction of S.380, Gross and his secretary, Miss Doris Phippen, were the only full-time occupants of Room 15A. Both of them were receiving salaries from the Navy Department under an arrangement originally worked out by Senator Murray for his War Contracts Subcommittee.[12] In the spring and summer of 1945, the Banking and Currency Committee borrowed additional staff from the executive agencies to assist Gross in his work on the Full Employment Bill. Senator Wagner requested and had made available to him personnel from the Reconstruction Finance Corporation, the Department of Labor, the Smaller War Plants Corporation, the Commerce Department, and O.P.A.

It is not easy in retrospect to impose any clear pattern on the variegated activities of the full employment staff during the long

12 *Congressional Record,* 79th Cong., 2d Sess., April 1, 1946, p. 2935.

fight for S.380. It is even more difficult to separate activities which stemmed directly from the creative minds of the staff, from those which were undertaken at the specific direction of the sponsors of the bill. There was nothing unusual in the formal relationship between Bertram Gross and Senator Wagner in the Banking and Currency Committee. It has been the standard practice for committee staffs to serve committee chairmen. What perhaps was unusual was the scope of initiative allowed Gross and his assistants in helping to plan and carry out the legislative campaign. In this sense, Gross was something of a *rara avis*. There was hardly a phase of the Full Employment Bill fight from the original drafting to final passage that Gross and his assistants failed to touch profoundly. To the details of this staff contribution we now turn.

### COLLECTION OF BASIC ECONOMIC DATA

No one who has dipped into the economic literature on employment policy can fail to recognize the technical complexities of the subject. One of the most significant contributions of the staff was the collection, analysis, and distribution of basic data about the background of full employment thinking in this and other countries. In the preparation of this material, Gross used all possible public and private resources: universities, private research organizations, the Legislative Reference Service, and many of the departments and agencies of the Executive branch.

Note some of these staff requests: to the Legislative Reference Service for a running bibliography of all recent books and articles on full employment and for "right to work" statements in the Constitutions of Brazil, Cuba, Estonia, Germany, Lichtenstein, Lithuania, Nicaragua, Paraguay, U.S.S.R., and Uruguay; to the Department of Labor for estimates of the postwar labor force, and for a study of the postwar employment survey made by the National Association of Manufacturers; to the Commerce Department for an explanatory statement on the background of the concept of Gross National Product, for a study of Sweden's full employment policy, and for a statement on the British reception of the White Paper on full employment; to the Department of Agriculture for the Secretary's opinion of certain amendments to S.380 offered by the Republican co-sponsors, and for a study of agriculture under conditions of full employment; to the Budget Bureau for an assembly of basic data on the experience of the past in respect to employment and production in the United States, and for a report on the extent to which the various statistical activities of the government now provided the basis for estimating future expenditures by consumers, business, and state and local governments, and what efforts were being made to develop a comprehensive system of estimating future expenditures.

One of the best examples of staff activity of this type was the preparation of a manual entitled "Basic Facts on Employment and Production." [13] The Budget Bureau with the assistance of the Census Bureau, the Bureau of Labor Statistics, the Bureau of Agricultural Economics, the Division of Research and Statistics of the Federal Reserve Board, the Treasury Department, and the National Bureau of Economic Research, organized the basic statistical data, and Sam Thompson, on loan to the Banking and Currency Committee from the Commerce Department, pulled the data together and with Bertram Gross prepared various notes commenting on special aspects of the material. This thirty-five page manual included "summary figures on population and the labor force; employment; production, income, and expenditures; productivity; prices; consumer credit; and liquid assets available for the transition from war to peace . . . the history of Federal Government receipts, expenditures, surpluses, deficits, and the public debt, and a presentation of the relative position of the United States in the world economy." [14]

To the sponsors of S.380 and to others interested in full employment, the material gathered and prepared by the staff was of unquestionable value. Some of the ablest experts on employment policy in and out of the government made their advice available to Congress through the requests of the staff. And when employment schemes rolled in on the tide of mail from special interest groups or individuals, this material was screened and analyzed and briefed for the consideration of the busy sponsors.

GHOST WRITING

A second important function performed by the staff was the preliminary drafting of speeches, articles, letters, press releases, memo-

13 U.S. Senate, *Report to the Committee on Banking and Currency*, Senate Committee Print No. 4, 79th Cong., 1st Sess., Sept. 1, 1945 (Washington, 1945).
14 *Ibid.*

randa, and reports for the various sponsors of the bill. A great deal
has been written in recent years about the profession of ghost
writing. The matter has often been misunderstood or misrepre-
sented. Every important public official in Washington gets dozens
of requests each year for speeches or articles or testimonial letters
on some current issue. Many of these requests are welcomed, for
they provide an opportunity to inform the public about pressing
governmental issues. They also serve as a means of building political strength. But writing is a laborious business. From the standpoint of his personal reputation a government official cannot afford
to turn out sloppy, inaccurate, or jejune public statements. Oftentimes, therefore, he is forced because of lack of time into allowing
subordinates to draft in rough outline (sometimes in almost finished
form) his public papers and addresses. Usually the official goes over
the draft before it is issued in final form. This was always the case
with Senators Murray and Wagner in relation to the full employment material prepared by the staff in Room 15A. In many cases
Murray and Wagner specifically laid out new approaches or called
for rephrasing.

Knowing that sponsors would be called upon to give floor
speeches, testimony, and public addresses, and to write articles and
testimonials, the staff as early as February 10, 1945, prepared a preliminary outline of a series of speeches and articles on "Full Employment in a Free America." Initially twelve titles were listed:

Full Employment and the Future of America
Full Employment and American Democracy
Full Employment and Business
Full Employment and Agriculture
Full Employment and Foreign Affairs
Full Employment and Basic Fiscal Problems
Full Employment and the West
Full Employment and the South
Full Employment and Housing
Full Employment and Social Security
Full Employment and Education
Full Employment and Public Works

Not all these titles were worked up into speeches, but some of
them were, and other topics were added as the need arose. Between
January, 1945, and February, 1946, Senator Murray alone issued
over twenty-five long statements—written and oral—on full employment. These included statements on the floor of the Senate,

testimony before the Banking and Currency Committee, and speeches before such diverse groups as the Chicago Reconversion Conference of the National Association of Manufacturers [15] and the Hosiery Wholesalers National Association.[16]

Murray received requests from and wrote articles for the *American Political Science Review*,[17] *Collier's*,[18] the *International Teamster*,[19] *Independent Women*,[20] the *New Republic*,[21] and the *Retail and Wholesale Employee* [22]—to name but a few. Many of the other sponsors of S.380 in the Senate and the House made use of similar opportunities. Some of them drafted their own speeches and articles, some used the talent of liberal pressure organizations, but many of them looked to the full employment staff for aid. In the fall of 1945, for instance, when the House steering committee on the Full Employment Bill was working out political strategy, a decision was made to have almost daily one-minute speeches and weekly major statements delivered in the House chamber by various House sponsors. The staff set to work to prepare drafts of these speeches—in itself an enormous job.

### LETTER PROGRAM

One of the most interesting and perhaps significant activities of the staff was the development of a direct-mail technique which Gross had first explored in his work with the War Contracts Subcommittee. It may be remembered that the job of the War Contracts Subcommittee was to work out legislation which would systematize and expedite the handling of canceled war contracts after the end of hostilities. As staff director of the subcommittee, Gross, under the direction of Senator Murray, was in constant correspondence with many business and industrial groups who would be especially affected by contract termination legislation. Drafts of proposed sections were distributed broadly in order to get the considered reaction of all interested parties. The result was that, when the Contract Termination Bill came out on the floor, it was fully known to hundreds of business and industrial leaders.

[15] May 24, 1945.                        [16] Jan. 22, 1946.
[17] "Maintaining High-Level Production and Employment: a Symposium," XXXIX, No. 6, December, 1945, pp. 1119-1126.
[18] "Jobs for Everybody," Oct. 6, 1945, pp. 33-34.        [19] August, 1945.
[20] September, 1945.        [21] "A Plan for America," Jan. 21, 1946, pp. 75-79.
[22] Labor Day Issue, 1945.

When Gross began to work on the Full Employment Bill, he recalled the value of this consultation by correspondence. With Senator Murray's support, he chose 200 names from the contract termination mailing list and in February, 1945, sent out copies of the Full Employment Bill along with a covering letter from Murray. The comments and criticisms of the businessmen were solicited, and a number of replies were received. Most of the letters were unfavorable to S.380, so that, although they were studied carefully by the sponsors of the bill, they were not given wide publicity. Later, in March and April, this consultation-by-mail technique was extended to include 1,500 public opinion formers all over the United States. Covering letters this time were sent out over Senator Wagner's signature. The organizations and individuals canvassed included representatives of business, labor, and agriculture; public organizations, including religious, health, education and research, minority, welfare, public education, and civic groups; international and peace organizations; women's groups; veterans' organizations; local government officials, columnists and editors, and experts in the social sciences. Senator Wagner in his letter of transmittal requested answers to four specific questions:

What should be the basic responsibilities of the Federal Government in the maintenance of continuing full employment after the war?

What specific improvements in S.380 might be considered by the Banking and Currency Committee?

If you believe S.380 should not be enacted, what alternative can you suggest?

If S.380 were to be enacted, could the cooperation between industry, labor, agriculture, Government, and other groups which would be essential to the bill's successful operation be obtained? [23]

About one-fifth of those canvassed sent full and careful replies, and as Senator Wagner said in his covering letter to the members of the Senate Committee on Banking and Currency when he transmitted these replies: "Months of hearings would have been required to elicit the information contained in their letters, and it is doubtful if hearings in Washington would ever have engendered the wide-spread discussion and analysis represented by this correspondence." [24] The dominant motive in sending out the letters

[23] *Hearings before a Subcommittee of the Senate Committee on Banking and Currency, on S.380,* 79th Cong., 1st Sess. (July, August, September, 1945), pp. 973–974.
[24] *Ibid.*

was undoubtedly to get some idea of the reaction which the sponsors could expect from the public. But the staff and the sponsors were also eager to get specific comments and criticisms on the details of the bill, and of course they could not have been blind to the educative value of the letter program in stimulating public thought and interest. The 350-odd letters received in response to this canvass were studied and summarized by the staff and were entered in the appendix of the published Senate Hearings where they were available for study by all members of Congress and the general public.[25]

A similar step toward eliciting opinion on the Full Employment Bill was taken in regard to the major agencies of the federal government. Each agency was asked the following four questions:

If we were assured of continuing full employment after the war, what might the effect be on the sectors of our economy with which your agency is concerned?
If S.380 were enacted by the Congress, what might be the role of your agency in helping to achieve continuing full employment?
In the present planning of your agency's postwar activities, what assumptions, if any, have you made with regard to the postwar level of the gross national product, the national income, and employment?
What specific improvements in S.380 might be considered by the Banking and Currency Committee? [26]

In following up this letter, the full employment staff worked closely with the Legislative Reference Division of the Budget Bureau, which has as one of its continuing responsibilities the job of analyzing the comments which various Executive agencies are called upon to submit on pending legislative issues, to see whether or not such comments are or are not in accord with "the program of the President." The full employment staff also spent time with the individual agencies in order to insure that the collective impact of their statements would have optimum effect on Congressional opinion. On June 18, 1945, a summary of the replies from thirty-three agencies was transmitted to the Committee.[27]

By these and other devices the staff rapidly increased the ferment of discussion on the full employment issue in and out of Washing-

25 *Ibid.*, pp. 999 ff.
26 U.S. Senate, "Summary of Federal Agency Reports on Full Employment Bill," *Report to the Committee on Banking and Currency*, Senate Committee Print No. 1, 79th Cong., 1st Sess., July 12, 1945 (Washington, 1945), p. 27.
27 *Ibid.*, pp. 1–26.

ton and was able to provide the sponsors of the bill with intellectual ammunition and support.

STAFF WORK ON SENATE HEARINGS

Much of the staff work on the Senate hearings was of course routine: answering requests from the scores of people who wanted to testify, sending out letters and telegrams to potential witnesses, preparing time schedules, and handling requests for information and printed and mimeographed material from individuals and organizations specially interested in the hearings. However, the staff worked closely with Senator Wagner in selecting witnesses and in preparing data and drafts for the testimony of Senators Murray, Thomas, O'Mahoney, and Patman. As early as March, 1945, the staff had outlined a preliminary schedule of hearings which ran as follows:

    I. Opening statement by Wagner:
        Significance of postwar employment issue
   II. Full presentation of bill by sponsors:
        Murray, Thomas, O'Mahoney, and Patman
           Employment and production—yesterday, today, and tomorrow
           The facts on the Full Employment Bill
           The issues on the Full Employment Bill
  III. Veterans
  IV. Business
   V. Agriculture
  VI. Labor
 VII. Church
VIII. Professional—economists, educators, lawyers
  IX. Government—state and local
   X. Government—federal
  XI. Miscellaneous
 XII. Summation by Wagner

When the hearings finally took place in July and August, some slight modifications had been made in the schedule. But the basic conception that the witnesses should represent a wide cross-section of groups and interests was followed faithfully.

POLITICAL STRATEGY

What we have considered so far in this chapter represents a sizable service to the Banking and Currency Committee and the sponsors of the Full Employment Bill. But it does not represent the central contribution of the staff. Their most significant service was in thinking through and organizing broad political strategy. This did not mean direct participation in internal Congressional affairs —a field of necessity reserved for the political leaders in the Senate and the House. It did mean, however, the analysis and use of external political forces which indirectly but nonetheless forcefully bore upon the legislative process. This work was done with the knowledge and permission and guidance of Wagner and Murray, but only the staff had the time, the undivided attention, and the mobility to follow through on details.

The proponents of S.380 were from the beginning conscious of the fact that they had an uphill fight on their hands. The war was still on and public attention was riveted to military news. Labor and liberal organizations, although interested in full employment as a goal, were split on methods and divided among themselves institutionally and power-politically. Opposition to S.380 was to be expected from a large part of business, conservative farm organizations, to a lesser extent from the old-line veterans' organizations, and strangely enough from an influential left-wing group in C.I.O.[28] Strategically, therefore, the proponents of the Full Employment Bill had three major jobs on their hands outside of Congress: (1) to arouse public interest, (2) to mobilize and unify the friends of the Full Employment Bill, and (3) to split the opposition.

*Arousing Public Interest.*—We have already discussed some of the steps taken to arouse public interest in the Full Employment Bill—speeches, articles, letter campaigns. Besides these, the staff used every possible device to get the full employment issue before the people. They worked closely with the press, especially with commentators and reporters whose liberal position could be trusted; [29] they gave full cooperation to radio forums interested in securing speakers to debate the full employment issue; they made contact with the *March of Time* in the hope that a movie short would be made on the whole subject of postwar employment; they worked with state legislators and legislative representatives of liberal pressure groups in preparing "Little Murray Bills" which were to be introduced in the state legislatures along with a statement memori-

[28] See below, p. 80.
[29] Particularly Nathan Robertson of *PM*.

alizing Congress to support the National Full Employment Bill.[30] In short, they tried through every possible channel to get facts and arguments circulating on the full employment issue.[31]

*Unifying Support.*—Mobilizing and unifying the efforts of potential friends of S.380 was a difficult and time-consuming assignment. On this, however, the staff had help. For a period of ten months they had at their service virtually the entire resources of the Union for Democratic Action, a liberal organization which assumed the job of spearheading the liberal-labor fight for the Full Employment Bill. The Union for Democratic Action provided a full-time Washington representative in the person of Paul Sifton, formerly with the National Farmers Union, to work in the closest possible relation with the staff and the sponsors of S.380 in building a strong liberal front for the passage of the bill. The details of this story must wait until a later chapter. It is only necessary to mention here that a great deal of time and effort on the part of Gross and Sifton was necessary to keep the potential supporters of the Full Employment Bill informed and enthused to the point where they were willing to forget past and present differences long enough to rally in support of S.380. By the time the Senate hearings were held, Gross and Sifton, with the active support of Senators Wagner and Murray, had organized an informal Continuations Group which met weekly to discuss liberal strategy for passage of the bill. At the heart of this Continuations Group were representatives of the following organizations: the American Federation of Labor; Americans United for World Organization; Brotherhood of Maintenance of Way Employees; Brotherhood of Railway Trainmen; Businessmen of America, Inc.; the Congress of Industrial Organizations; the Council for Social Action of the Congregational Christian Churches; the Independent Citizens Committee of the Arts, Sciences, and Professions; the National Association for the Advancement of Colored People; Y.W.C.A.; National Catholic Welfare Conference; National Conference of Jewish Women; the National Farmers Union; National Women's Trade Union League of Amer-

[30] See, for example, "Statement of Dewey Anderson before the Committee on Governmental Efficiency and Economy of the California Legislature Urging Passage of Assembly Bill 2136, Introduced March 7, 1945 by Mr. McMillan at the Request of the Entire Delegation of Democratic Assemblymen" (mimeograph).

[31] The extent to which widespread public interest in S.380 was actually aroused is discussed in Chapter X, and elsewhere.

ica; Railway Labor Executive Association; Union for Democratic Action; and the National League of Women Shoppers. Other organizations like the American Veterans Committee and the Southern Conference for Human Welfare joined in occasionally.[32]

Besides organizing the Continuations Group which met weekly from June to December, 1945, Sifton and Gross called three large pep meetings, one in April, one in July, and one in September which served to bring together an even larger representation of national organizations. These larger meetings were addressed by Murray or others of the important Congressional leaders and were forums for the exchange of opinion and the mobilizing of pressure resources. Not all the organizations went "all-out" behind S.380, but most of them served as media for the transmittal and publicizing of material worked up by U.D.A. and the full employment staff, and many of them did follow through with pressures on Congress. At any rate, the lining up of a strong phalanx of liberal forces was considered to be politically necessary, and in truth it is doubtful if S.380 would ever have passed, even in modified form, without the active support of these liberal organizations.

*Splitting Business Opposition.*—Early in the fight, Gross wrote to various liberal businessmen in New York and New England who had supported Roosevelt in the 1944 election. He asked them for names of other businessmen and industrialists who might be sympathetic to the Full Employment Bill. Through these and other contacts, relationships were established with two small business organizations: Progressive Businessmen, Inc., and Businessmen of America, Inc. (later known as the New Council for American Business).

It is not fair to say that either of these groups represented the general run of business opinion, but their support and the qualified support of a small number of influential businessmen like Beardsley Ruml and Ralph E. Flanders made it possible for the sponsors of the bill to claim that ". . . small businessmen want full employment. . . . Enlightened big businessmen want full employment." [33]

On the other hand, the most vigorous conservative business opposition to the bill was carefully dissected by the staff and featured

32 See U.S. Senate, "Assuring Full Employment in a Free Competitive Economy," *Report to the Committee on Banking and Currency,* Senate Subcommittee Print, 79th Cong., 1st Sess., Sept. 18, 1945 (Washington, 1945), pp. 18–19.
33 *Senate Hearings on S.380.*

by Senator Murray as "a small but vocal minority who are against the Full Employment Bill because they are against full employment. . . ." [34] On June 30, 1945, the staff issued a four-page mimeographed document called "Major Issues on the Full Employment Bill" which listed a series of objections to S.380. These were drafted by the staff as being generally representative of conservative opinion. This was all part of the strategy to split the opposition and to convince Congress and the general public that the major reason for any business opposition to the bill was the desire of a small, backward-looking group to maintain "a pool of unemployed to regulate wages and keep labor efficient." [35]

Taking note of the powerful business pressures which finally mobilized against S.380, it is fair to say that the proponents of the Full Employment Bill were never able effectively to cleave the business community. What they were in part able to accomplish, however—particularly during the Senate fight—was the creation of a symbolic identity between "selfish business interests" and anti-Full Employment Bill pressures.

*Splitting Agriculture.*—The National Farmers Union was of course strongly behind the Full Employment Bill, and the work of the Department of Agriculture through such people as Secretary Anderson, James Maddox, and Mordecai Ezekiel, was able to some extent to balance off the heavy opposition lined up by the American Farm Bureau Federation.[36] The National Grange was generally opposed to the bill, but the Grange statement before the Senate Committee was so ambiguous that a debate occurred on the Senate floor as to whether the Grange was actually for or against the measure. Where the opposition forces in agriculture made their greatest gains was in the House Committee on Expenditures where there was no real chance for the supporters of the bill to operate. During the months before the Senate hearings, the full employment staff maintained constant contact with representatives of the Na-

[34] *Ibid.*, p. 16.    [35] "Major Issues on the Full Employment Bill," Sec. 1(d).

[36] Ezekiel, particularly, had been fighting the battle for a number of years. During the early years of the war he gave a number of speeches on such subjects as "Jobs Mean Markets," "Making the War Worth Winning," "Establishing and Maintaining a Full Employment Economy in the United States." At a more technical level, he presented papers before the American Farm Economic Association, and wrote articles on Keynesian theory for the *American Economic Review*.

See U.S. Department of Agriculture series, *What Peace Can Mean to American Farmers,* especially Miscellaneous Publication Nos. 562, 570, and 582 (Washington, 1945).

tional Farmers Union and with strategically placed men in the Department of Agriculture in an attempt to educate the farmers to their "real" interest in full employment.

*Splitting Veterans.*—Realizing the growing power of the veteran in national affairs, the sponsors of the bill, largely through the staff, tried to gain the support of the leading veterans organizations. As early as February, 1945, Senator Murray wrote a letter to the American Legion suggesting consultation on the objectives of full employment. This brought no response. Later in April, however, Paul Sifton made contact with Millard Rice of the Disabled American War Veterans. This proved to be advantageous. Rice testified before both the Senate and House Committees on behalf of the objectives of the bill, although he asked for amendments to strengthen the position of disabled veterans. The strongest veteran support of all came from the newly formed American Veterans Committee, which gave unqualified backing to S.380. Charles Bolte, Chairman of A.V.C., stated his organization's support in a letter to Senator Wagner on June 7, 1945,[37] and Gross was quick to follow this up with an invitation to have Bolte testify before the Senate Committee. The two important old-line veterans organizations, the Legion and the Veterans of Foreign Wars, did not support the bill, and it is possible that they made their opposition felt in the Veterans Administration. It is interesting to note that General Omar Bradley shied away in hearings from giving the bill any endorsement at all.[38]

### THE IMPORTANCE OF ROOM 15A

The type of activity carried on by the staff in Room 15A was not unique. Nor was it, nor is it, indicative of the general level of staff activity on Capitol Hill. The imaginative, strategy-oriented, staff expert is rare at all levels of government. Such staff assistance can be of signal value to busy political officials if properly utilized and if clear lines of political responsibility are maintained. In the case of the Full Employment Bill, the staff became the central mechanism for mobilizing widely-dispersed intellectual resources and a coalition of pressures, public and private, behind the legislation. This was no small assignment. That S.380 emerged at all from the legislative maze was in no small measure due to the tireless efforts of the Senate staff in Room 15A.

[37] *Senate Hearings on S.380*, p. 1012.  [38] *Ibid.*, pp. 144–147.

# The Lib-Lab Lobby

. . . there can be no doubt that the
power of the lobbyist consists in part
. . . in the facility afforded him by the
Committee system.—Wilson, *Congressional Government*, p. 189.

THE TITLE of this chapter was chosen with more in mind than a
flippant alliteration. It is true that we are about to study the combined pressures of liberal and labor organizations in relation to the
Full Employment Bill. It is also true, however, that there is a striking parallel between the aims and methods of these organizations,
and the aims and methods of the so-called "Lib-Labs" of late nineteenth century Britain. The latter represented a coalition of reform
interests which had as their objectives: ". . . to secure the return of
workingmen to Parliament, to promote the registration of working-
class voters throughout the country 'without reference to their
opinion or party bias,' and to recommend to the support of the
working-class electors, candidates whose attitudes on labour questions commended them to the movement." [1] There was no thought
of a third party. "The working-class candidates desired to run as
Liberals, and, if elected, to sit as Members of the Liberal Party." [2]

Although the latter-day Lib-Labs in America have not been
particularly concerned with electing workingmen to Congress, they
have been concerned with "getting out the vote" and electing to

[1] G. D. H. Cole, *A Short History of the British Working Class Movement 1789–1937*
(London, 1937), p. 113.
[2] *Ibid.*

office men of progressive sympathies. Generally, they have looked to the Democratic Party as the party of progress. Certainly in 1945 there was little talk of a third party movement. The C.I.O. Political Action Committee was flush with happy memories of its part in the 1944 Democratic campaign; the A.F.L. was satisfied with its continuing application of Gompers' philosophy of political action —"reward your friends and defeat your enemies"; and the myriad liberal organizations which grouped politically under the tattered New Deal–Democratic banner, looked forward with confidence to the endless rule of President Roosevelt. The war was still on in early 1945, and the Communist issue which was to split the American left wing into bitter camps within two years was largely dormant.

There were of course nettling differences within the liberal movement and major institutional splits in organized labor. But under all of this was an almost universal faith in Roosevelt and a general agreement about the broad pattern of postwar goals. The loss of Wallace as Vice-President in 1944 had been a blow to some, and there was little reason for liberals to be sanguine about the make-up of the 79th Congress with Southern Democrats and Northern Republicans holding the balance of power. But a number of New Deal Congressmen remained, and it was felt that under Roosevelt's leadership a fighting chance existed for a progressive postwar program.

Granted this general optimism, it may seem strange that the news of an incipient Full Employment Bill was not greeted with universal acclaim by the Lib-Lab lobby in November and December of 1944. The reasons for the cool reception, however, are not difficult to discover. In the first place, the jealous staff of the Kilgore War Mobilization Subcommittee attempted to influence the minds of certain key liberals against the bill. In the second place, the left wing of the C.I.O., remembering Senator Murray's lukewarm support of the Kilgore reconversion bill and wanting an "Industry Council" approach to full employment, was highly suspicious. And finally, the A.F.L. somehow hit on the wild idea that the bill had been inspired by the C.I.O. and reacted accordingly.

Aside from the National Farmers Union, the only liberal organization which was initially excited about the embryonic bill was the Union for Democratic Action.

In December, 1944, the Union for Democratic Action found itself in an unhappy plight. It had been organized in 1941 for the major purpose of uniting labor and liberal groups behind an aggressive anti-Fascist foreign policy. While the statement of objectives mentioned a "fight for Democracy here and abroad," the initial interest of the organization was limited to combating isolationism and lethargy in respect to the European War. Pearl Harbor cut the ground out from under the U.D.A. as originally constituted.

During the war years under the leadership of Reinhold Niebuhr, James Loeb, Jr., and a board of directors composed of a variety of professional liberals and union leaders, the U.D.A. managed to eke out an existence as a catalyst for the formulation of progressive postwar aims. It also tried to point up the moral issues of the war and expose what it considered to be reactionary American trends in domestic and foreign affairs.

In 1944, the U.D.A. worked with other liberal organizations, like the National Citizens Political Action Committee, for Roosevelt's reelection, but after the campaign a growing hostility developed between the U.D.A. and the N.C.P.A.C. over the issue of the future of the latter organization.[3] The details of this split need not concern us here. It is sufficient to say that the U.D.A. leadership found itself after the 1944 election cut off from the militant P.A.C. crowd and with no program of continuing action of its own. It was at this juncture in the affairs of the U.D.A. that it learned of the Full Employment Bill. In terms of recouping lost prestige, raising money, and developing a positive liberal program, the Full Employment Bill seemed the answer to a prayer. The leadership of the U.D.A. reasoned that sparking the Lib-Lab fight for the passage of the Full Employment Bill would solve most of the internal problems of the organization and would perform a signal service for the entire liberal cause.

As soon as the *Year-End Report* of the War Contracts Subcommittee was issued in late December, 1944, James Loeb, Jr., Executive Secretary of U.D.A., got in touch with Senator Murray and Bertram Gross. He outlined U.D.A.'s interest and pledged the full

[3] James Loeb, Jr., in an interview, Washington, D.C., July 22, 1947; and Dwight Bradley, of N.C.P.A.C., in an interview, New York City, March 1, 1946.

resources of the organization to help fight for full employment legislation. Murray and Gross welcomed this unsolicited support and pledged their aid in return.

In order to keep in close touch with the legislative fight, U.D.A. established a small Washington office under the direction of Paul Sifton, a roving liberal with a cunning and flamboyant pen, who was borrowed for this express purpose from the National Farmers Union.

For a solid year, U.D.A. put its heart and soul and resources into the fight for the Full Employment Bill. When funds ran low it sponsored a dinner with a "name" speaker and passed the hat. Under the leadership of Loeb and Sifton, it became the keystone in the arch of Lib-Lab support for the passage of S.380. The job was not easy. Some C.I.O. and A.F.L. leaders were afraid that the bill would turn out to be a "pie-in-the-sky-by-and-by" affair, and would drain off support from more immediate issues like unemployment compensation, minimum wages, and fair employment practices legislation.[4] And of course there was the standing difficulty of the institutional and personality divisions within the labor movement.

*Gad-fly.*—For the first few weeks after the introduction of S.380 in January, 1945, Paul Sifton spent most of his time laying the groundwork for the U.D.A. campaign. He became a familiar figure in Room 15A where he and Gross thrashed out problems of organizing Lib-Lab support. Sifton helped Gross in preparing or selecting useful documents for the *Congressional Record* and for the enlightenment of friends of the bill. He also acquainted himself with the details of S.380 and the supporting staff documents. But Sifton did not confine himself to studying and writing. He spent hours in conversation with potential Lib-Lab allies, trying to convince them that "from here on, Full Employment is the main event in the home front fight to win a just and lasting peace."[5] His rounds included dozens of lobbying offices of liberal and labor organizations in Washington.

Sifton's technique was composed of cajoling and badgering. If he failed by direct salesmanship to get promises of support, he would get it by making life miserable for the recalcitrant. The

[4] James Loeb, Jr., in an interview, Jan. 15, 1946, Washington, D.C.; and Paul Sifton, in an interview, May 1, 1946, Washington, D.C.

[5] Union for Democratic Action, "Editorial Note" accompanying literature on Full Employment Bill, U.D.A. National Office, Washington, D.C. (1945).

lukewarm liberal lobbyist soon found himself deluged with telephone calls in his office or at home, buttonholed in restaurants or outside committee rooms in the Senate Office Building, or on the street. And the director of the U.D.A.'s Washington office had a way of lashing out with a salty phrase which both annoyed and fascinated his victims. Whether liked or disliked, Sifton could not be ignored.

*Public Education.*—Without question, Sifton's mightiest weapon was the pen, and he wielded it like a machine gun. Starting with a *Full Employment Kit* in March, 1945—a compilation of basic material on the Full Employment Bill—Sifton continued for the following eight months to write supplementary "news flashes" and special studies which fairly exploded with Siftonian phrases. A fair example was his critical analysis of a Chamber of Commerce bulletin *Can Government Guarantee Full Employment,* written by Emerson P. Schmidt.[6] One section of Sifton's essay reads:

> Up against the necessity for describing the alternative to a Full Employment Bill, the Chamber of Commerce pamphlet in its Summary Appraisal . . . takes refuge in a hodgepodge of stratospheric mysticism and escape clauses concealed in footnotes in fine print. After saying
>
>> "Were there no other reasonably satisfactory solution to the problems of unemployment, we all might embrace the new philosophy,"
>
> a footnote breaks the news in a whisper that
>
>> "under a free voluntary society, no one class or group is responsible for jobs. The job-making process depends on the maintenance of profit expectations and this, in turn, rests on a vast complex of forces and factors."
>
> This footnote makes an important confession: that the "job-givers" who have been given semi-divine status in page advertisements from coast to coast, really can't give jobs. Footnotes is a game that two can play at: we offer a footnote of our own.[7]

The written material prepared and disseminated by U.D.A. went to a mailing list of ten to fifteen thousand, including union locals, independent liberal associations, business groups, farm groups, religious organizations, professional societies, and a host of editors

6 U.S. Chamber of Commerce, "Postwar Readjustments," Bulletin No. 13, Washington, March, 1945.

7 Paul Sifton, "Some Observations on the United States Chamber of Commerce Postwar Adjustments Bulletin No. 13, 'Can Government Guarantee Full Employment,' by Emerson P. Schmidt, Director, Economic Research Department," U.D.A. National Office (mimeograph), Washington, D.C., July 9, 1945, pp. 2-3.

and columnists and other "public opinion formers." As word was circulated that U.D.A. was spearheading the fight for the Full Employment Bill, numerous requests for material were received from a variety of sources.

*Action Techniques.*—The U.D.A. was interested in public education for public action. In their *Full Employment Kit* which was prepared in March, 1945, they included an Action Bulletin which is worth including at this point in order to illustrate their pressure methods and goals.

### ACTION PAGE

#### WHAT TO DO ABOUT IT

1. *Write your Senators and Congressmen for information* about the Full Employment Bill. (Don't try to put them on the spot by asking them to commit themselves for or against this Bill now.)

2. *Study the provisions of the Bill, the need for it,* so that you can make up your mind and know what you are talking about when you discuss it with others.

3. *Talk about the Bill* at every opportunity, at home, at work, at meetings or organizations to which you belong.

4. *Ask that it be brought up at meetings of your organization* for thorough analysis and discussion.

5. *Organize discussions.*

6. If you favor the Bill, *try to get your organization to take action in support of it* by resolutions to be forwarded to Senators and Members of Congress and to the press.

7. *Arrange discussions between representatives of your organizations and other organizations* likely to give active support to the Bill. (Such organizations include labor unions, such farm organizations as the Farmers' Union, the state and local units of the Grange and Farm Bureau, cooperatives, church, parent-teachers groups, civic associations, chambers of commerce, and postwar planning committees.)

8. *Arrange for public meetings,* including qualified speakers from Congress, the Executive Branch, State and local governments, labor, business, and agriculture who can discuss various phases of the postwar employment problem and the Bill's method for meeting it.

9. Interest your local newspapers in this subject by furnishing them with news of your discussions and action, notices of meetings, *advance* texts of speeches at such meetings, etc.

10. Individually, and as members of Full Employment Committees of Correspondence, *watch for employment items in the press and use them in writing letters to the editor* in support of the Full Employment Bill.

11. Later, when the Bill comes up for hearing in each House, *write the Chairman and Members of the Committees* in support of the Bill, stating why you and your organization are for it. (List of members of the Senate Banking and Currency Committee and the House Committee on Expenditures in the Executive Departments follows.)

12. Later, as the hearings become a matter of news and general public interest, *begin correspondence with your Senators and Congressmen,* making them *aware of the back-home interest in the Bill.*

13. At the same time as #12, *step up local activity on support of the Bill by means of meetings, resolutions,* etc. so that your representatives will become aware of public sentiment for the Bill. (They read their hometown papers as carefully as letters and telegrams.)

14. *Whenever you need further information and other material in support of this Bill, please feel free to call or write to the Washington Bureau of the National Office of the Union for Democratic Action for help.* We will service you quickly.

15. The Washington Office of the U.D.A. is trying to arrange for a *speakers panel* of Senators and Congressmen willing to give A-1 priority for requests for speakers on the Full Employment Bill. We will do our best to service such requests for speakers. . . .[8] [Sifton wrote original drafts of a number of full employment speeches delivered by members of Congress.]

### THE CONTINUATIONS GROUP

In the preceding chapter brief mention was made of the Continuations Group organized by Sifton and Gross with the active support of the Congressional sponsors of S.380. The work of this group gives an unusually clear picture of the lobbying methods employed by a sizable bloc of liberal and labor organizations, and indicates the close practical relations which existed in 1945 between Congressional leaders and friendly pressure groups on questions of legislative strategy for the Full Employment Bill.

The Continuations Group met almost weekly on Capitol Hill from June to December, 1945. Their activities reflected three main interests: (1) educating the public on the issues of full employment; (2) influencing members of Congress by direct lobbying; and (3) influencing members of Congress by carefully conceived indirect pressures.

*Educating the Public.*—Attempts of the Continuations Group to educate the public were not significantly different from, and in part

---

[8] *Union for Democratic Action Kit on Full Employment,* Section 4, Washington, D.C., March, 1945, pp. 31–32.

were indistinguishable from, similar efforts by the U.D.A. and by the staff in Room 15A. Material initially prepared by Sifton and/or Gross explaining and defending the bill was often routed through the pressure group representatives who made up the Continuations Group. Such material was mailed out from Washington to the far-flung local organizations of the Lib-Lab lobby and was used in forums, discussion groups, union meetings, radio talks, professional journals, and directly or indirectly, by local newspapers.

Besides serving as a channel for U.D.A. and staff material, the Continuations Group served to encourage its member organizations to work up full employment pamphlets and releases on their own.

An important part of the educational campaign was the calling of two conferences in Washington in July and September, 1945. The plans for these meetings were worked out jointly by Congressional leaders, Gross, and the Continuations Group. For the meeting on July 26, invitations were sent to some 60 organizations, 42 of which sent representatives.[9] Both Senator Murray and Senator O'Mahoney addressed the meeting, exhorting the members to work for the passage of the bill. Murray stated that "we can never achieve and maintain full employment unless the plain people of America, small businessmen, farmers, etc. join in a great crusade." [10] O'Mahoney hoped that "this conference would be successful in organizing support for this legislation which would save business in America." [11] Representatives of various organizations were then called upon to state their position on the bill and to indicate positive steps being taken to support their position. Some of the statements are illuminating.[12]

*Lewis G. Hines, Legislative Representative of the A.F.L.:* Mr. Hines stated that President Green has already expressed himself as supporting the Bill, and plans are under way to reach the six million members to win support and bring about passage of the Bill.

*Robert K. Lamb, Chairman of the Subcommittee on War Production and Reconversion, C.I.O.:* Mr. Lamb reported that C.I.O.[13] has gone on

---

[9] "Report on Meeting of National Organizations on Full Employment Bill," U.D.A. National Office (mimeograph), Washington, D.C., July 26, 1945.

[10] *Ibid.*, p. 1.                    [11] *Ibid.*                    [12] *Ibid.*, pp. 2-4.

[13] The fact that the A.F.L. and the C.I.O. were both represented in the Continuations Group is not without significance. Although the two organizations had previously conducted parallel activities on behalf of a single piece of legislation, this was one of the first occasions when representatives of the two groups had met in common council.

record in favor of the principles of the Bill at a recent Executive Board meeting. Each of the international unions will prepare an analysis of problems of unemployment and all of these statements will be incorporated in testimony at the hearings on the Bill. The C.I.O. has authorized the C.I.O.-P.A.C. to follow the current pamphlet on reconversion with one on Full Employment. C.I.O. expects to hold meetings around the country during the summer and will be glad to cooperate with other organizations and local meetings.

*Lt. Robert Bangs, American Veterans Committee:* Lt. Bangs stated that the A.V.C. supports the Full Employment Bill and its National Planning Committee is continuing its campaign to acquaint their members with details of the Bill. Their attitude is implied in the plank: "jobs for veterans."

*Mrs. James Irwin, Young Women's Christian Association:* Mrs. Irwin said that the Y.W.C.A. is very interested in the Bill and is publicizing it throughout their membership.

*Reverend George Higgins, National Catholic Welfare Conference:* Father Higgins said that the Social Action Department of the N.C.W.C. is wholeheartedly in favor of the objectives of the Bill. The N.C.W.C. will do whatever it can to inform its own membership about the bill.

*Mrs. Olga Margolin, National Council of Jewish Women:* Mrs. Margolin said that the Council has endorsed the Bill, plans to prepare an article in the forthcoming issue of their magazine, and that they will do everything possible for public campaign.

*Judge William Hastie, National Association for the Advancement of Colored People:* Judge Hastie said that the N.A.A.C.P. is on record in favor of the Bill. The Negro has the most to lose if the objectives are not achieved. The fact must be brought home to minority groups that they will never be able to make progress unless there are adequate jobs for the people. The N.A.A.C.P. will make every effort to cooperate in order that the full support of the Negro might be mobilized behind this and all other important legislation. The N.A.A.C.P. has a mailing list of over 500,000 who receive information once a month and more comprehensive reports are sent to 700 chapters.

*James Loeb, Jr., for Russell Smith, National Farmers Union:* Mr. Loeb reported that N.F.U. is the originator of the Full Employment movement, has published a very fine supplement on the Bill, and is working actively to win support.

*Benedict Wolfe, National Lawyers Guild:* Mr. Wolfe stated that the Guild is making a study of the Bill which will be sent to all Chapters with the suggestion that the study be made the subject of local conferences. Only by getting into various localities where we will be able to get enough pressure to put the Bill across. [*sic*]

Mr. Wolfe said that one of the Guild's objections to the Bill is that it does not provide for full employment, but that it will be impossible to achieve employment unless the Bill is passed because this is the essential "first step."

The Full Employment Conference called on September 12 had a slightly different representation and purpose. Final Senate action on the bill was only days away. This second conference was an example of pressure strategy geared into the timing of legislative action. At the conclusion of its proceedings, the Conference drew up a resolution urging Congress to pass a Full Employment Bill which would include basic provisions concerning (1) the right to work, (2) the responsibility of the federal government to assure employment opportunities for all, and (3) the stimulation of private enterprise backed by federal investment when necessary.[14]

The September Conference had a morale function as well, however. The conferees were told that Senate floor action was but the first major hurdle. The more difficult problem of shepherding the bill through the House remained, and the Lib-Lab lobby was urged to continue the good fight.

*Direct Lobbying Activities.*—In July, 1945, Paul Sifton prepared a mimeographed list of all Senators and Representatives, giving in the case of the latter the principal cities and towns in each Congressional district, and indicating by asterisks the members of the two standing committees charged with responsibility for the Full Employment Bill.[15] This list was studied carefully at meetings of the Continuations Group and names were parceled out to those lobbyists who might have optimum weight with particular Senators or Congressmen. The Independent Citizens Committee, with strong Hollywood support, was to get after Senator Sheridan Downey of California; the Railroad Brotherhoods and the Southern Conference for Human Welfare were to approach the Alabama Senators; the National Farmers Union was to put pressure on Senator Butler of Nebraska; and so on. Direct lobbying of this sort was all in a day's work for most of the members of the Continuations Group, and represented orthodox pressure activity.

During the Senate hearings on the Full Employment Bill, the Continuations Group kept careful track of the attitudes of the mem-

14 "A Resolution in Support of Early Enactment of an Effective Full Employment Bill," Proposed for Adoption at a Meeting of National Organizations, Washington, D.C., Sept. 12, 1945.
15 Union for Democratic Action National Office, Washington, D.C., July 23, 1945.

bers of the Banking and Currency Committee with a view to concentrating pressure where it might be most needed. Attention was also paid to possible "strengthening amendments" to the bill which might be offered by supporting organizations during the course of the hearings. There was strategy even in this. The minutes of one Continuations Group meeting read in part:

It was suggested that supporting organizations who have amendments strengthening the bill should offer them to the committee in the course of the hearings. *Some may be adopted; all will tend to offset opponents' proposals of amendments to weaken or pervert the bill.* (Emphasis supplied.) [16]

The relationship between the Continuations Group and the Lib-Lab witnesses who testified before the Senate committee was intimate. Almost all organizations represented in the Continuations Group sent witnesses to testify before the Banking and Currency Committee, and one of the standard jobs of Washington lobbyists is to advise and help prepare testimony for those officials of their respective organizations who are asked to appear on such occasions.

After a modified version of S.380 had been passed in the Senate by an overwhelming 71–10 vote, the Continuations Group shifted its direct pressures to the House Committee on Expenditures in the Executive Departments. There was little change in technique, except that the Group developed close working relations with Congressman George Outland, who was chairman of a Steering Committee of House sponsors of the bill. As in the case of the Senate fight, "organizations agreed to list members whom they would be responsible for contacting and to start work at once." [17] Strong pressure was exerted on the six co-sponsors of the bill who were on the House Committee, to persuade them "to make attendance and active participation in all hearings and executive sessions of that Committee their first responsibility." [18] This was considered of prime importance because of the markedly conservative weighting of membership in the Expenditures Committee.

Late in the fall of 1945, it became obvious that the bill was either going to be killed or amended beyond recognition by the opposi-

16 Union for Democratic Action, "Roundtable Meeting of August 27" (mimeograph), Washington, D.C., Aug. 29, 1945.
17 *Ibid.*, "Report of Meeting of October 1" (mimeograph), Washington, D.C., Oct. 3, 1945.
18 *Ibid.*

tion forces in the House committee. The Continuations Group exerted what direct pressures it could, but it fought a losing battle in relation to House strategy and action. After an emasculated substitute bill was passed by the House on December 14, the final efforts of the Continuations Group were centered on the Conference Committee and the President. Letters signed by most of the participating organizations of the Continuations Group were sent to the Conference Committee and to President Truman, urging that the House substitute be rejected in Conference, that something close to the original bill be reported out, and that if this were not done, the President should veto the Act. The final meeting of the Continuations Group was held on February 5, 1946. The Conference Bill was explained to the Group by Senator Murray and Bertram Gross, and a letter was presented for ratification urging President Truman to sign the Employment Act of 1946.

*Indirect Pressures.*—Mention has been made earlier of some of the indirect pressures which the Continuations Group was instrumental in bringing to bear on Congress (see above, pages 85–88).

The group tried at every turn to match their direct lobbying with more diffuse pressures from the field. The action steps listed by U.D.A. in their Full Employment Kit of March, 1945, were essentially those followed by the member organizations of the Continuations Group. The Group did work out certain refinements, however. In the minutes of one of their meetings the following appears:

The importance of letters from back home to House Members was stressed, also the character of such letters. It was stated that identical letters, either mimeographed or identical in language though individually written, have little or no value. On the other hand, as few as 15 letters, each one obviously the independent expression of opinion of a constituent, have been known to persuade a Member to change his position on a pending issue.[19]

Perhaps the most vivid illustration of the relationship between a member of Congress and the Continuations Group in the formulating of plans for indirect pressures on behalf of the Full Employment Bill is to be found in the minutes of a meeting on October 15, 1945. The minutes read in part:

[19] *Ibid.*, p. 2.

2. Congressman George E. Outland, Chairman of the Steering Committee of Co-sponsors of HR 2202, was a guest at the meeting and presented a program which he hoped would be followed by the supporting organizations within the next few weeks.

3. Mr. Outland asked that *supporting organizations call upon their local chapters and membership throughout the country to write to President Truman immediately urging him to do everything he can to persuade Democratic members of the House Committee on Expenditures in Executive Departments to report out soon and favorably on the Full Employment Bill, HR2202.*

*Emphasize that this Bill is an integral part of the reconversion program as submitted to Congress last fall.*

Point out that *there must be immediate action—before a Christmas recess.*

Let him know that *your organization will support* a strong bill without emasculating amendments.

. . .

6. *When the Bill reaches the Floor, it is important that all Members of the House be made aware of the country-wide support for the Bill. Letters from local chapters and from constituents in Congressional Districts will be of the greatest value in advising them of the interest in and support for the Bill and the vital necessity for its early passage.*[20]

A final brief example of indirect pressure strategy on the part of the Continuations Group will suffice. In the minutes of the Group's November 5 meeting the following appears:

Arrangements were made for representatives of church and other organizations to discuss the Bill with Congressman Whittington for the purpose of emphasizing the importance of keeping in the Bill certain basic principles and procedures. [Whittington is one of Mississippi's leading Baptists.][21]

*Evaluation.*—In terms of Lib-Lab pressure, the Continuations Group bore the brunt of the in-fighting. Under the leadership of the U.D.A., the Group worked hard to develop a pressure strategy which would insure the passage of the Full Employment Bill. It was, of course, only partially successful. The bill originally backed by the Group was a far cry from the bill finally passed. Some observers on the periphery of the Group's activities have suggested that the defeats suffered by the bill were to a large extent due to the disharmony within the Group itself and to the piddling means

---

20 Union for Democratic Action (mimeograph), Washington, D.C., Oct. 23, 1945.
21 Union for Democratic Action (mimeograph), Washington, D.C., Nov. 8, 1945.

employed to further the desired ends. It is true that there were at times awkward disagreements among the members of the Group. It is also true that Sifton and Gross had to fight certain widely shared opinions, such as a belief that the bill would not work without provisions for a full-blown planning staff like the National Resources Planning Board. Finally, it is true that certain organizations within the Group failed to give substantial support to the struggle for the bill's passage, especially after the relatively minor setbacks suffered in the Senate. But after these qualifications have been made, the fact remains that the Continuations Group did spearhead the fight, and that a bill of sorts was finally passed. The evidence seems at least to support the thesis that without the work of the Continuations Group, the Congressional sponsors of S.380 would have had even rougher sledding than they in fact encountered.

In a final tribute to the members of the Continuations Group, Senator Murray said on February 5, 1946, "The work of the liberal groups contributed more to the passage of the Employment Act of 1946 than the boys in the Senate and House. Without you, success could not have been achieved." [22]

In one sense this was a tribute to the work of all the Lib-Lab pressures, but in a special sense it was an expression of particular gratitude to the U.D.A.-sponsored Continuations Group.

### ORGANIZED LABOR

It was not long after the introduction of the Full Employment Bill that the leadership of organized labor realized it could not afford to ignore the proposed legislation. This conviction grew during the spring and summer of 1945 as the result of a number of factors: (1) the failure of the Kilgore subcommittee staff to produce a substitute bill; (2) growing rank and file sentiment behind the bill largely as a result of the Wagner letter campaign organized by Gross in the spring; (3) fear on the part of both the A.F.L. and the C.I.O. that the other might give strong support to the bill and gain adherents thereby; (4) the work of Sifton and the Continuations Group; (5) the death of Roosevelt and the consequent realization on the part of labor leaders that a fight for any progressive postwar legislation would be an uphill battle; and (6) the speedy end of the

---

[22] I was present at this final meeting and attempted to take down Senator Murray's words verbatim.

war, which caused legitimate labor fears about widespread unemployment.

*Publications.*—By late summer and early fall of 1945, labor journals began to espouse the cause of S.380. In August, 1945, the *American Federationist* ran a favorable although rather lukewarm editoral. The *C.I.O. News* in the same month carried a story which reflected the impact of V-J Day on unemployment:

A prairie fire unemployment crisis this week swept across the U.S. from New York to California. Men and women thrown out of work swarmed into U.S. Employment offices seeking jobs or unemployment compensation. Meanwhile in Washington the C.I.O. urged passage of the Full Employment Bill as an aid to averting a jobless crisis that might become as bad as the 1929 depression—unless Congress acts at once on legislation designed to cushion the shock of reconversion.[23]

About the same time, C.I.O.–P.A.C. printed a pamphlet-of-the-month called *The Answer Is FULL EMPLOYMENT* which was a slightly diluted plea for the Murray Bill "as a good stride forward in the right direction." [24] The whole tenor of the pamphlet was that only the total C.I.O. program, including adequate wage rates, annual wage guarantees, minimum wages, price control, ability-to-pay taxation, unemployment compensation, social security, community development, aid to education, planning for leisure, good race relations, and freedom of political action would bring full employment. The pamphlet reflected a widespread fear among labor leaders that the Full Employment Bill would attract too much rank and file support, to the possible detriment of the other programs sponsored by the C.I.O. leadership. In the pamphlet's own words, "This Bill is not a perfect instrument. It is not a cure-all. This Bill by itself is not a guarantee of everlasting prosperity and economic security. But this Bill is needed to supplement the C.I.O. 12-point Full Employment program." [25]

On the whole, however, the C.I.O. stand was stronger than that of the A.F.L.[26] The P.A.C. pamphlet was circulated widely. Suffi-

[23] Quoted in the Providence *Journal*, Aug. 28, 1945.
[24] Joseph Gaer and Robert K. Lamb. *The Answer Is FULL EMPLOYMENT*, C.I.O. Political Action Committee Pamphlet of the Month No. 4 (New York, 1945), p. 14.
[25] *Ibid.*
[26] According to the Providence *Journal*, Aug. 28, 1945, the Full Employment Bill was not included on the A.F.L. list of "must" legislation as outlined by President William Green. The A.F.L. emphasis was on "emergency unemployment compensa-

cient copies were printed to enable the *Nation* magazine to send it to its entire subscription list. And of course there was the regular C.I.O. and National Citizens' Political Action Committee mailing list which directly and indirectly reached millions of American citizens.

It has been estimated that there are about 800 regularly published labor papers in the United States with a combined readership of some 15,000,000 families.[27] The *C.I.O. News* alone has a circulation of nearly half a million.[28] Even though some of the top leaders of the large labor organizations were at no time fully dedicated to S.380, most of labor officialdom gave some support to the bill, and through their various journals they had the means of keeping the full employment issue alive among the rank and file. It must also be noted that moderate support from the top was often recharged by the enthusiasm of local labor organizations.

*Oral and Written Testimony.*—In response to the letter campaign organized by Wagner's staff in April, 1945, about fifty important labor organizations submitted written endorsements of the purposes behind the Full Employment Bill. Many of these responses were hedged with minor qualifications about particular sections of the bill, but there were a few blanket endorsements. All these letters were published in the printed Senate Hearings and were there available to interested legislators.[29]

Six important representatives of organized labor testified before the Senate Committee on Banking and Currency: William Green for the A.F.L., Philip Murray for the C.I.O., John L. Lewis for the United Mine Workers, George Harrison for the Railway Labor Executives' Committee, L. E. Keller for the Brotherhood of Maintenance of Railway Trainmen and Martin H. Miller for the Brotherhood of Railroad Trainmen. In terms of labor pressures, these men represented the heaviest artillery in the country. While agreeing in their testimony that S.380 was no cure-all, they gave the basic principles of the bill strong endorsement, and left no doubt

---

tion, an increase in the minimum wage, a postwar housing bill, and the Wagner-Murray-Dingell Bill."

[27] Victor Riesel, "Labor Is Big Business," *Readers Digest*, January, 1946, p. 120.

[28] *Ibid.*

[29] *Hearings before a Subcommittee of the Committee on Banking and Currency, on S.380*, 79th Cong., 1st Sess. (Washington, 1945), pp. 977 ff.

as to the stand of organized labor on the issue of government responsibility in respect to widespread unemployment.

There was a basic similarity underlying the testimony of all the labor representatives. The following general pattern is observable in the six separate labor statements:

(1) A statement of need for full employment legislation based upon the experience of the organization and its fears about postwar unemployment;
(2) A general endorsement of the purposes of S.380;
(3) Suggestions for amendments or additions to the bill based upon the peculiar interests of the organization testifying;
(4) Strong endorsement of other legislation of interest to labor as a whole, and the organization testifying in particular.

With minor differences in emphasis similar testimony was introduced in the House hearings by second-string representatives of the C.I.O., A.F.L., and the Railway Brotherhood.[30] In the House hearings, however, the labor representatives were badly shaken by the cross-questioning of conservative Congressmen.

*Activity of Locals.*—No story of labor pressures for S.380 would be complete without mention of the activities of the locals. Partly as a result of the Wagner letter campaign, partly as a result of the work of the Continuations Group, the U.D.A., and the P.A.C., a great deal of local activity was carried on for the cause of S.380. This took the form of action groups for full employment, letters and telegrams to Congressmen, mass meetings, and forums. The amount of heat engendered was substantial. Mr. Manasco as chairman of the House Committee was deluged with mail and visiting labor delegations. During the presentation of the C.I.O. testimony before the House Committee, Representative Clare Hoffman of Michigan stated, "We are receiving letters and telegrams from local C.I.O.'s, and the national C.I.O. all the time." [31]

Some of this pressure was a little naive. Hundreds of duplicate C.I.O.–P.A.C. postcards reached Mr. Manasco's office one day, telling him that if he did not use his influence to report out a strong Full Employment Bill, the signatories would vote against him in the next election. Manasco, who comes from the 7th District in

---

[30] *Hearings before the Committee on Expenditures in the Executive Departments, on H.R.2202*, 79th Cong., 1st Sess. (Washington, 1945).
[31] *Ibid.*, p. 349.

Alabama, noted with interest that the cards were postmarked Brooklyn, New York.[32] The labor delegations (mostly C.I.O.) often showed a similar lack of finesse in dealing with Congressmen face to face. Unless there is a reasonable chance that a pressure delegation can deliver on its threats, the use of threatening language does little except to stiffen the resistance of the Congressman. But with these necessary qualifications, there is little doubt that the energy and enthusiasm of local labor groups had an effect on rank and file opinion, on the national officers of the big labor organizations, and on some Congressmen.

MISCELLANEOUS LIBERAL SUPPORT

Only a word need be said about the various non-labor liberal organizations and spokesmen. The work of U.D.A. has already been mentioned, and brief allusions have been made to other groups like the Independent Citizens Committee of the Arts, Sciences, and Professions; the Y.W.C.A.; the American Veterans Committee; the National Catholic Welfare Conference; and the National Association for the Advancement of Colored People. A study of the Senate and House Hearings indicates that support for S.380 came from a variety of non-labor and non-governmental sources: university professors; representatives of religious, racial, and educational groups; veterans; welfare workers; the National Farmers Union; the National Lawyers Guild; and various independent businessmen.

Separately, except in certain localities, none of the miscellaneous supporting organizations or spokesmen were comparable in power to organized labor. But collectively they represented a sizable bloc of pressure opinion, and it was not by accident that their aid was sought by the Wagner staff and by U.D.A. The parochialism of much of their testimony was offset by the sheer spread of support which their participation represented. Religious and racial groups particularly are often able to make a deep impression on Congressmen and Senators who are forced to weigh the possible political impact of minority coalitions in urban constituencies.

Liberal journals like the *New Republic* and the *Nation,* and liberal newspapers like the *Chicago Sun, PM,* and the *New York*

[32] Representative Carter Manasco, in an interview, Washington, D.C., Feb. 20, 1946.

*Post* did their best to keep their readers informed about the issues of full employment and the legislative course of S.380.[33]

## THE IMPACT OF THE LIB-LAB LOBBY

No complete evaluation is possible of the contributions of the disparate organizations and individuals who worked for the passage of S.380. In terms of substantive changes in the bill itself, the contributions were meagre. Liberal pressures killed the policy statement in Section 2(b) of the bill, as introduced, which read in effect that those having "full-time housekeeping responsibilities" were to be exempt from the right to employment. Liberal pressures were also responsible for suggesting certain changes in the federal spending sections of the bill—changes which were incorporated in the Senate version as passed.[34] The Employment Act of 1946, however, carried no direct substantive evidence of the impact of the Lib-Lab lobby.

Furthermore, it would be difficult to prove that the direct pressures of the Lib-Lab lobby changed a single Congressional mind. By and large, the members of Congress who listened with any semblance of receptivity were friends of the liberal cause to begin with. Most of those against S.380 had little or nothing to fear from the Lib-Lab lobbyists, whose power was largely confined to the urban-industrial centers of America.

This is not to suggest, however, that the Lib-Lab lobby was an unimportant factor in the history of the Full Employment Bill. Senator Murray was not just being polite in his tribute to the work of the liberal organizations. An Employment Bill *was* passed, and the Lib-Lab lobby was in no small measure responsible.

Liberal and labor supporters of the bill made at least three major contributions. In the first place, they served as channels of information to and from a large and politically important segment of the public. Whether a member of Congress is sympathetic or unsympathetic to a particular bill, widespread public concern about an issue is bound to have an important effect on a member's willingness to force the issue to some type of legislative decision. In terms of the enthusiasms it aroused and the controversies it started, the Lib-

[33] The most complete newspaper coverage of the legislative history of the bill is to be found in *PM*, 1945–1946; note especially the articles by Nathan Robertson.

[34] See below, Chapter Six.

Lab lobby helped to keep the full employment issue alive in the minds of a large section of the American public and representatives in the national legislature.

In the second place, the Lib-Lab lobby strengthened the hands and stiffened the backs of its friends in the Legislative and Executive branches of the government. A thousand interests compete for the attention of a single Congressman or Senator, and unless sustained outside pressure is exerted on behalf of a particular piece of legislation, a legislator finds it almost impossible to avoid mental diffusion. The same may be said of the President of the United States. There is at least circumstantial evidence to prove that President Truman was sensitive to the proddings of the Lib-Lab lobby in connection with the progress of the Full Employment Bill in the House and in Conference.

Finally, a number of liberal and labor organizations willingly cooperated with the political strategists on Capitol Hill, playing the game as the sponsors and the staff wanted it played. This theme has been touched on already and will recur occasionally throughout the balance of the study. It is only necessary to recall at this point the relationship of Bertram Gross and Representative George Outland to the U.D.A. and the Continuations Group. This two-way relationship between Congress and pressure groups has not received the attention it deserves from students of government.

CHAPTER SIX

# The Senate Approves

> Nowadays many of the Senators are, in-
> deed, very rich men, and there has come
> to be a great deal of talk about their
> vast wealth and the supposed aristocratic
> tendencies which it is imagined to breed.
> But even the rich Senators cannot be said
> to be representatives of a class.—Wilson,
> *Congressional Government*, p. 225.

IT WOULD DO considerable violence to history to suggest that the
Senate as a whole, or the Senate sponsors of S.380 in particular,
spent most of their working hours in 1945 worrying about the Full
Employment Bill. During the first session of the Seventy-ninth
Congress, which lasted from January 3 to December 21, 1945, the
Senate passed 1,005 bills and resolutions, voted for 23 investigations
of which nine were by special committees, handled 11,056 Presidential nominations, and filled up 5,960 pages of the *Congressional
Record* with its proceedings.[1] Besides full employment, the Senators
among themselves, in committee, or on the floor, had such weighty
matters to discuss as the extension of the reciprocal trade agreements, the organization of the United Nations, the death of Roosevelt, the Bretton Woods agreement, the end of the war, the Civil
Aviation Treaty, the atomic bomb, the extension of war powers,
the return of the United States Employment Service to the states,

[1] Floyd M. Riddick, "The First Session of the Seventy-Ninth Congress," *The American Political Science Review*, Vol. XL. April, 1946, *passim*.

the extension of O.P.A., and appropriations to the Fair Employment Practices Commission, to name only a few.

If one judges by the number of pages in the *Congressional Record*
devoted to debate, however, the Full Employment Bill was by no
means an unimportant issue. Only six measures received more
attention,[2] and from August 21 to September 28, many of the members of the Senate Banking and Currency Committee spent a substantial amount of time on S.380, in hearings, in executive session,
and in floor debate. It may of course be argued that twelve days of
committee hearings, a few days of closed committee sessions, and
four days of floor debate are hardly adequate for a full discussion
of America's future employment policy. But that is only to rail
against one of the facts of American political life: that Congress
has too much to do and too little time in which to do it. The Senate
of the United States is supposed to be the greatest deliberative body
in the world, but its majority leader in 1945 felt constrained to
make the following comment:

I do not know what has happened to the Senate of the United States. I
regret to say what I am going to say, but it seems to me that it has reached
an all-time peak in irresponsibility of attendance on the floor of the
Senate. We can get but few Senators to come here while there is under
consideration one of the most important matters that will be before the
Senate in weeks, involving billions of dollars worth of property; and
when the debate has been concluded Senators will come trooping in,
asking somebody at the door what the Senate is voting on and how they
should vote. It does not present a very encouraging picture of delibera-
tion in the Senate of the United States.[3]

The diffusion of interest forced upon individual Senators means
of course that the fate of an issue depends to a shocking extent upon
a handful of men who take special interest in the pending legislation in committee. For that reason, proper committee referral is
a matter of high strategy for the proponents of a controversial bill.
It was not by accident that S.380, which logically could have been
sent to any one of a half-dozen committees, was referred to the
Senate Committee on Banking and Currency.

2 *Ibid.*, p. 259; cf. *Congressional Record*, 79th Cong., 1st Sess., Sept. 25–28, 1945.
3 *Ibid.*, p. 261.

### THE SENATE BANKING AND CURRENCY COMMITTEE

As has been noted earlier, the chairman of the Banking and Currency Committee was Senator Robert A. Wagner of New York. Roland Young has described the importance of committee chairmen as follows:

The chairman is powerful because he can call committee meetings whenever he wishes, because he has a large amount of freedom in preparing the legislative agenda for the committee, and because he is officially consulted on questions relating to the committee . . . more than that, he has a status with Congress, with the bureaucracy, and with the general public.[4]

It should also be noted that committee chairmen have a determining voice in the selection of witnesses for committee hearings. Wagner was, of course, a co-sponsor of the Full Employment Bill and a man with enormous prestige in the field of social legislation —state and national. At least one close observer of the history of the Full Employment Bill believes that Wagner's work for S.380, as chairman of the Banking and Currency Committee, was the most important single factor in pushing the bill through the Senate.[5]

Without denying for a moment the importance of Senator Wagner's position and prestige, the fact should also be noted that the membership of the Banking and Currency Committee was weighted by a close margin in Wagner's favor. Out of twenty members of the committee, six could be counted on to follow Wagner's lead almost without question.[6] There was better than a fifty-fifty chance of holding five more,[7] and only eight could be definitely pigeonholed as probably hostile.[8] In other words, the strategists recognized that in case of a showdown they could count on a solid bloc of seven votes, and that the doubtful votes were weighted in Wagner's favor.

At the very beginning, however, there was hope that a showdown would not be necessary; that with careful handling, the bill might be made to appeal to most if not all of the conservatives on the committee. The strategists reasoned that an almost unanimous report from the powerful Banking and Currency Committee would insure an almost unanimous final vote in the Upper Chamber.

[4] Roland Young, *This Is Congress* (New York, 1943), p. 108.
[5] Paul Sifton, in an interview, Washington, D.C., May 1, 1946.
[6] Barkley, Downey, Murdock, McFarland, Taylor, and Mitchell.
[7] Fulbright, Carville, Tobey, Glass, and Bankhead.
[8] Radcliffe, Taft, Butler, Capper, Buck, Millikin, Hickenlooper, and Capehart.

All these considerations were in the minds of the Senate sponsors and the staff when the question of committee referral arose—a fact not readily appreciable to the casual reader of the *Congressional Record* who finds the simple notation on January 22, 1945, "The bill [S.380] . . . was read twice by its title, referred to the Committee on Banking and Currency, and ordered to be printed in the Record." [9]

### FIGHT OVER WALLACE CONFIRMATION

The fight over the confirmation of Henry Wallace as Secretary of Commerce is only tangentially related to the Full Employment Bill. But it deserves mention at this point because the confirmation was a Senate affair, it took place less than a week after the introduction of S.380, and Wallace fought his case on the grounds that the Reconstruction Finance Corporation and the Department of Commerce should be used "to help carry out the President's commitment of 60,000,000 jobs." [10] It is interesting to note that the members of the Banking and Currency Committee split on Wallace in about the same proportions as they split eight months later in closed committee sessions on various amendments to S.380. The nature of the fight over Wallace was an advance warning to the Senate sponsors of the Full Employment Bill that the future was not to be entirely smooth sailing.

### "FULL EMPLOYMENT" AT SAN FRANCISCO

If the sponsors needed any further reminder of the struggle ahead, they had it later in the spring when rumors began to trickle back from the San Francisco United Nations Conference that a back-stage battle had occurred over the use of the words "full employment" in the United Nations Charter. The story is much too complicated to be reported in full, [11] but the gist of it is that Senators Vandenberg and Connally took violent exception to the use of the term "full employment." According to Drew Pearson, "both said that the Senate would turn down the Charter if 'full employment' were inserted." [12] Dean Gildersleeve, who was on the drafting committee for that particular section of the Charter, was ordered to

[9] *Congressional Record,* 79th Cong., 1st Sess., p. 377.
[10] Paul Sifton, "Henry Agard Wallace," published in J. T. Salter, ed., *Public Men in and Out of Office* (Chapel Hill, 1946), p. 95.
[11] See "Washington Merry-Go-Round," Washington *Post,* June 3, 1945.     [12] *Ibid.*

press for the substitution of the words "high and stable levels of employment." "Full employment" was finally retained by a vote of the polynational drafting committee, and a face-saving device was worked out by the American delegation. But the whole affair was no encouragement to the sponsors of the Full Employment Bill back in Washington.

### REPUBLICAN CO-SPONSORS

Part of the strategy of the original sponsors of the bill and of their staff was to "split the opposition." This was attempted in regard to business, agriculture, veterans—and the Republican Party.

The possibility of gaining Republican support was dramatized the day the bill was introduced. After Senator Murray had presented the bill and spelled out the reasons behind it, Senator Wayne Morse, junior Republican Senator from Oregon, crossed the Senate floor and congratulated him warmly. Murray did not forget this, and he and Gross were finally able to persuade Morse to join up. Morse, in turn, put pressure on Senator Langer of North Dakota who, according to the *New Republic* supplements, had a consistently liberal voting record on domestic issues.[13]

Senator Aiken of Vermont was approached through Russell Smith of the National Farmers Union. Aiken was at first reluctant. He believed that the bill failed to go far enough. He also demurred on the grounds that he was afraid of becoming a "perpetual cosponsor." Smith finally convinced him, however, and Aiken lined up his New Hampshire friend, Senator Charles Tobey, who was engaged at the time in a passionate fight for the Treasury-sponsored Bretton Woods agreement.

Although the Republican co-sponsors had been approached in the late spring, the official announcement of their co-sponsorship came on July 28, 1945.[14] With this announcement, the four Republicans issued a statement containing four amendments for committee consideration. These amendments provided for mandatory rather than permissive consultation by the President with industry, labor, agriculture, and state and local governments, a detailed policy

---

13 See James G. Patton and James Loeb, Jr., "Challenge to Progressives," *New Republic*, Feb. 5, 1945.

14 U.S. Senate, "Assuring Full Employment in a Free Competitive Economy," *Report from the Committee on Banking and Currency*, 79th Cong., 1st Sess., Senate Report No. 583, Sept. 22, 1945 (Washington, 1945), p. 36.

on stabilization of agriculture, a safeguard against achieving or maintaining full employment by the use of measures injurious to other countries, and a precise definition of the terms "full employment" and "Federal investment and expenditures."

As originally planned, Senate hearings on S.380 were slated to begin in late April or early May, 1945. The Banking and Currency Committee, however, found itself tied up with the Bretton Woods agreement and with O.P.A., until late June. Since the Senate had agreed to a summer recess beginning around August 1, the Senate sponsors of S.380 had to make a ticklish tactical decision; should they attempt to rush the hearings through before the summer recess —permitting a long hiatus between the hearings and final action, or should they postpone the hearings until October, risking delaying tactics on the part of the opposition which might result in no action being taken before the next session of Congress? A compromise decision was reached to split the hearings. Preliminary hearings were set for July 30 and 31 with the understanding that full public hearings would be the order of business after the Senate reconvened in the fall. The Banking and Currency Subcommittee appointed to handle the hearings was composed of Senator Wagner, chairman, and Senators Radcliffe, Murdock, Taylor, Fulbright, Mitchell, Tobey, Taft, Buck, and Hickenlooper.

*Preliminary Hearings.*—Seven members of Congress—five Senators and two Representatives—presented statements before the Banking and Currency Subcommittee on July 30 and July 31. Much of this material had been prepared by the committee staff with the cooperation of Executive branch economists. Senator Wagner led off with a general statement of the importance of domestic full employment to world peace and prosperity, and the need of the bill as a framework for a specific and effective full employment program.

Senator Murray then traced the history of the bill, stressed the urgency of advance planning against depression, and of overriding the special interests of a small minority opposed to full employment.

Senator O'Mahoney summarized the weakness of our economic system in the past, and presented factual data and charts to illustrate the significance to business of mass markets and adequate purchasing power, and the prospect of postwar inflation, deflation, and mass unemployment if the government should fail to exercise its responsibilities.

Senator Morse interpreted the British election as an indication that to preserve our system we must make private enterprise work, and warned that the people are demanding employment. He also outlined the four amendments proposed by the Republican sponsors of the bill.

Representative Patman outlined and explained in detail the provisions of the bill.

Senator Thomas (Utah) discussed the historical, legal, political, and ethical significance of the concept of "the right to work," emphasizing that it has been universally accepted as a basic human right.

Representative Outland described what full employment would mean to veterans, business and professional men, farmers, workers, state and local governments, and to the social structure.

The preliminary hearings represented a straight selling job. There were no opposition witnesses, and the cross-examination of the sponsors by Senators Taft and Radcliffe was mild.

Essentially, the sponsors attempted to promote three ideas through the medium of these early hearings: (1) that there was an overwhelming need for and demand for full employment, (2) that there was a need for a government policy and a government plan, such as was outlined in S.380, for assuring full employment and the right to work, and (3) that the opposition to S.380 was made up of a small and selfish minority who did not "really want a stable and expanding economy." [15] In terms of strategy, the sponsors and the staff were obviously interested in creating a symbolic identity between a desire for full employment as a goal, and S.380 as the means. If you weren't for S.380, you were obviously one of the small and selfish minority who did not want full employment at all. As we shall see, this process of "naming your enemies" was a constant theme throughout the Senate fight, and was such a successful technique that businessmen shied away from testifying against the bill for fear that they would be charged with favoring unemployment.[16]

[15] *Hearings before a Subcommittee of the Senate Committee on Banking and Currency, on S.380*, 79th Cong., 1st Sess. (Washington, 1945), p. 83.
[16] Emerson P. Schmidt, U.S. Chamber of Commerce, in an interview, Washington, D.C., Feb. 4, 1946.

Initially there was some disagreement between the staff and some of the sponsors about the use of this technique, some of the sponsors believing that the idea should be fostered that *everyone* was for full employment. The staff idea prevailed, however, that psychologically it would be more potent to face the opposition with the dilemma of backing a bill with which they were not in entire agreement, or being publicized as "the exceptions . . . who do not want all Americans to have the right to work, who do not want continuing full employment." [17]

*Full Hearings: Timing.*—When the preliminary hearings were completed on July 31, a subcommittee adjournment was scheduled until October 9.[18] With the sudden and dramatic end of the Japanese war on August 15, however, the Senate recess was cut short and full public hearings on the Full Employment Bill were rescheduled for August 21. The haste in getting hearings under way was largely the result of President Truman's concern over reconversion dislocations and his realization that the Democrats were shy on pending postwar legislation. On August 16, the New York *Post* carried a story with a lead statement which read, "President Truman, concerned over the prospect of 5,000,000 people out of work by November, today said a bill now in Congress, designed to steer the country into full employment, was 'must' legislation." Truman made this clear to his Democratic Congressional leaders, and within a week Senate hearings were resumed on S.380.

The natural uncertainties which came with the end of the war were aided and abetted by a series of gloomy prognostications, made by a number of Washington economists, to the effect that the spring of 1946 would see eight to ten million unemployed.[19] The estimates of course were wrong, but there is little doubt that, projected against the background of immediate postwar uncertainties, they established for the hearings and the Senate debate a climate of opinion which was unusually favorable to the sponsors of the bill.

*Full Hearings: Choice of Witnesses.*—The abrupt change in the dates for the full hearings placed a heavy burden on the staff in Room 15A. In a period of a week, witnesses had to be selected, notified, and scheduled. Sixty-seven witnesses testified between

---

[17] *Senate Hearings on S.380*, p. 83.          [18] *Ibid.*, p. 141.
[19] See L. R. Klein, "A Post Mortem on Transition Predictions of National Product," *Journal of Political Economy*, August, 1946, pp. 289–308.

August 21 and September 1, and, since no hearings were held on Saturday, Sunday, and Monday (August 25–27), that meant an average of seven and a half witnesses per day. Many more people asked to testify than could possibly be accommodated, with the result that a number of statements had to be submitted in writing to be included at the end of the printed hearings.

Of the 67 witnesses who appeared in person before the committee, only four were strongly opposed to the bill.[20] Of the fifteen businessmen who appeared, only three were in fundamental opposition.[21] The witnesses fell into the following groups: 10 government officials, 3 mayors, 2 university professors, 4 representatives of religious groups, 6 of labor, 7 of veterans, 7 of welfare organizations, 2 of farmers, 2 of education, 1 lawyer, 8 members of Congress, and 15 businessmen.

The one-sidedness of the testimony was not the design of the sponsors and the staff, although it would seem that way at first glance. Attempts were made to solicit testimony from a number of businessmen "who had publicly expressed their position against the bill, or who were regarded as possible opponents of the bill." For one reason or another most of these businessmen did not accept the invitation. Furthermore, Senator Wagner asked Senator Taft to secure opposition witnesses, but the Ohio Senator, the ranking spokesman for the Republican minority, failed to do so. In actual fact, the failure of more opposition witnesses to appear during the hearings was not as serious as it might seem. Scores of opposition letters were published in the appendix of the printed hearings, and there was a growing amount of anti-S.380 material in the press and in pressure literature. Members of Congress had ample opportunity to hear more than one side of the issue.

*Full Hearings: the Cross-Examination.*—That the subcommittee proponents of the bill were prosecutors as well as judges is amply illustrated in the text of the hearings. In general, whenever a witness was testifying *for* the Full Employment Bill, he received comfort and encouragement from the subcommittee majority or from visiting sponsors like Senator Murray. Whenever a witness testified

[20] Willford I. King, chairman, Committee for Constitutional Government; William L. Kleitz, vice-president, Guaranty Trust Company, New York; Ira Mosher, president, National Association of Manufacturers; James L. Donnelly, executive vice-president, Illinois Manufacturers Association.

[21] Kleitz, Mosher, and Donnelly.

*against* the bill, the hearings turned into a kind of modern inquisition. Two brief examples will suffice.

After Clarence Avildsen, chairman of the board of the Republic Drill & Tool Company of Chicago, had made a statement in strong support of S.380, the hearing continued as follows:

*The Chairman* (Senator Wagner): Well, I can say for myself, that is a very splendid statement.
*Mr. Avildsen:* Thank you.
*The Chairman:* It ought to be distributed to all the businessmen of the country.
*Mr. Avildsen:* Thank you.
*The Chairman* (turning to Senator Murray): Senator?
*Senator Murray:* I do not think the statement calls for any questioning on my part. . . .
. . . It is your judgment, as a liberal businessman, that it is necessary for the Government to take a hand in this situation and undertake to aid and encourage business in bringing about the highest possible production and employment?
*Mr. Avildsen:* Absolutely, and I think it is the only way we can do it. I think this is something that should have been done a long time ago.
*Senator Murray:* If we had such a measure as this in existence in the late twenties or during the period following the last war, we could have avoided the very serious depression that came on following the crash in Wall Street in 1929.
*Mr. Avildsen:* Absolutely.[22]

The remaining two pages of cross-examination consist of questions fed by Senators Murray and Wagner and invariably answered by Mr. Avildsen with the words, "absolutely" or "That is right."

On the other hand, when William Kleitz, vice-president of the Guaranty Trust Company of New York, issued a strong statement on the defects of the bill, he was met by a withering blast. Kleitz has just completed that part of his testimony dealing with the New Deal's "drastic and experimental changes in the economic environment" which created a "pervasive fear and uncertainty" when Senator Murray interrupted to ask:

Did you oppose those activities on the part of the Government at the time or did you feel they were unwarranted?
*Mr. Kleitz:* As I recall it, at that time we were not invited to express our opinion, sir.
*Senator Murray:* Why do you select this period, the two periods, the

[22] *Senate Hearings on S.380,* pp. 418–419.

twenties and the thirties, to illustrate the points you wish to illustrate here? It seems to me that those were two unusual periods in the history of our country. In the first place, the twenties was a period of inflation brought on by American business. Then the 1930's was another unusual period in the history of the country in which there was an effort to bring back employment in the country. Why couldn't you select some other period in the history of the United States that could illustrate the point that you wish to illustrate here?

*Mr. Kleitz:* Well, if we say the 1920's was a period of inflation, of course an inflation is the hardest thing in the world to define. I am not sure I know what the definition is.

*Senator Murray:* Do you approve the rapid rise in stocks and securities during that period and the manipulations that took place on the stock exchanges of the country which were afterwards investigated by the Banking and Currency Committee, shown to be fraudulent and dishonest?

*Mr. Kleitz:* No sir; I certainly do not condone anything fraudulent or dishonest.

*Senator Murray:* You realize that in the period of the 1920's that the manipulations that were going on were draining the country of its wealth. You were manipulating these stocks and securities, running them up to a fictitious value and getting the people to purchase them, and they were afterwards defrauded. Isn't that true?

*Mr. Kleitz:* You say "You were doing that."

*Senator Murray:* Well, you represent the banking and financial fraternity down in Wall Street. You are coming here to oppose this bill, and I say you represent them down there and you represent their philosophy.

*Mr. Kleitz:* May I say, with all due respect, that I am coming here because Senator Wagner telegraphed and asked if we would have a representative come to this hearing.[23]

*The Function of Hearings.*—Although it is obvious to anyone who reads Congressional hearings that they are not limited in design to the shedding of light, it would be a mistake to write them off as unimportant sideshows. Not only do hearings serve to keep issues alive in the press and in the minds of the interested public, they often serve busy legislators by clarifying and high-lighting differing points of view and by exposing overlooked defects or values in pending legislation. This is not to say that the main function of a Congressional hearing is to enlighten judicious and detached Congressional minds. It is to say that hearings frequently have valuable by-products. Their chief function, of course, is to

[23] *Ibid.*, pp. 524–525.

further or block a particular legislative or personal cause. Strategy is central. If the Senate hearings on S.380 are unconvincing in this respect, the House hearings which are discussed in a later chapter will dispel all doubts.

EXECUTIVE SESSIONS AND COMMITTEE REPORTS

Between September 1 and September 20, after the completion of the public hearings, a number of executive (closed) sessions were held by the subcommittee and by the full membership of the Banking and Currency Committee.[24]

In the subcommittee sessions, which were held immediately after the close of the hearings, Wagner, Tobey, Murdock, Taylor, Taft, and Radcliffe were in regular attendance. Barkley attended "when needed." Other members of the subcommittee either did not attend at all, or appeared sporadically.

Senator Wagner submitted for committee consideration what amounted to a substitute version of S.380. This revised bill was the work of Bertram Gross, Edward Pritchard (an assistant of Fred Vinson), and Leon Keyserling, and had been developed in consultation with a number of agency economists.

The three-man redrafting team of Gross, Pritchard, and Keyserling had at their disposal a substantial volume of opinion on the subject of S.380—even prior to the Senate hearings. Gross had gone through the letters which had been submitted in response to the Wagner letter campaign in the spring; the federal agencies and departments (often with Gross's aid) had submitted statements on the bill; [25] a number of pressure groups had made their opinions on the bill known, either by direct lobbying or by circulating written statements; [26] the press and various journals of opinion had taken positions; and finally, economists and political scientists in and out of the government had taken considerable interest in the bill and had made their views known through articles or through direct

[24] There are some persuasive reasons for maintaining the institution of closed committee sessions, but to the student of the legislative process they are a tantalizing and frustrating phenomenon. It is possible by sleuthing and careful deduction to get part of the story, but at best the reporting on this vitally imporant part of the legislative process is bound to be meagre.

[25] See U.S. Senate, "Summary of Federal Agency Reports on Full Employment Bill," *Report to the Committee on Banking and Currency*, Senate Committee Print No. 1, 79th Cong., 1st Sess., July 12, 1945 (Washington, 1945).

[26] See below, Chapter VI.

contact with the three members of the redrafting team.[27] It should be noted, of course, that Gross, Keyserling, and Pritchard, and the Senate sponsors had themselves developed over a period of months an appreciation of certain limitations in the bill as originally introduced.

In redrafting the Full Employment Bill, therefore, the three-man team had in mind a wide variety of comments and criticisms. A glance at the tentative committee prints which were prepared between August 19 and September 20, 1945, gives some indication of the intellectual gyrations of the redrafters. Three things are immediately apparent. The first is that in the early stages of redrafting, the three-man team was acutely conscious of the business opposition to the bill. The August 19 committee print, for instance, included a long section which was obviously written for the purpose of mollifying business opinion. Two examples of these new provisions will suffice. Section 3(b) (1) of the August 19 print reads:

(b) . . . Federal economic policies and programs shall be formed and executed so that

(1) with allowance for changing conditions, maximum stability, consistency, and public knowledge with respect to what the Government is doing and planning to do *will create an atmosphere in which private enterprise and other non-Federal activities can go forward most confidently;*

And Section 3(b) (7) reads:

the regulatory activities of the Government shall be evaluated not only in terms of the abuses which they prevent, *but also according to their effect upon private employment.*[28]

Upon further consideration, the redrafters deleted these sections, but their appearance in at least one committee print is not without

27 See, for instance, John H. G. Pierson, "National Budget as an Aid in Reducing Deficits under Assured Full Employment," *Monthly Labor Review*, August, 1945, pp. 210–214; William Stix Wasserman (affirmative) and Harley L. Lutz (negative), "Should the Government Guarantee Employment," *Modern Industry*, June 15, 1945, pp. 117, 124; Charles I. Gragg and Stanley F. Teele, "The Proposed Full Employment Act," *Harvard Business Review*, Spring, 1945, pp. 323–337; "Post-War Jobs," Parts I, II, *Press Research Inc.* (Washington, 1945); Leo Barnes, "The Anatomy of Full Employment," *Nation*, May 26, 1945, pp. 593–597; Seymour E. Harris, "The Way to Full Employment," *New Republic*, June 4, 1945, pp. 783–786; Stanley Lebergott, "Shall We Guarantee Full Employment," *Harper's Magazine*, February, 1945, pp. 192–202.

28 U.S. Senate, S.380, Confidential Committee Print. 79th Cong., 1st Sess. Italics added.

interest. The sponsors and proponents of the bill knew quite well that widespread business support for the bill would insure its passage, but they also developed a firm conviction that business support could be bought at too high a price. The fact that the "appeasement" clauses of the August 19 draft were deleted within a matter of days [29] is sufficient evidence that the redrafters wavered only temporarily.

The second obvious change which strikes the reader of the revised drafts is the new emphasis given to agriculture. This reflected a belated recognition on the part of the sponsors that insufficient attention had been given previously to attracting the pressure support of the big farm organizations. The Republican sponsors added one amendment concerning agriculture, but the redrafters experimented with a number of others.

Finally, the redrafts reflect a major preoccupation of the authors with the more technical economic sections of the bill. Not only were simple terms substituted for complex ones, but the economic studies proposed under the National Employment and Production Budget were limited to "present and foreseeable trends," [30] in an attempt to answer criticisms to the effect that the original bill promised to make impossible economic forecasts. In addition, following the suggestion of certain labor lobbyists,[31] the spending provisions of the bill were made an integral part of a continuing governmental "tool-kit" for combating depressions. In the original bill they had been mentioned only as a last resort to be considered after everything else had failed.

There were other minor changes: the policy declaration was simplified; specific references to the Congressional committees to be represented on the Joint Committee were deleted; the Morse-Tobey-Aiken-Langer amendments dealing with agriculture, full employment without economic warfare, and mandatory consultation with economic groups were added. But at the heart of the work of Gross, Keyserling, and Pritchard, and the various government economists they brought in partly for advice but largely to insure continuing agency interest in the bill, was an attempt to smooth

[29] The Confidential Committee Print of Aug. 26, 1945, is almost totally free of these clauses.

[30] U.S. Senate, S.380, Confidential Committee Print, 79th Cong., 1st Sess., Aug. 26, 1945.

[31] Robert Lamb of the C.I.O. was particularly influential.

the technical edges of the original draft and broaden its appeal. Between August 19 and September 22, Gross and his fellow workers turned out nine different drafts. It was S.380 in advanced stages of revision which Senator Wagner submitted early in September, 1945, to the Banking and Currency Subcommittee for consideration in executive session.

*The Senate Opposition.*—The executive sessions of the Banking and Currency Subcommittee and full Committee saw the first real indications of minority opposition. This opposition, which had been only mildly encountered during the hearings, was led by Senators Taft, Radcliffe, and Hickenlooper. Their position on S.380 can be summarized roughly as follows: (1) they were agreed that some sort of governmental planning mechanism to study the economy was probably desirable; (2) they disliked the term "full employment"; (3) they disliked any hint of a government "guarantee" or "assurance" of the right to work, or of full employment; (4) they objected to the bill's ultimate reliance on "federal investment and expenditure." [32]

Holding to these beliefs, they proposed a number of amendments in subcommittee which, as we shall see, were later voted on in full committee, and which later still were introduced on the floor of the Senate.

It is perfectly clear all the way through the Senate fight that the major interest of the opposition leaders was in destroying what they considered to be the dangerous psychological underpinning of the Full Employment Bill. To this we shall return.

*The Subcommittee Report.*—By the middle of September, the Banking and Currency Subcommittee had completed its deliberations and on September 18, Wagner issued a subcommittee report which had been prepared by the staff.[33] The report was something of a departure from ordinary procedures. It is quite common for a full committee to submit majority and minority reports to the Senate; it is most unusual for a subcommittee to submit to the full committee a printed report for public release. The subcommittee

---

[32] See U.S. Senate, "Assuring Full Employment in a Free Competitive Economy," *Minority Views from the Committee on Banking and Currency*, Senate Report No. 583, Part 2, 79th Cong., 1st Sess., September 24 (legislative day, September 10), 1945 (Washington, 1945).

[33] U.S. Senate, "Assuring Full Employment in a Free Competitive Economy," *Report to the Committee on Banking and Currency*, Senate Subcommittee Print, 79th Cong., 1st Sess. (Washington, 1945).

report was drafted as the personal statement of the chairman, although the second and third paragraphs make the following elaboration:

The following report represents the view of the chairman and the other members of the subcommittee who believe that the bill should be reported to the Senate without further change.

The remaining members of the subcommittee have joined in reporting the bill, as amended, but have reserved the right to propose additional amendments in the full committee.[34]

No minority report was written at this stage.

The subcommittee report was an attempt to keep the public informed about the progress of the bill, as well as an attempt to influence the decisions of the full committee in executive session. In spite of the fact that the subcommittee report was prepared by the staff in extreme haste, it is one of the most comprehensive and carefully organized documents which came out of the long struggle for the Full Employment Bill. As a selling brochure it is something of a minor classic.

Within the compass of 25 pages, the report (1) outlined the need for the Full Employment Bill, pointing up the dangers of unemployment to our institutions, to our economic health, and to world peace; (2) outlined the principles of the Full Employment Bill, supporting each section with judiciously chosen quotations from such respectable figures as Msgr. John O'Grady, Bishop G. Bromley Oxnam, Mr. Stettinius, businessman Ralph Flanders, National Grange Master Albert Goss, James F. Byrnes, Governor Dewey, Harold Smith, Dr. Ernest Minor Patterson of the Wharton School of Finance and Commerce, William Green, and small businessman Harry Golden; (3) pointed up the flexibility of the bill, indicating that many types of programs were possible under it; (4) emphasized the widespread support for the bill, listing forty organizations which had endorsed it and stating that its principles "have also been strongly endorsed by innumerable businessmen, experts, religious leaders, farm leaders, and labor leaders," by "the majority of the witnesses who testified before the subcommittee," by "the great majority of correspondents whose letters appear in the record," and by "members of both the Democratic and Republican Parties"; [35] (5) criticized the opposition amendments, introducing this section with the words:

[34] *Ibid.*, p. 1                              [35] *Ibid.*, pp. 18–19.

Because of the widespread support for the Full Employment Bill throughout the country, the opponents of the measure have ceased to argue that it should be defeated.

Knowing that it will be enacted in one form or another, they now favor amendments which would eliminate or weaken one or more of its basic principles.[36]

(6) gave a synopsis of amendments offered and the arguments against their adoption; and (7) outlined the major differences between the bill as reported and the original bill, showing in detail why each change was made.

The report also included 44 pages of appendixes including a list of witnesses who testified on S.380; excerpts from the committee testimony on "the right to employment," "the government's responsibility to assure continuing full employment opportunities," the policy on "federal investment and expenditure," the "national production and employment budget," and the "joint committee on the national budget"; major differences between the Full Employment Bill and the Employment Stabilization Act of 1931; and a long "Statement of Essential Human Rights Drafted by a Committee Representing Principal Cultures of the World, Appointed by the American Law Institute." This last, prepared by a distinguished list of international lawyers and educators, included the "right to work" as its Article 12.[37]

The subcommittee report was another major step on the part of the sponsors and the staff in carrying out a carefully organized strategy to insure favorable Senate action.

*The Full Committee Executive Session.*—On September 19 and 20, the Banking and Currency Committee met to discuss and vote on a series of amendments to S.380 which were offered by various members. These sessions were well attended, and the discussions were marked by that combination of camaraderie and earnest disagreement which is one of the hallmarks of democracy. On September 19, the opposing teams lined up as follows: for the bill without change as reported from the subcommittee: Wagner, Glass (by proxy given to Wagner), Barkley, Murdock, McFarland, Taylor, Mitchell, Tobey, and Downey. Against the bill, unless amended substantially: Taft, Thomas (Idaho) (by proxy given to Taft), Radcliffe, Butler, Capper, Buck, Millikin, and Hickenlooper. Floaters: Fulbright and Carville.

36 *Ibid.*, p. 20.    37 *Ibid.*, p. 58.

Senator Downey arrived a little late on the morning of September 19, so that the division on the first two amendments found only eighteen voting. The remaining nine amendments, however, were voted on by 19 out of the 20 Senators on the committee. John Bankhead was ill and his proxy was not received by Wagner until the following day.

The division on the amendments illustrates the rather sobering fact in a democracy that the fate of a piece of legislation may depend on the action of one or two strategically placed individuals. The committee division on nine of the eleven amendments to the Full Employment Bill ran: 9–9, 8–10, 8–11, 7–12, 9–10, 10–9, 8–11, 9–10, and 8–11. If Carville and Fulbright had voted consistently with the conservatives, the Full Employment Bill would have received an unfavorable committee report, and might possibly have been killed summarily on the Senate floor.

The substance of most of the proposed amendments need not concern us here. The most important of them were reintroduced during the Senate debate. Two minor amendments, however, were accepted in committee without objection.[38] The only amendment which was passed over the objections of the sponsors was one by Senator Fulbright which struck out the phrase in Section 2(a) reading "all Americans have a right to opportunity for employment" and substituted "all Americans . . . are entitled to . . . etc."

What must be emphasized at this point is the importance of the full committee session as a major hurdle which the Senate sponsors had to clear in their struggle for favorable consideration of the bill in the Upper Chamber. On September 20, a motion by Radcliffe to report the bill without a favorable recommendation was defeated by the narrow margin of 8 to 11. The final motion by Murdock to report out the bill with a favorable recommendation was carried 13 to 7.

*The Majority Report of the Full Committee.*—Aside from a full printing of S.380 as reported by the committee, the only major difference between the majority report of the full committee and the previous report of the subcommittee was the addition in the former of a 13-page section called "The Opposition to the Full

[38] One by Fulbright which added the word "education" before the word "housing" in Section 2(d); and one by Senator Taylor on behalf of Senator Downey which provided for the possible use of Federal old age pensions, in Section 2(d)(3).

Employment Bill—and the Answers." [39] The obvious inference of this section was that no one could possibly be opposed to S.380 unless he held that full employment was either "impossible" or "undesirable," or that "the responsibility of the government should be limited to the relief of destitution." [40] To some extent this was a repetition of the strategy referred to earlier—an attempt to identify all opposition to the bill with an extreme, conservative minority. The featured statements of Ralph Blodgett and Carlyle Fraser [41] to the effect that depressions should not be abolished "for they have many desirable features" and "private capitalism requires a floating number of unemployed" were representative of extreme business opinion only. The position taken by the Chamber of Commerce of the State of New York in its March, 1945, Bulletin to the effect that depressions are "the price we pay for freedom" [42] was a more widely accepted business belief, but was by no means held universally by the business community. Of significance is the fact that a good deal of moderate business opposition to the bill was totally ignored by the drafters of the committee report. If the report is viewed as a weapon of psychological warfare, this omission is understandable.

*The Minority Report.*—The Minority Report of the full committee was presented by Mr. Radcliffe "for himself, Mr. Taft, Mr. Thomas of Idaho, Mr. Butler, Mr. Capper, Mr. Buck, and Mr. Hickenlooper." [43] In eight pages the minority attempted to sell its position to the Senate by emphasizing the following points: (1) that it concurred "fully in the stated goal of the so-called full-employment bill" [44] and agreed with the bill's provisions "directing the President to submit a national budget and program to prevent unemployment and establishing a joint congressional committee to consider the President's program"; [45] (2) that it disagreed "with some of the methods prescribed to achieve the goal of full employment" and believed "that, if adopted, far from preventing unem-

---

[39] U.S. Senate, "Assuring Full Employment in a Free Competitive Economy," *Report from the Committee on Banking and Currency*, Senate Report No. 583, 79th Cong., 1st Sess., Sept. 22, 1945 (Washington, 1945), pp. 20–32.

[40] *Ibid.*, p. 20.          [41] *Ibid.*, p. 23.          [42] *Ibid.*, p. 21.

[43] *Ibid.*, p. 1. There is no indication that the minority had any staff assistance comparable to that provided by Gross for the majority. George Smith, secretary to the Republican Steering Committee, gave some research aid to Taft and may have helped in the drafting of the Minority Report.

[44] *Ibid.*          [45] *Ibid.*

ployment [the provisions] would only lead to inflation followed by depression and unemployment"; [46] (3) that several amendments offered to the bill in Committee were voted down by the slim margin of 9–9 and 10–9. In this connection the minority stated, "We think it fair to say that on the question of eliminating the provisions which require compensatory deficit spending, the committee is evenly divided"; [47] (4) that the bill's opening statement of policy was not legally binding, and that there was some question about "the wisdom of Congress adopting declarations of policy having no legal effect, [although] there is some psychological advantage at this time in affirming our interest in securing full employment"; [48] (5) that the National Budget should be prepared by an Office of Director of the National Budget, which would be "responsible to the Congress and the people, as well as to the President," and that the director of that Office should be appointed with Senate confirmation; [49] (6) that the "unlimited government spending" policy of the bill was dangerous, and was in reality "the so-called compensatory spending theory, advanced by Lord Keynes, Stuart Chase, Sir William Beveridge, and Mr. Henry Wallace"; [50] (7) that of course the government could guarantee full employment if it were prepared to set up a totalitarian government ("Hitler did it. Stalin does it."); [51] (8) that a number of amendments should be offered to qualify the spending policy and the government assurances of full employment; (9) that the bill "neglects the situation of the farmer or the individual businessman and deals solely with those seeking employment" and that "the American Farm Bureau Federation is definitely opposed to the bill in its present form." [52]

Implicit in the minority attack was the charge that the bill contained unsound principles and untried theories which, unless modified, would destroy freedom itself. Omitting any references to the widespread support which the bill had received in the United States, the minority attempted to tie the bill to a series of names (Keynes, Beveridge, Chase, Wallace, Hitler, and Stalin) which might evoke a negative response from many of their colleagues. It also attempted to line up farm area votes by high-lighting the opposition of the Farm Bureau.

46 *Ibid.*          47 *Ibid.*          48 *Ibid.*, p. 2.
49 *Ibid.*          50 *Ibid.*, p. 4.      51 *Ibid.*
52 *Ibid.*, p. 8.

### THE SENATE FLOOR DEBATE

Although Senate action on the bill was an unpredictable skirmish, the strategy of the floor fight can be summarized very easily. The supporters of the bill wanted to block as many amendments as possible and sell the bill as a package to the Senate. The opposition wanted to emasculate the policy declarations and the "investment and expenditures" sections of the bill, leaving only a planning mechanism which Congress could control. Neither side succeeded fully in accomplishing its goal. The policy underpinnings of the bill were seriously eroded, but the substantive program was left almost completely intact.

*The Sponsors' Strategy of Presentation.*—Although the Senate proceeded to a consideration of the Full Employment Bill on September 24, 1945, the full dress debate did not begin until the following day. On September 25, 27, and 28, the sponsors deployed their heavy artillery and fired four oratorical salvos. Senator Wagner led off with an analysis of the provisions of the bill and a blast at the bill's opponents, repeating many of the statements included in the subcommittee report.[53] After a brief debate, Senator Murray followed with a speech on the implications of the bill for business, adding an attack against the minority amendments, and stating that "the rank and file of businessmen, especially small businessmen," repudiate the doctrine of the opposition.[54]

Then, after a full day of debate on the first Radcliffe amendment, the high point of the sponsors' strategy was reached in the dramatic speech of Senator O'Mahoney.[55] It is rare that a speech on the floor of the Senate actually changes stubborn Senate minds. O'Mahoney's presentation was an exception. It is generally conceded by friend and foe alike that the Wyoming Senator's dramatic, illustrated lecture on the economics of S.380 had a marked effect on the final vote. With the use of charts and graphs placed in the well of the Senate floor and against the back wall of the chamber, O'Mahoney breathed economic respectability into the pending legislation. With the attitude of a patient professor he explained technical economic concepts to his colleagues, emphasizing that he was opposed to deficit spending and that was why he was supporting the bill. He

---

[53] *Congressional Record*, Sept. 25, 1945, pp. 9099–9102.  [54] *Ibid.*, pp. 9106–9111.
[55] *Congressional Record*, Sept. 27, 1945, pp. 9197–9211.

pulled out all the stops in the semantic organ: "I am arguing for the investment of private capital under a free enterprise system, and the elimination of deficit spending"; [56] or again, "The chart (on the back wall) was not prepared by any 'leftists.' It did not come from any organization interested in Federal spending. It came from the Cleveland Trust Company of Cleveland, Ohio"; [57] or finally, "There is nothing in this bill which is in any way antagonistic to big business or to wealth." [58]

He flattered the collective ego of Congress:

Mr. President, this is a bill to vest in Congress the power and the responsibility of meeting the issue, instead of continually delegating the power to the executive branch of the government. This, Mr. President, is a bill to restore the functions of Congress.[59]

At the close of O'Mahoney's presentation, Senator Taft addressed the chair with the words, "Mr. President, I think that I can agree with about 90 percent of everything which the Senator from Wyoming has said." [60] Aging Senator Bailey walked out of the Chamber shaking his head and saying, "If I'm ever tried for treason, I hope Joe O'Mahoney can defend me."

The careful strategy of co-sponsorship developed by Senator Murray and Bertram Gross ten months before had paid off.

The final major speech on behalf of the bill was delivered by Senator Wayne Morse on the last day of the Senate debate.[61] It was largely a rebuttal to various opposition arguments and charges. Perhaps typical was Morse's comment about the "compensatory spending" allegation in the Minority Report:

Mr. President, in my opinion that is merely an argument by invective. I think it is a non sequitur. As one of the co-sponsors of the bill, I assert that my judgment has not been influenced one iota with regard to similar views held by other persons in this country or abroad. I think it is fallacious reasoning to object to this bill because of an allegation which, in my judgment, cannot be substantiated in fact, namely, that the roots of the bill are found in the philosophy of Keynes, Chase, Beveridge, or Wallace.[62]

That the Morse speech was part of a total strategy is a matter of record. At the beginning of his address, Morse stated:

56 *Ibid.*, p. 9205.         57 *Ibid.*, p. 9200.         58 *Ibid.*, p. 9211.
59 *Ibid.*, p. 9204.         60 *Ibid.*, p. 9211.
61 *Congressional Record*, Sept. 28, 1945, pp. 9265–9275.         62 *Ibid.*, p. 9272.

. . . I suggested to my co-sponsors of the bill that we might very well forego my discussion today. However, it was the judgment of those supporting the bill that in order to complete the record this speech should be made a part of the record because of the emphasis which I shall give to certain features and objectives of the bill.[63]

*The Fight over the Amendments.*—Eleven amendments were offered to S.380 on the floor. Of these, six represented minor changes in the language of the bill and were adopted by voice vote. Debate centered around the first Radcliffe amendment, the Hatch substitute amendment, the Taft amendment, and the two Hickenlooper amendments.

The Radcliffe amendment sought to replace the provision in Section 2(4) for whatever federal investment and expenditure might prove necessary to assure full employment with the following statement:

In furtherance of the objective of full employment and to supplement investment and expenditure by private enterprises, State and local Governments, the Federal Government shall, consistent with its needs, obligations, and other essential considerations of national policy, proceed with a comprehensive program of public works and other expenditures so planned that they can be speeded up and enlarged when other employment decreases or retarded when full employment is otherwise provided.[64]

The part of the amendment which seemingly enraged the sponsors was the phrase: "consistent with its needs, obligations, and other essential considerations of national policy." Radcliffe stressed the fact that that phrase was objected to again and again by the committee, a fact which he could not understand. That some of the sponsors of the bill were not so much worried about this particular language as they were about "giving in" to Radcliffe was made abundantly clear in the record by the fact that an identical "consistent with" clause was included in the Hatch substitute amendment which was adopted two days later by voice vote.[65] Senator Murdock reflected the attitude of his colleagues when he stated:

Mr. President after my experience with the subcommittee it seems to me that the opposition to the bill in the subcommittee will not stop at any language until the entire philosophy and theory of the bill are sabotaged. They say "Yes; we earnestly believe in full employment, but . . ."[66]

[63] *Ibid.*, p. 9265.
[65] *Ibid.*, Sept. 28, 1945, p. 9284.
[64] *Congressional Record*, Sept. 26, 1945, p. 9172.
[66] *Ibid.*, Sept. 27, 1945, p. 9198.

O'Mahoney reinforced Murdock and high-lighted the strategy
of the sponsors with the charge that in committee "every concession
that was made by the sponsors of the bill was met by another amendment on the part of those who opposed it." [67]

In other words, the delaying tactics of the sponsors which even-
tuated in the dropping of the Radcliffe amendment and the substitution of a compromise amendment by Senator Hatch was an attempt to contain what was considered to be the ambitions and strategies of the bill's opponents. It was felt that ready agreement to
the Radcliffe amendment might encourage a flood of opposition
amendments which would be difficult to stop.

The Hatch compromise which was readily agreed to by most of
the bill's sponsors replaced both the Radcliffe amendment and
Paragraph 4, Section 2 of the bill. As finally adopted by voice vote,
this amendment read:

(4) to the extent that continuing full employment cannot otherwise be
attained, [the Federal Government shall] consistent with the needs and
obligations of the Federal Government and other essential considerations of national policy, provide such volume of Federal investment
and expenditure as may be needed, in addition to the investment and
expenditure by private enterprises, consumers, and State and local
governments, to achieve the objective of continuing full employment.[68]

The only supporter of the bill who objected strongly to the Hatch
amendment was Senator Glen Taylor of Idaho. His remarks are
worth attention for they epitomized the feelings of a number of
liberal supporters of the original bill, and they pointed up what
amounted to a fundamental change in the minds of the bill's
strategists which had taken place sometime between the end of the
committee sessions and the passage of the Hatch amendment.

After pointing out that there was nothing in the Full Employment Bill which specifically provided for jobs for anybody, Taylor
continued rather bitterly:

Yet I feel that the bill has value. I consider that there is a psychological
value in the bill as it is now written, but not as it will appear if the pending amendment is agreed to. The bill says emphatically that the Federal
Government does assume the ultimate responsibility to see that everybody in America who desires work has an opportunity to work. The
language which is proposed to be inserted waters that down until it

[67] *Ibid.*, p. 9199.          [68] *Ibid.*, Sept. 28, 1945, p. 9276.

would say, "We will see that you have a job if something does not interfere."

Mr. President . . . the people of America have confidence in the
Congress of the United States. It is their ultimate recourse to come to
Congress. . . . They feel that if the Congress says "There will be a job"
there will be a job. But if we say "There are going to be jobs—perhaps,"
this bill will not be worth the paper it is written on, because there is
nothing to it other than a declaration of principle. On the other hand,
if the people can have confidence in it, it will mean something. It will
give them confidence that there will be jobs; they will go ahead and
spend the money they have saved during the war which will start the
wheels turning again and businessmen will have confidence.[69]

In their agreement to the Hatch amendment, the sponsors made
it unmistakably clear for the first time that their major interest
was in an economic planning mechanism, and that if anything had
to give under conservative pressure it would be the very statements
of obligation and assurance which had originally caught the
imagination of liberal and labor supporters. The gradual erosion
of the emotional heart of the bill which began with the Hatch
amendment continued until the final adoption of the Employment
Act of 1946.

The Taft amendment, which was adopted by a roll call vote of
82–0, started out as an attempt to insist that any program of federal
investment and expenditure would have to be accompanied by a
program of taxation "designed and calculated to prevent any net
increase in the national debt"[70] over a reasonable period of years.[71]
From the standpoint of intelligent economic debate, the discussion
of the Taft amendment probably represented the high-water mark
of the entire struggle over S.380.[72] As Professor Hansen has pointed
out, "the level on which the debate took place, in contrast with earlier ones, is highly encouraging. And the progress that has already
been made in fiscal thinking in this country will not stop where this
debate left off."[73] After ascertaining that Senator Taft did not mean
that budget balancing should be the only criterion of fiscal policy,
the agreement of the sponsors was assured when the words "without interfering with the goal of full employment" were added.[74]

[69] *Ibid.*, p. 9278.                          [70] *Ibid.*, p. 9284.
[71] Actually, the day before, Taft had specified nine years. See *Congressional Record*,
Sept. 27, 1945, p. 9217.
[72] *Congressional Record*, Sept. 28, 1945, pp. 9284–9290.
[73] Alvin Hansen, *Economic Policy and Full Employment* (New York, 1947), p. 118.
[74] *Congressional Record*, Sept. 28, 1947, p. 9288.

There was some disagreement between the sponsors and Taft as to what this appended phrase meant, but the shut-out vote is indicative that the ambiguity did not seriously bother either side.[75]

The two Hickenlooper amendments, one admonishing the federal government not to engage in commercial activities in competition with private enterprise,[76] and the other a vague declaration against "unnecessary Government restrictions," [77] were defeated by margins of 49–30 and 44–35 respectively. Little time was given to debating either amendment, but they are of particular interest because they represent the only divisions during the Senate fight which were roughly along party lines. The first Hickenlooper amendment was voted on according to the following party division: [78]

|  *Against* |  *For* |
|---|---|
| Democrats, 38 | Republicans, 24 |
| Republicans, 10 (11, including Progressive LaFollette) | Democrats, 6 |

The second Hickenlooper amendment had the following tally: [79]

|  *Against* |  *For* |
|---|---|
| Democrats, 37 | Republicans, 27 |
| Republicans, 6 (7 including Progressive LaFollette) | Democrats, 8 |

The fact that the final vote on the Senate bill was by an overwhelming 71–10 makes the division on the Hickenlooper amendments the only real indices of party feeling towards the Full Employment Bill in the Senate. By and large, the Republicans tried to modify the bill in a conservative direction; the Democrats tried to stand pat on a liberal version. Roughly a fifth of the Senate membership crossed party lines. Attempts to secure party discipline were made by President Truman through Majority Leader Barkley on the Democratic side, and Senator Taft and ex-Senator Danaher of the Republican National Committee on the Republican. Taft held a Republican conference before the floor fight and asked support of his colleagues in backing the minority amendments which would be offered; [80] Danaher roamed around the Senate chamber

[75] *Ibid.*, p. 9287.        [76] *Ibid.*, p. 9296.        [77] *Ibid.*, p. 9302.
[78] *Ibid.*, p. 9300.        [79] *Ibid.*, p. 9302.
[80] Kingsport (Tennessee) *Times*, Sept. 23, 1945. The A.P. release used by the Kingsport *Times* points out that Senator Morse objected strenuously to Taft's attempt to line up the Republicans behind the conservative minority amendments.

and in the lobbies attempting to secure some sort of agreement on a "Republican" position.[81] But complete uniformity was impossible in either party. Both parties had a liberal wing and a conservative wing, and these wings broke with the party majority with impunity. Party loyalty is only one of a number of influences which impinge upon a legislator's mind when it comes to voting, and whereas it would be wrong to suggest that there is no difference between the economic ideology held by the majorities of the two major parties, there is no doubt that both parties have their own internal divisions. Democratic Senator Radcliffe found himself closer to Republican Senator Taft on matters of economic policy than did Republican Senator Wayne Morse.

### THE FINAL VOTE

The Senate approved the amended bill on September 28 by the whopping vote of 71–10.[82] A number of factors contributed to this overwhelming support—factors which can be listed even if they cannot be weighed. Many of them have been mentioned already: the tireless and productive work and strategic planning of the staff and the sponsors, the strong Lib-Lab pressures, Wagner's leadership as chairman of the Banking and Currency Committee, the psychological impact of the end of the war and the dire predictions of the economists about coming unemployment, the subcommittee and committee reports, the dramatic presentation made by O'Mahoney on the floor of the Senate.

To these must be added the support given the bill by powerful Republican leaders like Taft and Vandenberg, once they were assured that certain governmental commitments had been tempered. At one point in the Senate debate after Senator Capehart of Indiana had questioned the real value of the bill, Senator Vandenberg said:

It seems to me that one of the replies to the able Senator from Indiana is that the answers we have made to depressions heretofore have been

[81] Floyd McCaffree, Republican National Committee headquarters, in an interview, Washington, D.C., April 11, 1946. Actually, some of the sponsors of the Full Employment Bill were sure that Danaher was "telling" the Senators how to vote. The National Committee, of course, does not have that kind of power.

[82] *Congressional Record,* p. 9304. The dissenters were: Buck (R), Delaware; Byrd (D), Virginia; Gerry (D), Rhode Island; Gurney (R), South Dakota; McClellan (D), Arkansas; Millikin (R), Colorado; Moore (R), Oklahoma; O'Daniel (D), Texas; Robertson (R), Wyoming; and Wherry (R), Nebraska.

hit-and-miss answers, they have been spasmodic answers, they have been expedients, whereas the pending measure contemplates a plan with respect to depressions.

If the Senate will permit, I should like to testify that that prospectus has from my point of view very honorable Republican roots. When I came to the Senate in 1928 the first bill I ever introduced in the Senate, as reported in the *Congressional Record* for May 17, 1928, was a plan for a "prosperity reserve," which is an even better term than "full employment." It sought the orderly planning of useful public works, and provision in advance for their financing, to be used in time of depression, to cushion, so far as possible, the impact of the depression. I still believe in planning in 1945, just as much as I did in 1928.[83]

It is impossible to estimate the impact of this type of statement on the rank and file of Republican (and Democratic) Senators, but few would question that such a statement carried considerable weight. Busy legislators tend to gravitate around legislative leaders, and often vote uncritically on the basis of respect for a leader's opinion. This is something quite different from simple party loyalty.

The charge has been made by several friends of the bill that one reason for the size of the favorable Senate vote was the realization of the conservatives that the bill would be cut to pieces in the House. They could vote for the bill with impunity, capitalizing on the political support which a favorable vote might bring, with the assurance that House action would render the bill meaningless. There is no real evidence to support this contention, although it should not be ruled out as a possibility.

Two final factors should be noted. The first is that the Senate as a body has been generally more liberal than the House of Representatives since 1938. This is partly a result of the six-year terms which began or fell due and were renewed, in the Presidential years of 1936, 1940, and 1944, when the magic of Roosevelt's name carried a number of sympathetic Senators into power. More fundamental perhaps is the fact that most Senators have at least one urban area in their constituency to worry about. As we shall have reason to note, the majority of Congressional districts are rural and small town. As the political power of organized labor has grown (a phenomenon limited largely to the last decade), and as population movements into the cities have increased, it has become increas-

[83] *Congressional Record*, Sept. 28, 1945, p. 9268.

ingly difficult for Senators and Congressmen-at-Large to ignore the
interests and demands of the urban worker. A Representative from
the 17th District in Illinois, for instance, may find it possible to
disregard the voice of the urban worker; a Senator, representing
the entire state, would do so only at considerable peril to his political future. This reflects an important change in the foundations
of American politics, and helps to explain the Senate vote on S.380.

Finally, the conservative business opposition to the bill was late
in mobilizing. It was not until after the Senate vote that outside
opposition pressures turned on their big guns. If the barrage had
hit the Upper House, it might have had some effect. In point of
time it passed over the heads of the Senators and landed with full
force on the House of Representatives.

INTERPRETATIONS OF THE SENATE-PASSED BILL

We have suggested above that the Senate bill as passed was a
modified version of the original bill as far as the statements of policy
were concerned, but that the substantive provisions were hardly
touched. We have also noted Senator Taylor's reaction to the Hatch
amendment. The fact is that four separate interpretations of the
meaning of the Senate bill developed. Interpretation number one,
held by the most conservative group, was that the bill was still extremely dangerous, and that every effort should be made to kill it
or modify it drastically in the House.[84] Interpretation number two,
held by a number of moderate conservatives, was that the wings
of the original bill had been clipped, that it was no longer dangerous, but that any further modifications in the House would be welcomed.[85] Interpretation three, held by a large block of liberal supporters, was that the Senate bill was a *good* bill, that the important
provisions had been kept, and that in many ways the version passed
by the Senate was sounder than the original. As one proponent put
it, "We retreated from weakness to strength." [86] This group felt,
however, that no further modifications could be made in the bill
in the House without grave danger of rendering the legislation
meaningless. And finally, interpretation number four, held by a
number of liberals of the Senator Glen Taylor stripe, held that

[84] For the pressure organizations which accepted this position, see the following
chapter.
[85] This was essentially the position taken by Senator Taft.
[86] This became the official position of the sponsors.

the most important parts of the original bill—the unequivocal statements of policy regarding the right to work and the government assurance of full employment—had been lost in the shuffle, and that, with their loss, nothing of any real importance remained.[87] Those sharing this opinion tended to lose enthusiasm for the fight ahead.

In actual fact, the real struggle over the bill which developed after the Senate action was a conflict of forces between those who accepted interpretation one and those who accepted interpretation three. To this struggle we now turn.

[87] Senator Barkley commented that the Senate version "promised anyone needing a job the right to go out and look for one." He of course did his best in conference committee, four months later, to salvage all that could be salvaged of the Senate bill.

CHAPTER SEVEN

# Conservative Pressures

> . . . it is still politically unorthodox to
> depart from old-time phraseology in
> grave discussion of affairs.—Wilson, *Con-*
> *gressional Government*, p. 6.

THE CONSERVATIVE pressure organizations in America today represent a complex phenomenon. They are extremely powerful, but
the nature of their power is largely misunderstood. They are not
unified under the tight control of any one organization, and they
often work at cross purposes, yet they present a united front on
many public issues. They are generally identified with business,
yet in terms of direct legislative influence one of the most powerful
conservative organizations in America is the American Farm
Bureau Federation.

## THE NATURE OF THE OPPOSITION TO S.380

The pressures which most actively opposed the Full Employment
Bill are easily identified. Among the more important were the
National Association of Manufacturers and its constituent organizations, various Chambers of Commerce, the Committee for Constitutional Government, and the American Farm Bureau Federation. Before turning to a study of the activities of these groups, it
is important to make clear the stated reasons for their opposition to
S.380. Not all the following objections were endorsed by all opposition pressures, but they do represent the arguments which appeared
most frequently in the press, in pressure literature, in letters, and
in the hearings.

*Full Employment Cannot be Guaranteed in a Free Society.*— The argument that full employment and freedom were incompatible took a number of forms. Some opponents adopted the simple syllogism: Russia is a tyranny, there is full employment in Russia, full employment means tyranny.[1] Others quoted from Sir William Beveridge's *Full Employment in a Free Society*—particularly those sections which dealt with possible extension of governmental controls over prices, investment, the location of industry, and the mobility of labor, if full employment was to be insured.[2] Still others felt that "there is an implicit threat that if 'free private enterprise' cannot supply jobs, then the task will be taken over by the government. The final step would be for the government to provide all the employment there is." [3]

*Initiative Would Be Killed by the Adoption of S.380.*—The theme of paternalism and loss of initiative recurred frequently. The position is summed up in a letter written to Senator Wagner by Joseph D. Brown of the Kem Manufacturing Company:

It is not good business for labor, business, or the farmer to depend upon the Government to do their thinking and financing. American history teaches us that our success is due largely to independent thinking and financing. It is only human for people to lose their initiative when they feel that there is always someone to pull their chestnuts out of the fire, so as to speak.[4]

*Government Spending Undermines Business Confidence.*—One of the most persistent opposition attacks was aimed at the spending provisions of the bill. Walter H. Wheeler, Jr., president of Pitney-Bowes, stated:

A large segment of business believes that under this bill, if enacted into law, the Government would immediately seek to effect by its own spending a state of employment at least somewhat comparable to that existing during the past few years, with continued heavy deficit financing, and no long-term budget balancing. This, to my mind, would be a serious mistake, and I do not believe it is contemplated, but there is absolutely no

[1] See, for instance, Citizens National Committee, Inc., *Full Employment and the National Budget*, Research Report No. 2–417 (Washington, 1945), p. 19, and H. W. Prentiss, *Competitive Enterprise versus Planned Economy*, National Association of Manufacturers (New York, August, 1945), p. 13.

[2] *Hearings before a Subcommittee of the Committee on Banking and Currency, on S.380*, 79th Cong., 1st Sess. (Washington, 1945), pp. 540–541.

[3] Gould Lincoln in the Washington *Star*, Sept. 8, 1945.

[4] *Senate Hearings on S.380*, pp. 1018–1019. See also the testimony of Albert Goss, Master of the National Grange, *ibid.*, p. 591.

assurance now in the bill to so indicate. In fact, quite the contrary is a more legitimate assumption; and if it is not corrected, the measure might well cause such a lack of confidence as to result in more unemployment rather than less.[5]

*Economic Forecasting for Over-all Employment Planning Impossible.*—The conservative pressures concentrated heavy fire on those sections of S.380 dealing with the preparation of the National Production and Employment Budget. Perhaps typical was the statement of Ralph E. Flanders:

A dangerous feature of the bill is the proposal that this information [reports on economic conditions] be used as the basis for determining what shall be done throughout the following fiscal year. It involves the element of prophecy. I seriously doubt if prophecy is possible. We cannot prophesy clearly enough to make these advance determinations.[6]

Closely associated with this argument was the further charge that the economic prognostications of the government would by themselves have an unwholesome effect upon our economic life. If the President announced for instance that a depression was in the offing, the announcement itself might bring on a depression.[7]

*S. 380 Would Lead to Inflation.*—Finally, a number of attacks were made on the inflationary implications of the bill. It was argued that "it does not follow that unemployment can be eradicated by simply spending more until full employment is reached. Long before that point is reached, inflationary price rises would be produced."[8]

This by no means exhausts the list of arguments leveled against S.380.[9] Some extreme conservatives talked about the desirability of "riding the business cycle,"[10] others advocated a "floating pool

[5] *Ibid.*, p. 603. For a comparable statement, see article by Dr. Walter E. Spahr in the *Commercial and Financial Chronicle*, Sept. 28, 1945.

[6] *Senate Hearings on S.380*, p. 1067. See also Citizens National Committee, Inc., *Full Employment and the National Budget*, Research Report No. 2-417 (Washington, 1945), p. 16, and the testimony of James L. Donnelly, *Senate Hearings on S.380*, p. 666.

[7] *Hearings before the Committee on Expenditures in the Executive Departments, on H.R. 2202*, 79th Cong., 1st Sess. (Washington, 1945), p. 305.

[8] G. Habeler, Professor of Economics, Harvard University, in a letter to Senator Wagner, May 18, 1945, printed in *Senate Hearings on S.380*, pp. 1092-1093.

[9] See *Senate Hearings on S.380*, especially the Appendix, for additional criticisms.

[10] Ralph B. Blodgett, "We Need Those Depressions," University of Illinois Bulletin, Aug. 24, 1945, quoted in U.S. Senate, "Assuring Full Employment in a Free Competitive Economy," *Report from the Committee on Banking and Currency*, Senate Report No. 583, 79th Cong., 1st Sess., Sept. 22, 1945 (Washington, 1945), p. 23.

of unemployed." [11] But such ideas, even if shared among certain limited groups, were, for obvious reasons of public relations, not widely publicized.

In general, the analysis which the conservative pressures presented to the public and Congress was that S.380 was totalitarian and un-American in implication, destructive of free enterprise, and dangerous or impractical in its underlying economic theories. Some of the more moderate conservative spokesmen, as we shall see in the following chapter, were willing to accept the bill if certain qualifying amendments were adopted. The Committee for Economic Development particularly followed this line.[12] But the most powerful voices of the right wanted the bill destroyed, or severely emasculated.

How then did the conservative pressures attempt to sell their ideological wares? Space prohibits a detailed consideration of more than a few organizations, but these few were important.

### THE NATIONAL ASSOCIATION OF MANUFACTURERS

David Cushman Coyle, writing in *Harper's Magazine* about the conservative businessman, makes the following analysis:

He loves free enterprise, private business, the Constitution, and the American Way of Life. But most of his opinions about politics are sold to him by the larger organizations in business and finance, among whom the monopolists have most to gain by political action, and therefore do the fastest game of propaganda.[13]

One of the most powerful of these organizations is the National Association of Manufacturers. Represented on the 1945 N.A.M. Executive Committee, which comprises a type of inner sanctum of the Board of Directors, were such industrial giants as the National Cash Register Company, E. I. duPont de Nemours, the California Packing Corporation, Swift and Company, the Chrysler Corporation, the Borden Company, the Sun Oil Company, and the Mon-

[11] Mr. Carlyle Fraser, Atlanta Chamber of Commerce, quoted in Senate Report No. 583, p. 23.

[12] See *Senate Hearings on S.380*, pp. 356–366 and 393–399. See also the testimony of Walter H. Wheeler, *ibid.*, pp. 602–607. The C.E.D. is not included as a "pressure" group because it made no attempt to *initiate* direct or indirect pressures on legislators. It testified when called upon, and, at Will Whittington's suggestion, submitted a bill draft which was important in the history of S.380 (see Chapter VII). But it has intentionally stayed as far away as possible from conventional pressure activities.

[13] "Planning Is a Fighting Word," June, 1946, p. 557.

santo Chemical Company.[14] Although some of these are not strict monopolies, they are all powerful enough to exert monopolistic pressures in their respective industries.[15]

The pace of N.A.M.'s campaign against the Full Employment Bill was forced by the sudden shift of the hearing schedule from October back to late August, 1945. Senator Wagner's request for N.A.M. testimony resulted in a hurried meeting of the Executive Committee in New York, and swift action on the part of the N.A.M.'s research staff to prepare testimony for Ira Mosher, president of the association.[16] In addition, the N.A.M. developed by August 28—the date of Mosher's appearance before the Senate committee—a "Program for Permanent Prosperity" which was filed with the committee for insertion in the printed hearings.[17]

*Testimony.*—One cannot get a true picture of the N.A.M.'s attitude toward the Full Employment Bill from the Senate hearings alone. Recognizing that the Senate subcommittee would be weighted against him, Ira Mosher with the aid of N.A.M. research and public relations specialists, drew up a statement which was a masterpiece of moderation and conciliation. The technique is reflected in Mosher's opening words:

My purpose in appearing before you today is fourfold:
1) To endorse the objective—full employment—to which these hearings are directed;
2) To compliment the sponsors of S.380, the proposal which you currently are considering, for the open-minded manner in which they have solicited and considered all varieties of opinion on the measure they propose;
3) To raise certain questions about the practical operation of the bill as now written; and
4) To suggest an alternate approach which manufacturers believe is far more certain to assure full employment than the proposal now under consideration.[18]

In the House hearings, however, under the friendly stimulation of the House committee members, Mr. Mosher changed his approach:

---

[14] National Association of Manufacturers, June 15, 1945 (mimeograph).
[15] See Clair Wilcox, *Competition and Monopoly in American Industry*, T.N.E.C. Monograph No. 21 (Washington, 1940), *passim.*
[16] Miss McKane, N.A.M., in an interview, New York City, Feb. 28, 1946.
[17] See *Senate Hearings on S.380*, pp. 490–500.     [18] *Ibid.*, p. 460.

It is my private opinion that the bill is nothing more nor less than a plain Government-spending bill.[19]

. . . there could be no greater discouragement to business [than this type of legislation].[20]

. . . if depression unemployment occurs . . . the Federal Government [should] make such contributions to the States as necessary to enable them to provide the needed relief [direct relief or W.P.A.].[21]

The positive program for full employment submitted by N.A.M. included recommendations for (1) creation of a committee of experts to study money and credit,[22] (2) a major revision in our tax laws and general governmental policies which would promote confidence among investors,[23] and (3) the elimination of all special favors and all special privileges.[24] The last included among other things more vigorous enforcement of the anti-trust laws, labor curbs, a progressive but gradual reduction in tariffs, and international agreements to end cartels.[25]

*Educational Campaign.*—Although N.A.M. pressures against the Full Employment Bill did not reach top efficiency until after the Senate fight, an educational campaign aganst the bill was started soon after the bill's introduction.

On January 25, 1945, three days after S.380 was introduced, H. W. Prentiss, president of Armstrong Cork and former president of the N.A.M., attacked the bill in a speech before a Cincinnati businessmen's association.[26] N.A.M. printed Prentiss's address and gave it wide distribution. What wide distribution means can be judged from the following letter which Senator Murray received from a constituent:

Dear Senator Murray:
The enclosed pamphlet, in which H. W. Prentiss, Jr., states that your Full Employment Bill would lead to "state socialism" was placed in the box in which each teacher receives official school notices, etc. in the office of the Fergus County High School at Lewistown, Montana.
Other pamphlets put into the boxes, apparently with official sanction by the school's authorities (and certainly with no protest on their part) included these titles: *The American Triangle of Plenty*, by F. C. Crawford; *What Bureaucracy Means to You: Prices, Profits, and Production*, by Charles S. Davis, President, Borg-Warner; *Jobs and the Woman*, by

---

[19] See *Senate Hearings on S.380*, p. 556.          [20] *Ibid.*, p. 576.
[21] *Ibid.*, p. 575.          [22] *Senate Hearings on S.380*, p. 464.
[23] *Ibid.*, pp. 466–467.          [24] *Ibid.*, p. 465.          [25] *Ibid.*, pp. 493–496.
[26] The speech was in connection with the Golden Anniversary of the N.A.M.

Ruth M. Leach, v.p. International Business Machines Corporation. All of the pamphlets are published and distributed by the National Association of Manufacturers. All are biased, political tracts.

They were given me by one of the teachers who received them. I thought it would interest you to know of this instance of interference with the freedom of teaching in a Montana high school. I hope you can take steps to have the practice discontinued.[27]

This letter which hints at the ubiquitous coverage of N.A.M.'s informational services supplements the findings of the LaFollette Committee in 1939, which listed some of N.A.M.'s media for disseminating ideas and information: "Radio speeches, public meetings, news, cartoons, editorials, advertising, [and] motion pictures. . . ."[28]

To its own membership of 16,000 and to a wide mailing list, N.A.M. circulated its *N.A.M. News* of September 1, 1945, which carried summary statements of Ira Mosher's testimony on S.380 and the N.A.M.'s "Program of Permanent Prosperity." In October, 1945, to 2,500 columnists and editorial writers over the nation, went N.A.M.'s "Industry's Views." This one-page flyer was called "The Full Employment Record of Private Business" and included a chart, the burden of which was that private enterprise had maintained full employment until the federal government stepped in in 1930 and began a program of deficit financing. Under the chart were the words, "Mats of this chart may be had on request to the Distribution Section, National Association of Manufacturers, 14 West 49th Street, New York 20, N.Y."

This attention to "mats" brings up the services supplied by N.A.M. to rural newspapers. The Association circulates a clip sheet which "feeds stuff all ready to go to print to 7,500 weekly newspapers."[29] Even a hasty glance through Senator Murray's press clipping notebooks on S.380 reveals that this material was not circulated in vain. In Chapter X below, more specific mention is made of this, but it is important to mention here that through this service to the rural press, and through its "Farm and Industry," a release sent to 35,000 farm leaders, N.A.M. pays considerable attention to opinion in rural and small-town America.[30] Over a period of years,

27 This letter was shown to me by a staff member of the Banking and Currency Committee.
28 Quoted in V. O. Key, *Politics, Parties, and Pressure Groups* (New York, 1946), pp. 130–131.
29 *Trainmen News*, June 24, 1947.
30 *Ibid*. N.A.M. is not alone in this. The money of the Pew family of Pennsylvania

N.A.M. helps to shape the climate of opinion of a vast segment of our population—general attitudes toward labor, business, and federal policies. Together with other conservative pressures, N.A.M. attempts to insure that an identity will be created between the interests of business and the interests of agriculture. The politics of full employment cannot be understood without a clear recognition of this fact.

*General Motors and James C. Ingebretsen.*—N.A.M.'s influence is often reinforced by the separate activities of some of its largest contributors.[31] Perhaps the most striking job undertaken by the opponents of S.380 was sponsored by Donaldson Brown, vice-chairman of the General Motors Corporation, and a member of the 1945 N.A.M. Board of Directors.

Sometime in September, 1945, Donaldson Brown received a Washington news-letter which suggested that the Full Employment Bill would probably pass because of the sparseness of business opposition. Brown became excited and talked with Leonard Read of the National Industrial Conference Board. Brown indicated that he wanted to testify against the Full Employment Bill in the House and asked Read's advice about a possible research man who could prepare material for him. Read suggested a Los Angeles lawyer by the name of J. C. Ingebretsen who had done a considerable amount of legislative reporting for the Los Angeles Chamber of Commerce. Brown wired Ingebretsen, brought him on to New York, and set him up in Room 2400 of the Waldorf Astoria hotel. When Ingebretsen arrived, he told Brown that he would need some assistance on the technical economic aspects of S.380. Through Leonard Read, contacts were made with Dr. Jules Backman of the New York University School of Commerce. Backman had previously done work for the National Retail Dry Goods Association against O.P.A.

For over a month in September and October, 1945, Ingebretsen and Backman labored on the compilation of anti-Full Employment Bill material for Donaldson Brown. Early in this period, Ingebret-

is behind the *Farm Journal* and the *Pathfinder*, the top farm magazines in America from the standpoint of circulation. Frank Gannet, spark plug of the Committee for Constitutional Government, is the owner of a string of rural newspapers in upper New York state and publisher of the *American Agriculturalist*.

[31] The following story is based upon interviews with James C. Ingebretsen, Washington, D.C., March 26, 1946; Representative Carter Manasco, Washington, D.C., Feb. 20, 1946; John Costello, Washington, D.C., Feb. 15, 1946; and Dr. Jules Bachman, New York City, Feb. 28, 1946.

sen made frequent trips to Washington and through John Costello, Los Angeles Chamber of Commerce Washington representative and former Congressman, Ingebretsen was introduced to Carter Manasco, chairman of the House Committee on Expenditures. Manasco told Ingebretsen of the trouble the committee was having in lining up opposition witnesses to the Full Employment Bill and solicited Ingebretsen's aid. Ingebretsen returned to New York, talked with representatives of the N.A.M., the Commerce and Industry Association, Charles Eaton, Jr., of the National Association of State Chambers of Commerce, and other business leaders. Through these contacts, Ingebretsen prepared a list of opposition witnesses which he submitted to Manasco. The latter used the list as the basis for selecting many of the witnesses who testified against the bill in the House committee hearings.

Among the opposition witnesses scheduled to appear, of course, was Donaldson Brown. Two weeks before he was to testify, however, Brown went riding, fell off his horse, and broke his collarbone. In order to make sure that Ingebretsen and Backman had not labored in vain, Brown, through the New York offices of General Motors and N.A.M., saw to it that the prepared material was mimeographed for distribution to the other opposition witnesses. Some of this material was also sent through John Costello to "friendly" House committee members.

The bulk of Ingebretsen's and Backman's labors were contained in two sizable mimeographed documents. The first began with a "Bibliography of Critical Comments and Analyses," continued with an outline of "Main Criticisms of Full Employment Bill" and then proceeded to spell out "Types of Questions Directed to Opposition Witnesses and Suggested Answers." The questions were abstracted from the cross-examination in the published Senate Hearings.

The second publication was called *A Compilation in Excerpt Form of Statements and Expressions of Views Exposing Inherent Fallacies and Contradictions of the So-Called "Full Employment" Bill, S.380.* It was divided into eight sections:

Section 1: The Full Employment Bill (S. 380) Means Government Controls.
Section 2: The Full Employment Bill (S. 380) Destroys Private Enterprise.

Section 3: The Full Employment Bill (S. 380) Will Increase Powers of
the Executive.
Section 4: "Full" Employment Guaranteed—Criticisms—Terms.
Section 5: The Full Employment Bill (S. 380) Legalizes a Compensatory
Fiscal Policy—Federal Spending and Pump Priming.
Section 6: The Full Employment Bill (S. 380) Leads to Socialism.
Section 7: The Full Employment Bill (S. 380) is Unworkable, Imprac-
tical, and Promises Too Much.
Section 8: The Full Employment Bill (S. 380) Items for Ridicule.

Section 8 represented an interesting device. It included seven
items for ridicule, a typical example of which is the following:

### RIDICULE AND LAUGH AT THEM:

The Majority Report Observes:
"Witnesses before the subcommittee and correspondents whose letters
are in the Record emphasized that the present postwar outlook is *as
unstable as our past experience.*" (Senate Report on S.380, p. 2.)
    What! In the face of the abundant life brought in by the New Deal?
    What! After fifteen years of super-efforts of the New Deal for "recov-
ery and reform?"
    What! After spending $23 billions of government money in peacetime
and over $250 billions in war?

Altogether, the work of James C. Ingebretsen and Dr. Jules Backman on behalf of the vice-chairman of General Motors represented
a sizable contribution to the chairman and conservative members
of the House Committee. Congressmen like Carter Manasco and
Will Whittington had no Bertram Gross, but they were obviously
not without staff assistance. In preparing for the hearings they had
the assistance of General Motors. In redrafting the legislation, as
we shall see, they had the assistance of the Machinery and Allied
Products Institute, the Committee for Economic Development, and
the Chamber of Commerce. In educating the public, they had the
assistance of the N.A.M., the Committee for Constitutional Government, and the American Farm Bureau Federation—to name but a
few.

### THE CHAMBER OF COMMERCE

The United States Chamber of Commerce is a federation of
1,700 business organizations—"state and local chambers of commerce, trade associations, and societies of businessmen not or-

ganized for private purposes." [32] Separate consideration must be given to its work and to that of its affiliates.

Its general activities and functions are too well known to need any detailed elaboration in a book of this type. V. O. Key has written the following summary:

It maintains a staff at its headquarters in Washington to conduct research and to make known the views of organized business to Congress and to administrative agencies. Its committees analyse issues as they arise and disseminate information to the membership and to the interested public outside. Its publicity staff prepares for release to the daily press and to specialized journals news about and views of the Chamber. Its official organ, *Nation's Business,* presents the Chamber's views to the membership and to the public. During Congressional sessions its staff follows closely the work of Congress and keeps the membership informed on legislative developments relevant to their interests.[33]

Probably the most influential man in the Chamber of Commerce from the standpoint of shaping business opinion about full employment was Emerson P. Schmidt, director of the Economic Research Department. One of the earliest full-fledged attacks on S.380 came from his pen in the form of a Chamber of Commerce *Post-War Readjustments Bulletin* published in March, 1945.[34] Although the Chamber made it clear that this *Bulletin* was "not a report of the Chamber of Commerce" and did not, therefore, necessarily represent its views, it is hardly likely that a study of this sort would have been distributed by the Chamber if it had represented alien views. Actually, the March, 1945, *Bulletin* was thirteenth in a series of identically sponsored studies to which reference was made in Chapter III.

Less than a month later, in April, 1945, *Nation's Business* carried a story on the Full Employment Bill, and from then until the final passage of S.380 the Chamber headquarters in Washington kept careful track of the legislation. After the passage of the bill in the Senate, the Chamber's Board of Directors at its meeting on November 30 expressed opposition to the Senate-passed version of S.380, and ordered that a report called "A Program for Sustaining Employment," which had been prepared by the Chamber's Committee on Economic Policy, be printed and distributed to the membership

[32] V. O. Key, *op. cit.,* p. 126.　　　[33] *Ibid.,* p. 128.
[34] "Can Government Guarantee Full Employment?"

as representing the views of their Committee.[35] Emerson Schmidt as Secretary of the Committee on Economic Policy had a large hand in the writing of this later report.

On December 7, 1945, the Chamber published a Special Number of their *Legislative Daily,* which was devoted to a comparison of the Senate-passed bill and the version of the bill reported by the House committee. In the eyes of the Chamber, the House bill was vastly preferable. The Special Number also contained an objective statement of the prinicipal arguments for and against the bill as passed in the Senate. It concluded with a section on the "Position of the U.S. Chamber" which began with the statement:

The Chamber deplores, and will actively oppose, any effort, whether direct or indirect, to substitute for our tried and proven American system of free enterprise either new or old theories of economics, regardless of the source of the effort or its Utopian objective.[36]

It is interesting to note, in light of what finally happened to the Full Employment Bill, that the Board of Directors of the Chamber expressed agreement with recommendations for the "creation of a permanent Economic Commission to make continuing studies and recommendations to achieve" the goal of "a high level of productive employment in a free voluntary society" and "of a Joint Congressional Committee to review the findings of the new Commission as a guide to future Congressional action." [37] A discussion of the contribution of the Chamber to the drafting of the House bill must wait until a later chapter, but it must be noted here that its clear preference for the House Committee's version as against the Senate-passed version of S.380, and its agreement with recommendations for some sort of governmental planning mechanism, were not lost on the conservative leaders of the House committee.

In view of this general hostility to the Full Employment Bill, it may be wondered why no representative of the Chamber testified before either the Senate or House Committee. The reason was that the then President, Eric Johnston, was *not* opposed to S.380, and although for reasons of institutional loyalty Johnston made no public statement endorsing the bill, he, as the logical representative of the Chamber, refused to testify against it.[88]

35 U.S. Chamber of Commerce, "Governmental Affairs," *Legislative Daily,* Vol. II, No. 255, Dec. 7, 1945, p. 5.
  36 *Ibid.*        37 *Ibid.*        38 *House Hearings on H.R.2202,* p. 441.

*State and Local Chambers of Commerce.*—The reaction of some of the state and local chambers of commerce to S.380 made the position of the national Chamber seem relatively mild. This is quite understandable when it is recognized that the national Chamber exerts no rigid policy control over affiliated organizations, but merely supplies such affiliates with information.

A comparison of the Chamber's *Legislative Daily* on S.380, referred to earlier, with the statements of various state and local chambers of commerce printed in the House *Hearings,* or with the Los Angeles Chamber of Commerce pamphlet, *The Economic Sentinel,*[39] would seem to indicate that more went into the formulation of local business opinion about the Full Employment Bill than national Chamber propaganda.

One of the most extreme diatribes against S.380 was a "Private Bulletin to Members" issued by the Ohio Chamber of Commerce on September 17, 1945, and inserted in the printed *Hearings* of the House Committee by Congressman Clare Hoffman of Michigan. After attacking what it called "Fake C.I.O.–P.A.C. 'Unemployment Crisis' Propaganda," the bulletin continued:

The Communist-sparked C.I.O.–P.A.C., aided by its political fellow-travelers, is now making the drive which has been in preparation for years. Everything that has happened up to now has been but a preliminary.

This is the hour, almost the moment, of historic decision. The basic goal of C.I.O.–P.A.C. is to overturn our system of competitive, private enterprise and substitute for it complete government control over capital and labor alike. . . .

Keystone of the new group of "crisis" legislative enactments, devised by the same cunning brains that have guided this boasted bloodless revolution, is the full employment bill, now being seriously considered in Washington.

Labeled in fraud and deception as a bill designed to preserve private enterprise, if enacted, it would be the scaffold on which private enterprise could be dropped to its death. . . . [40]

Then, after urging the members to collect facts about the existing labor shortage, and to "place these real facts in the hands of our elected public officials," the bulletin concludes: "If the C.I.O.–P.A.C. Federal legislative program succeeds, the Government moves in as the new management of your company." [41]

[39] "The Full Employment Act of 1945," Vol. III, No. 3, October, 1945.
[40] *House Hearings on H.R.2202,* p. 390.    [41] *Ibid.,* p. 391.

Most of the statements submitted by various state chambers of commerce to the House committee, and the testimony of Dr. Walter E. Spahr, Professor of Economics at New York University, on behalf of the National Association of State Chambers of Commerce, were not as extreme as the Ohio Chamber bulletin. But taken together, they represented a widespread and uncompromising business attack on the Full Employment Bill.

*The Significance of the Chamber of Commerce.*—Although the U.S. Chamber and various state chambers were of considerable assistance to the chairman and conservative leaders of the House committee, providing them with conservative ammunition against S.380, the main contribution of the various Chambers to the opposition cause was educational. If one takes into consideration the 2,000 organizations and the 15,000 business firms and corporations affiliated with the U.S. Chamber, and the 135,000 individual members of the U.S. Junior Chamber of Commerce,[42] it is obvious that a large section of business opinion is reached by Chamber activities. Small business in particular is at the base of the federation: leadership in small and medium-sized towns and cities throughout America is often exerted by the leading business or banking concerns in the locality, but the rank and file membership is composed of the shopkeepers, real estate dealers, insurance salesmen, lawyers, and bankers who make up the local business community. The ideas about national legislation which are formulated by the national Chamber and by committees of affiliated organizations permeate, in the long run, the minds of the vast majority of American citizens who identify themselves with business interests. And since one of the aims is to sell "business" and "free enterprise" to the public at large, the influence of the Chamber extends beyond business organizations per se. On August 28, 1945, the Cleveland *Plain Dealer* carried the following story:

William A. Porterfield, a leading Canton industrialist and a director of the Ohio Chamber of Commerce, spoke before the American Legion at a lunch today.

Asserting that forecasts of heavy unemployment in the reconversion period were misleading, Porterfield said that estimates running up as high as 10 million were particularly unfortunate and declared that they were made to "scare Congress and the Administration into poorly considered measures such as the Murray full employment bill."

[42] *The World Almanac 1946* (New York, 1946), p. 588.

In one minor job of public relations, the ideas of the Ohio chamber were transmitted to another pressure group, to the newspaper-reading public, and to the Ohio Congressmen and Senators who keep up with home-state news. It is this type of indirect pressure which makes the Chamber of Commerce a powerful influence on national policy.

### THE COMMITTEE FOR CONSTITUTIONAL GOVERNMENT

The story of the Committee for Constitutional Government has been told best by the Committee itself. In 1944 it published and circulated a pamphlet called, *Needed Now—Capacity for Leadership, Courage to Lead* [43] which spelled out the history of the organization from its inception in 1937. Started initially by a group of men opposed to President Roosevelt's Supreme Court "packing" plan, the Committee, under the leadership of Frank Gannett, Sumner Gerard, Dr. Willford I. King, and former Indiana Congressman Samuel Pettengill, has become one of the most remarkable (although perhaps overrated) "influence" groups in America. Dedicated to "the preservation and strengthening of constitutional safeguards," the Committee has fought such threats to Americanism as Roosevelt's Reorganization Plan of 1938, the Roosevelt "purge" of 1938, the "spend-lend" bill of 1939, the Wagner Health Bill, the third term, wartime limitations on salaries, and the Full Employment Bill. It has campaigned for a Constitutional amendment to limit "the power of Congress to impose income, inheritance, and gift taxes to a maximum of 25 percent." [44]

Harold Ickes once labeled the activities of the Committee "mail order government." [45] Some indication of its technique can be gleaned from its own description of the campaign against the Supreme Court "packing" plan.

During the first twenty-four weeks, 10,000,000 envelopes packed with arguments against the court plan cascaded into the mails. Every envelope went to a carefully chosen recipient.

Each recipient was a "leadership individual" in his locality—editor, physician, leader, professional man. There were educators, members of civic bodies or patriotic organizations, members of women's clubs, governors, mayors, commissioners, and contributors to party funds. Every mailing brought in additional names; men and women who became in-

[43] Committee for Constitutional Government, Inc., New York, 1944.
[44] *Ibid.*, p. 25.      [45] *Ibid.*, p. 11.

terested in the Committee's work suggested others in their communities. And so grew the permanent mailing list of key individuals which has enabled the Committee to project as quickly as it does an issue to the country.[46]

Between 1937 and 1944, "in mobilizing and educating public opinion on constitutional issues," the Committee sent out:

82,000,000 pieces of literature—booklets, pamphlets, reprints of editorials and articles, specially addressed letters and 760,000 books.

More than 10,000 transcriptions, carrying 15 minute radio talks on national issues, besides frequent national hook-ups for representatives of the Committee.

350,000 telegrams to citizens to arouse them to action on great issues.

Many thousands of releases to daily and weekly newspapers. Full page advertisements in 536 different newspapers with a combined circulation of nearly 20,000,000.[47]

Back in 1943 the Committee presaged its later attack on S.380 by circulating a leaflet called "Full Employment—Or Else!" a chapter from Henry Wriston's book *Challenge to Freedom*, in which Wriston attacked the goal of full employment as "a manifestation of sentimental humanitarianism."

In 1945, the Committee's main attack against S.380 was in the form of a pamphlet called "Full Employment and Freedom in America" which was an embellished condensation of an address by Virgil Jordan of the N.A.M.-sponsored National Industrial Conference Board.[48] Accompanying the condensation were cartoons showing bureaucrats telling workers where they must work and at what jobs, and telling consumers what they were allowed to buy. The pamphlet also included an article by Samuel Pettengill called "The Ancestry of the Bill" which traced the "family tree" back to the Constitution of Communist Russia. "This Russian spawn," according to Pettengill, "entered the womb of the National Resources Planning Board. . . . Then Henry Agard Wallace, four Senators, President Truman, and Sidney Hillman ordered long pants for the child and we find sonny-boy playing around in the halls of Congress." [49] According to Pettengill's somewhat compli-

[46] *Ibid.*, p. 6.                          [47] *Ibid.*, p. 30.
[48] Condensation by the Committee for Constitutional Government, Inc., of a statement by Dr. Virgil Jordan before the Controllers Institute of America, St. Louis, May 31, 1945.                          [49] *Ibid.*, p. 11.

cated metaphor, the uncles of the child were Adolf Hitler and
Benito Mussolini.

On the final page of the pamphlet, the Committee made a statement of its own:

> No Congress was ever confronted with such a barrage of socialist legis-
> lation as is now pending in Washington with the combined support of
> large groups of radicals, heavily financed pressure groups, backed by
> left-wing press and radio, and with C.I.O.–P.A.C. as the most formidable
> supporter.
>
> The Communist party says of the Murray "Full Employment" bill
> (S.380) "Congress *must* adopt this legislation." . . . If not amended,
> with its most dangerous features removed, this mislabeled "Full Em-
> ployment" bill (really bigger government—more debts—more taxes)
> may turn America permanently from constitutional private enterprise
> toward a system of collectivist statism.
>
> Make yourself a committee of one. Arouse members of your family,
> your associates, fellow workers in your unions, in service clubs. Give each
> a copy of this bulletin. Write your Congressmen and Senators. Tell them
> you will never forget how they vote on these bills, and will support them
> if they put the nation's interest above the selfish demands of pressure
> groups. Distribute this pamphlet widely.[50]

Circulated to a mailing list running into the hundreds of
thousands,[51] material of this sort unquestionably stimulated a certain amount of indirect pressure against the Full Employment Bill
and, of course, provided additional ammunition for the Congressional opponents of S.380.

An accurate evaluation of the impact of the Committee for Constitutional Government's activities on the history of S.380 is of
course impossible. The isolationist stand of some of their leaders
before Pearl Harbor reduced the organization's prestige, and of
course pressure of the sort exerted by the Committee inevitably
faces a kind of law of diminishing returns.[52] All that can be said
with any assurance is that the work of the Committee was an additional factor in building up the case of the conservative opposition.[53]

[50] *Ibid.*, p. 12.

[51] In the Committee's New York office, I was told that the regular mailing list was
550,000.

[52] See Estes Kefauver and Jack Levin, *A Twentieth Century Congress* (New York,
1947), Chapter XIII, for a discussion of the effect of this type of letter campaign on
Congressmen.

[53] Another organization which carried on a campaign similar to that of the Committee for Constitutional Government was the National Economic Council under

### THE AMERICAN FARM BUREAU FEDERATION

No story of the conservative pressures against the Full Employment Bill would be complete without some reference to the farm organizations. The American Farm Bureau Federation was not the only farm group which opposed the bill, but it was by far the most important.

In order to understand the position of the Farm Bureau on S.380 it is necessary to recognize two facts: (1) that big agriculture is big business; and (2) that regardless of claims that it represents 830,000 farm families in 45 states,[54] the Farm Bureau hews close to the viewpoint of the big commercial farmers.[55]

*The Farm Bureau and Business.*—The frequent identity of interest between the policy-makers in the Farm Bureau and those in the large business organizations is reflected in their parallel attitudes towards many controversial issues. For example, the Missouri Valley Authority was attacked by the Farm Bureau, the power companies, and the railroads; the Case Labor Bill was backed by the N.A.M., the Chamber of Commerce, and the Farm Bureau; the California Central Valley power development was fought by the California Power Company and the Farm Bureau; the Cooley Farm Security Adminstration Bill was opposed by the Farm Bureau and the American Bankers Association.[56] "Both the Farm Bureau and the Grange . . . are actively represented on the agriculture committee of the U.S. Chamber of Commerce." [57]

*The Activities of the Farm Bureau.*—The functions of the Farm Bureau have been summed up by Blaisdell in his T.N.E.C. Monograph on *Economic Power and Political Pressures.*

In striving for the realization of its program, the Farm Bureau acts as the national organization of local groups, brings pressure to bear on legislators in the determination of government policy, broadcasts its views on both general and particular issues, and unifies State Farm Bureau activ-

---

the direction of the egregious Merwin K. Hart. Vol. III, No. 12A, of the Economic Council's Papers (September, 1945) carried the headlines, "If you are Opposed to Communism—STOP THE FULL EMPLOYMENT BILL." An attached blue sheet called "See Here, Mr. Voter" concluded with the warning, "Don't send a copy of this pamphlet with your letter. State your own ideas in your letter."

[54] *House Hearings on H.R.2202,* p. 739.

[55] See Donald C. Blaisdell, *Economic Power and Political Pressures,* T.N.E.C. Monograph No. 26 (Washington, 1941), p. 177.

[56] *National Union Farmer,* April 15, 1946, p. 5.

[57] See Wesley C. McCune, *The Farm Bloc* (New York, 1943), pp. 8–11.

ities. In pushing its national program the A.F.B.F. is brought into close contact with Congress, the administrative agencies, and the Federal Courts. Also, it publishes a monthly magazine, a bi-weekly news letter, publicity releases, and special articles for farm journals, produces a monthly radio program, furnishes speech and program material, and performs other services of an informational nature.[58]

As recently as June, 1944, *Fortune* stated that "As matters now stand few things in politics are as certain as [Farm Bureau President] Ed O'Neal's ability to get votes." [59] *Fortune* listed five methods by which the Farm Bureau influences Congress:

1. It rewards its friends with reelection. Local Bureau organizations get out the vote.
2. It makes it very unpleasant for Congressmen who oppose its measures.
3. It defends Congress against the President, which is duck soup for Congressmen. Ed is a spectacular critic of the "bureaucrats."
4. It offers prominence and publicity to friendly legislators.
5. It is very skillful at log rolling and trading with other pressure groups.[60]

*The Farm Bureau and S.380.*—Like other conservative pressures, the Farm Bureau did not start its real campaign against the Full Employment Bill until relatively late. No representative of the Bureau testified before the Senate Committee, although President O'Neal sent a long telegram to Wagner on August 30, 1945, stating that the Farm Bureau's Board of Directors had just met in Chicago and were in definite opposition to S.380.[61] The full Board statement was also sent by mail to every Senator.[62]

During the House fight, the Farm Bureau exerted a substantial amount of direct and indirect pressure. Through their *News Letter* and their slick-paper *Nation's Agriculture* they publicized their opposition, and they followed this up with heavy personal pressure on key Congressmen like Carter Manasco and Will Whittington who came from strong Farm Bureau areas.[63] W. R. Ogg, director of the Farm Bureau's Washington office, testified before the House committee and presented a long statement of O'Neal's for inclusion in the printed hearings.[64] O'Neal's statement was quite similar to

[58] *Op. cit.*, p. 177.
[59] Quoted in Stuart Chase, *Democracy under Pressure* (New York, 1945), p. 97.
[60] *Ibid.*, pp. 97–98.   [61] *Senate Hearings on S.380*, pp. 830–831.
[62] James D. Parel, Washington Office of the American Farm Bureau Federation, in an interview, Washington, D.C., July 17, 1946.
[63] *Ibid.*   [64] *House Hearings on H.R.2202*, pp. 738–754.

the statements submitted by business organizations with one interesting exception: "The Farmers of the Nation resent not being able to hire help because relief projects in the community *can outbid them for labor*" (italics supplied).[65] In these few words, O'Neal suggested that one of the paramount reasons for Farm Bureau opposition to the Full Employment Bill was the big farmer's fear of losing cheap farm labor. This fear was echoed by many Congressmen, including the chairman of the House Committee, Carter Manasco, who asked Mr. Ogg the following rhetorical question:

Wouldn't it be necessary, ultimately, if this bill were put into effect, and implemented by the legislation necessary to carry it out, to carry out the commitments under the bill, for the government to freeze all men on the farm? Because if they started leaving the farms to work for these government projects, somebody would go hungry.[66]

In terms of direct pressures on key Southern and Midwestern rural Congressmen, it is probable that no organization was of more importance in the fight against S.380 than the American Farm Bureau Federation.

### EVALUATION OF THE CONSERVATIVE PRESSURES

Space has limited the study of conservative pressures to a relatively few organizations, but perhaps sufficient examples have been given to provide the reader with an appreciation of the scope and power of the opposition pressures which were mobilized late, but tellingly, against the Full Employment Bill. Through educational campaigns, testimony, and direct and indirect pressures on Congress, the conservative lobby made its weight felt.

But the short-run, overt influence of the conservative pressures pales before their long-run and less obvious influence. Through the considered use of word-symbols over a couple of generations; through the attention paid by business and big commercial agriculture to rural opinion; through the concerted drive of business organizations to convince the public-at-large that "What is good for business is good for America," the conservative pressures helped to shape the prepossessions which a majority of our national legislators brought with them to the 79th Congress. This educational campaign pays enormous dividends. Many legislators vote their own conscience and would be affronted by attempts of conservative or-

[65] *Ibid.*, p. 741.                    [66] *Ibid.*, p. 754.

ganizations to exert direct influence on their votes. What they fail to recognize is that their consciences have been previously conditioned by the climate of values assiduously cultivated by these same conservative pressures. It is there, not in campaign contributions, direct lobbying, and letter campaigns, that the real and enormous power of the conservative lobby rests.

# CHAPTER EIGHT

# The House Disapproves

> The committee reports, upon which the
> debates take place, are backed by neither
> party; they represent merely the recom-
> mendations of a small body of members
> belonging to both parties, and are quite
> as likely to divide the vote of the party to
> which the majority of the committee be-
> long as they are to meet with opposition
> from the other side of the chamber. If
> they are carried, it is no party triumph;
> if they are lost, it is no party discomfiture.
> —Wilson, *Congressional Government*,
> p. 96.

ON FEBRUARY 15, 1945, the Full Employment Bill as H.R.2202 was
introduced in the House of Representatives by Congressman
Wright Patman of Texas. The choice of Patman is another indication of the care exercised by the Senate sponsors in developing their
legislative strategy. Patman was a Southerner; he represented a
rural constituency; he had a liberal, but not *too* liberal, voting
record.[1] Had the Senate sponsors picked a Congressman from a
strong labor constituency in New York or Detroit or Chicago, or
a militant liberal like George Outland of California or Andrew

[1] On a number of important labor issues during the war, Patman had voted with
the conservatives. See *How Your Congressman Voted*, Research Institute of America
(New York, 1946), p. 30.

Biemiller of Wisconsin, H.R.2202 might have been identified from the beginning with the "New Deal" wing of the House. This the Senate sponsors wanted if possible to avoid.

## COMMITTEE REFERRAL

But at the very time that Senators Murray and Wagner and their staff assistant Bertram Gross were worrying about the strategy of House sponsorship, they overlooked another bit of strategy—a fact which was to cost them heavily. It will be remembered that the early draft of the Full Employment Bill which was published in the *Year-End Report* of the War Contracts Subcommittee in December, 1944, was written as an amendment to the Budget and Accounting Act of 1921. Although the bill as introduced in the Senate made no mention of the Budget Act, the earlier draft had obviously made sufficient impression on the House Parliamentarian so that when he was called upon to make a committee assignment [2] for H.R.2202 he referred it automatically to the House Committee on Expenditures in the Executive Departments—a venerable but relatively minor standing committee which had, among other things, jurisdiction over matters of special concern to the Budget Bureau. If Patman or the Senate sponsors had tried to guide, and had succeeded in guiding, Speaker Rayburn (and through Rayburn the House Parliamentarian) in the matter of committee referral, and if H.R.2202 had consequently been sent to the House Banking and Currency Committee or the House Labor Committee, the story of the Full Employment Bill might have been markedly different.

The House Committee on Expenditures was heavily weighted on the conservative side. Although the *New Republic* voting tallies may not be infallible indices of liberalism vs. conservatism in Congress, it is interesting to note the following *New Republic* record [3] of 16 of the 21 members of the Expenditures Committee on 24 important policy issues prior to 1945:

[2] The responsibility for the referral of bills rests with the Speaker, but in most cases the Parliamentarian makes the decision.

[3] James C. Patton and James Loeb, Jr., "Challenge to Progressives," *New Republic*, Feb. 5, 1945, pp. 189–193. Reprinted by permission of the publishers.

|                              | Plus (a liberal vote) | Minus (a conservative vote) | No Vote |
|------------------------------|:---------------------:|:---------------------------:|:-------:|
| Hoffman (Michigan)           | 0                     | 21                          | 3       |
| Church (Illinois)            | 4                     | 19                          | 1       |
| Elliott (California)         | 4                     | 14                          | 6       |
| Gibson (Georgia)             | 6                     | 12                          | 6       |
| Gossett (Texas)              | 7                     | 16                          | 1       |
| Manasco (Alabama)            | 8                     | 15                          | 1       |
| Judd (Minnesota)             | 8                     | 13                          | 3       |
| Mansfield (Texas)            | 9                     | 11                          | 4       |
| Randolph (West Virginia)     | 10                    | 11                          | 3       |
| Whittington (Mississippi)    | 11                    | 13                          | 0       |
| LaFollette (Indiana)         | 13                    | 10                          | 1       |
| Cochran (Missouri)           | 13                    | 0                           | 11      |
| Bender (Ohio)                | 15                    | 9                           | 0       |
| O'Toole (New York)           | 19                    | 0                           | 5       |
| Dawson (Illinois)            | 19                    | 1                           | 4       |
| Hart (New Jersey)            | 20                    | 1                           | 3       |

The other five members of the committee were newcomers to Congress in January, 1945, but their subsequent voting records [4] on ten major issues during the first session of the 79th Congress were as follows:

|                              | Plus (a liberal vote) | Minus (a conservative vote) | No Vote |
|------------------------------|:---------------------:|:---------------------------:|:-------:|
| Rich (Pennsylvania)          | 0                     | 10                          | 0       |
| Henry (Wisconsin)            | 2                     | 8                           | 0       |
| Latham (New York)            | 2                     | 7                           | 1       |
| Ervin (North Carolina)       | 5                     | 5                           | 0       |
| Resa (Illinois)              | 10                    | 0                           | 0       |

According to these *New Republic* tallies, only 7 out of the 21 members of the Expenditures Committee voted on the liberal side more times than on the conservative side. It is perhaps significant that of the 14 conservatives, eight came from Congressional districts which contained no city larger than 30,000 population.[5] Of the seven liberals, five represented tremendous urban concentra-

---

[4] "Elections: 1946," *New Republic*, Feb. 11, 1946, pp. 211–214. Reprinted by permission of the publishers.

[5] Hoffman, Michigan 3d; Elliott, California 10th; Gibson, Georgia 8th; Gossett, Texas, 13th; Manasco, Alabama 7th; Randolph, West Virginia 2d; Whittington, Mississippi 3d; and Rich, Pennsylvania 15th. Census: 1940 (pin-pointed on Rand-McNally Congressional District Maps).

tions: two in Chicago, two in metropolitan New York, and one in St. Louis.[6]

The then chairman of the House committee, Carter Manasco, represented one of the poorest districts in America, the Alabama 7th, but his voting record was almost consistently conservative on domestic issues. When the C.I.O. in August, 1946, evaluated the record of Congressmen on twelve key issues, Manasco's anti-C.I.O. score was 11–1.[7]

This, then, was the nature of the committee into whose hopper the House Parliamentarian dropped the Full Employment Bill. Granted the power of committees and committee chairmen in determining the fate of a piece of legislation, this referral was a major blow to the sponsors of S.380.

### HOUSE "CO-SPONSORS"

The problem faced by Patman in the House was considerably more complicated than the problem faced by the sponsors in the Senate. Besides the unfavorable committee referral, Patman had to consider the general conservatism of the Lower House,[8] and the simple problem of size. It is difficult enough, in order to assure a favorable majority, to line up 49 Senators behind an issue; in the House, a majority of 435 is 218. Although Patman could count on the Senate staff for speech-drafting and intellectual ammunition, the Senate side of the Capitol was not in a position to mobilize the type of House support which would be needed in a showdown floor fight.

In the early spring of 1945, Patman set about trying to secure House "co-sponsors" for H.R.2202. Technically, only one representative may introduce a bill in the Lower Chamber; but unofficially an unlimited number of Congressmen may register their support. In response to Patman's preliminary efforts, 65 Congressmen pledged themselves as "co-sponsors." By June this number had been increased to 72, and by the time of the floor debates in the House to 116.

The earliest 65 or 70 supporters of H.R.2202 were in general the

[6] Resa, Illinois 9th; Dawson, Illinois 1st; Hart, New Jersey 14th (Hoboken and Jersey City); O'Toole, New York 13th; and Cochran, Missouri 13th.
[7] Washington *Post*, Aug. 18, 1946. Manasco was defeated in the 1948 primaries.
[8] See below, Chapter Nine.

ones most passionately convinced of the bill's importance.[9] On May 22, 1945, they held an informal meeting and authorized Patman to name an executive committee which might act as a steering group for their activities.[10] On June 11, in Patman's office, the executive committee of the co-sponsors held its first official meeting. The members of the committee were: George Outland of California, chairman; Andrew Biemiller of Wisconsin, secretary; Walter Brehm of Ohio, John Fogarty of Rhode Island, Walter Granger of Utah, Estes Kefauver of Tennessee, Matthew Neely of West Virginia, Mary Norton of New Jersey, Luther Patrick of Alabama, George Sadowski of Michigan, Charles Savage of Washington, and Wright Patman, ex officio.[11] The geographic spread is noteworthy. It was not accidental. The nature of the leadership of the steering committee should also be noted. Outland, the chairman, had first been elected to Congress in 1942; Biemiller, the secretary, in 1944. Both were passionate liberals, but neither had had sufficient experience in Congressional strategy to enable him to channel his enthusiasm effectively. The fact that older hands were not chosen to direct the activities of the steering committee was probably a strategic error.

At this June 11 meeting, Patman gave a pep-talk which included such exhortative statements as "we must make this a great crusade for the most constructive single piece of legislation in the history of this nation." [12] The various committee members pledged their aid and promised to follow through during the summer in their own districts.

Some of them did follow through. George Outland, for instance, gave 22 speeches on the Full Employment Bill in his home state of California during the summer recess. While on the Coast he was kept informed of Washington developments on S.380 by Helen Gauntlet, who had joined Bertram Gross's staff in July, and who was specifically assigned to work with Outland and the House steering committee as they needed her.

When Congress reconvened after V-J Day, most of the heavy work for the House bill landed squarely on the shoulders of George Outland and Andrew Biemiller. They worked with friendly pressure groups, submitted names of possible witnesses to Carter

[9] Representative George Outland, in an interview, Washington, D.C., Feb. 22, 1946.
[10] Representative Outland, press release, June 11, 1945.     [11] *Ibid.*     [12] *Ibid.*

Manasco, distributed to their colleagues material for inclusion in the *Congressional Record,* and tried to keep up the enthusiasm and missionary spirit of the friends of the bill. Outland himself testified before the House committee, and later on, during the floor fight, he led the liberal forces in their vain attempt to kill the substitute House amendment.

The failure of Outland and the co-sponsors to force through a generous version of S.380 in the House was not for lack of effort. It is true that they lacked experience and adequate staff assistance, but what really beat them was a series of stubborn political facts, not the least important of which was that although 116 Congressmen became co-sponsors of the bill, 319 did not.

THE HOUSE HEARINGS

The hearings in the Expenditures Committee began on September 25 and continued off and on until November 7.[13] Whereas the Senate committee was concerned with only one bill, the House committee considered three: H.R.2202 as introduced, the Senate bill as passed, and a substitute bill numbered H.R. 4181 which had been submitted by Representative Charles LaFollette of Indiana. The latter contained all the language of H.R.2202, but included in addition certain words and clauses which LaFollette felt would strengthen and clarify the original bill. The LaFollette substitute received little attention in the process of the hearings, but technically it was a part of the committee's responsibility.

*Choice of Witnesses.*—Committee Chairman Carter Manasco managed, with the aid of suggestions proffered by James C. Ingebretsen and Congressman George Outland, to line up 40 witnesses: 14 representatives of business, 7 federal government officals, 5 Congressmen, 3 representatives of veterans, 3 of labor, 3 of agriculture, 1 college president, 1 college professor, 1 church leader, 1 representative of an educational association, and 1 social worker. A number of additional statements (mostly anti-H.R.2202) were submitted by various individuals and organizations and were selected by Manasco for inclusion in the printed hearings.[14]

As compared to the Senate hearings, there was a marked increase in the number of opposition witnesses. Of the 14 business repre-

---

[13] *Hearings before the Committee on Expenditures in the Executive Departments, on H.R.2202,* 79th Cong., 1st Sess. (Washington, 1945).
[14] *Ibid.,* pp. 1119–1163.

sentatives who testified on the bill in the House committee, only
one registered in favor of H.R.2202,[15] although two others, Ralph
Flanders for the Committee for Economic Development and George
Terborgh for the Machinery and Allied Products Institute, supported the idea of a substantially amended bill.

*The Cross-Examination.*—It will be remembered that the Senate
committee took care of 70-odd witnesses in eleven days of hearings
—an average of over six a day. The House committee, on the other
hand, heard 40 witnesses in 21 days, or an average of two a day. This
gives some indication of the time spent by the members of the Expenditures Committee on the cross-examination of witnesses. On
October 30, to take an extreme example, the committee cross-
examined Henry Wallace from 10:00 A.M. to 1:00 P.M. and from
2:30 P.M. to 6:20 P.M.[16]

The star conservative performers on the committee were Manasco, Hoffman, Whittington, and Rich. In defense of H.R.2202,
Congressman John Cochran of Missouri carried the lion's share.
Although Charles LaFollette and George Bender helped on occasion, the former was concerned with the fate of his own substitute
bill, and the latter was constantly voicing a pessimistic assertion
that the Senate-passed Full Employment Bill was a legislative
wraith, so why go on.

On the conservative side, Manasco and Hoffman did the most
talking. With the occasional aid of Ralph Church of Illinois and
Ed Gossett of Texas, Manasco and Hoffman carried on a cross-fire
of questions which even now cause the sensitive reader of the hearings to squirm with vicarious suffering. Listen to Clare Hoffman [17]
bearing down on Henry Wallace:

*Mr. Hoffman:* "All Americans have a right to employment." Do you
endorse that?
*Mr. Wallace:* I think they do.
*Mr. Hoffman:* Then that wouldn't exclude any man from a Federal
job created under this, because he didn't belong to a union would it? I
just want to know whether in your opinion it is a bill to relieve all who
are unemployed, or just the union unemployed.
*Mr. Wallace:* I have been over this a great many times, Mr. Congress-

15 James S. Schramm, co-owner and manager, J. S. Schramm Co., Burlington, Iowa.
*House Hearings on H.R.2202*, pp. 205–236.
16 *House Hearings on H.R.2202*, pp. 827–920.          17 *Ibid.*, p. 918.

man. The point which troubles you I don't believe belongs in this bill. I don't think it should be considered in this particular bill.

*Mr. Hoffman:* Then, Mr. Secretary, you do not approve of that language, "All Americans have a right to an opportunity for employment," do you?

*Mr. Wallace:* Yes; I do.

*Mr. Hoffman:* Then you wouldn't deprive a non-union man of a job created by the Federal Government.

*Mr. Wallace:* No; I wouldn't want to see a non-union man deprived of a job.

*Mr. Hoffman:* And you think that no construction could be placed on this bill that would deprive a non-union man of participation in a Federal-works program?

*Mr. Wallace:* I don't think that belongs . . .

*Mr. Hoffman:* Why don't you answer that right off? You do or you don't. You come here and endorse a bill which on its face, says that all Americans have the right to jobs. Now if you don't believe it, that is all right with me.

*Mr. Wallace:* I do believe it.

*Mr. Hoffman:* All right then. Then you don't believe that a man should be deprived of a job created by the Federal Government, and with tax money, just because he don't belong to a union; is that right?

*Mr. Wallace:* I think . . .

*Mr. Hoffman:* I want to say that for a man with your experience who has been so successful in the corn-breeding business, and in the Agriculture Department, and who has pleased so many farmers, I can't see why you should have so much difficulty with that little simple question.

*Mr. Wallace:* Your question is very complex.

This was typical Hoffman courtroom style: the unmerciful persistence, the attempt to catch the witness in a verbal trap, the almost complete irrelevance to the matter at hand.

Earlier, Henry Wallace [18] had rebelled at a question thrown by Representative Ervin:

*Mr. Wallace:* Frankly, I don't think this has anything to do with the bill. I think that question is completely beside the point, and, to use a lawyer's phrase, thrown in to befog the issue.

*Mr. Hoffman:* Now, I take exception to that, Mr. Chairman.

*Mr. Ervin:* Wait a minute. I can take care of myself.

*Mr. Hoffman:* I am not endeavoring to help you at all. I am just one-twenty-first of the committee, but I object to statements going in here that questions are just thrown in to befog the issue. I am sure that so far every Congressman has treated the secretary courteously and he has no

[18] *Ibid.,* p. 868.

right to question our right to ask these questions. We may be dumb, Mr. Secretary, but give us credit for being sincere.

*Mr. Wallace:* Yes, I will give the Congressman credit for being sincere, but I also think these questions are being thrown in to befog the issue.

*Mr. Hoffman:* That's all right; and I think many of your statements are thrown in for the same purpose.

*Mr. Ervin:* I refuse to yield.

*Mr. Hoffman:* You don't need to yield. I don't care whether you do or not.

*Mr. Ervin:* I can take care of myself.

*Mr. Hoffman:* I raise this question about proper assertions by Members of Congress.

*Mr. Wallace:* I don't know why a Congressman can't sincerely throw in a question to befog the issue, if he wants to.

Few of the witnesses had Wallace's temerity to challenge the nature of the questioning, but even he got tired before the inquisition had finished.

Similar tactics were of course used by the committee supporters of the bill. One of the most notable examples was Representative LaFollette's attempt to embarrass Dr. Walter E. Spahr by asking whether or not he agreed with statements made by his New York University colleague, Dr. Willford I. King.[19]

Matters became particularly warm when opponents *within* the committee met head on. When Representative LaFollette testified on behalf of his own version of the bill,[20] Representative Church of Illinois began to ride him on the subject of minimum wages:

*Mr. Church:* Do you think of a single industry that you would extend that act to?

*Mr. LaFollette:* . . . If you mean would I extend the provisions of the minimum wage, the answer is "yes."

*Mr. Church:* Upward from the present wage amounts.

*Mr. LaFollette:* That is right.

*Mr. Church:* And would you extend it to additional persons?

*Mr. LaFollette:* I have answered that twice, and my answer is I don't know. If I were on the labor committee, I would give you a damned good answer, but I am not.

*Mr. Church:* You don't want to enlighten us on that? I think that is very important here.

*Mr. LaFollette:* I am glad you do.

*Mr. Church:* If you are assuming that attitude, I won't ask you any more questions.

19 *Ibid.*, pp. 492–493.          20 *Ibid.*, p. 738.

*Mr. LaFollette:* I don't think you better. I never get much sense out of your questions anyway, and if you are going to be adroit with me, I am twice as smart as you are.

One of the few witnesses who seemed to be able to parry these thrusts successfully and without loss of humor was former Congressman, and at that time, Secretary of the Treasury Fred Vinson. At one point in his cross-examination by Representative Church, Vinson voiced what must have been silently harbored by dozens of other witnesses: "Ralph, you are an old-timer. You know all the tactics, fellow. Don't kid me." [21]

Not all of the cross-examination was carried on at this courtroom level. There were occasions when a committee member seemed genuinely interested in learning. Notable in this respect was Congressman Will Whittington of Mississippi, whose gentlemanly behavior during the hearings was often in sharp contrast to that of his more litigious colleagues. [22]

*The Level of Argument.*—The conservative committee majority reflected in general the position of business and conservative farm groups. There was little indication in the hearings, however, that very many of the committee members understood the economics which some of their more learned witnesses tossed at them. Chairman Manasco confessed that he was not an economist, [23] a fact which was made amply evident by his endorsement of bogus economic arithmetic. Time and time again, the chairman posed the following question to witnesses: "With 8,000,000 people unemployed next year, if the Federal Government were to furnish them with $3,000 a year, that would amount to $24,000,000,000 that would come out of the Federal Government, would it not?" [24]

There is no particular reason why a small-town Alabama lawyer should be acquainted with the economic concept of the multiplier, but Manasco's naïveté poses a fundamental question about the place of Congress in the policy-making process. The problem is not limited to the Lower House. When Senator O'Mahoney, in presenting his testimony to the Senate committee, referred to "frictional" unemployment, Senator Abe Murdock of Utah interjected:

[21] *Ibid.*, p. 985.
[22] Because of his habit of beginning a cross-examination with the phrase "with all due deference," Whittington was frequently referred to on Capitol Hill as "With-all-due-deference Will."
[23] *House Hearings on H.R.2202*, p. 368.         [24] *Ibid.*, p. 364.

"Well, in terms that a Senator can understand, is it . . . ?" [25]

Occasionally, in the House hearings technical questions were slipped to friendly Congressmen by visiting pressure representatives, but there were few cases of mature economic debate between a Congressman and a witness. Too often in the House committee, the full employment issue was argued out on the level of shibboleths, clubroom chatter, and irrelevancies. One has the feeling, after reading through the House hearings, that the wave of postwar strikes which developed across the nation during the period of the committee sessions, came in for as much attention as the contents of the bill.

### EXECUTIVE PRESSURES

We have referred earlier to the use made of the Executive departments and agencies by the Senate staff and the sponsors of S.380: the assistance of federal economists in the drafting process, the statements of departments and agency heads in response to staff questions, the testimony of Cabinet officers before the Senate and House committees. We have also noted the Roosevelt speeches in the 1944 campaign, and Henry Wallace's special efforts on behalf of the Full Employment Bill before and after its introduction.[26] The fate of the bill in the House cannot be understood, however, without a brief analysis of the relationship of the Executive branch to Congress in terms of direct political pressure.

*Roosevelt and Full Employment.*—Since the first two terms of Roosevelt's administration were concerned to a large degree with the enigma of unemployment, there is no reason to doubt the late President's vital interest in the problem. The question may consequently be asked why Roosevelt did not assume leadership in 1944 and 1945 for sponsoring an administration full employment bill. He had established the "Right to Work" as one of the clauses in his Economic Bill of Rights in January, 1944; he had dramatized the idea of 60,000,000 jobs in the 1944 campaign; he restated his concern with the problem in his message to Congress in January, 1945; his Executive office—particularly the Budget Bureau—co-

---

[25] *Hearings before a Subcommittee of the Committee on Banking and Currency, on S.380*, 79th Cong., 1st Sess. (Washington, 1945), p. 29.

[26] Wallace's book, *Sixty Million Jobs* (New York, 1945) was, of course, an additional contribution to the public debate on the full employment issue and received considerable attention in the House hearings.

operated intimately with the Senate staff. But at no time did Roosevelt specifically endorse the Murray bill, and he made no effort to sponsor a separate bill.

Actually, the late President's hands-off policy is not hard to understand. In the summer of 1944, a group of Washington economists led by Alvin Hansen and Gerhard Colm drew up, on an informal interdepartmental basis, a confidential American "White Paper" on full employment which they presented to Roosevelt early in the fall of that year. That is as far as it got. Recognizing the importance of Congressional unity in terms of his dreams for a United Nations Organization, the late President obviously felt that his endorsement of a specific full employment plan might muddy the water, and that specific plans for full employment had better come from Congress itself. Roosevelt followed this hands-off policy until his death.

*Truman and Full Employment.*—In President Truman's second press conference after his assumption of office, in response to a question, he told reporters that he was not familiar with the Murray Full Employment Bill.[27] Although this was taken by certain columnists to mean that the President was heading toward the right wing, since they were convinced he *must* have been familiar with the bill, in actual fact the President was probably speaking the truth. As we have seen, although he had "signed" the *Year-End Report* of the War Contracts Subcommittee back in December, 1944, when he was a member of that subcommittee, he was away from Washington when the report was issued, and a member of his office staff had given Senator Murray permission to use Truman's signature. By the time the bill was introduced, Truman was Vice President.

With the end of the Japanese war, however, Truman called in his legislative lieutenants and indicated that he wanted full speed ahead on full employment legislation. On September 6, he reinforced his position by sending to Congress a 21-point message on needed legislative action which included the following statement:

A national reassertion of the right to work for every American citizen able and willing to work—a declaration of the ultimate duty of Government to use its own resources if all other methods should fail to prevent prolonged unemployment—these will help to avert fear and establish full employment. I ask that full-employment legislation to provide these vital assurances be speedily enacted.[28]

[27] Fred Perkins's column in the Washington *News*, May 3, 1945.
[28] *Congressional Record*, 79th Cong., 1st Sess., Dec. 14, 1945, p. 12267.

Truman followed up this message by assigning to John Snyder, chief of the Office of War Mobilization and Reconversion, the responsibility for lining up various Cabinet members to maintain relations with Congress in connection with each section of his 21-point program. For applying pressure on full employment legislation, Snyder recommended a four-man Cabinet committee made up of Secretary of the Treasury Fred Vinson, chairman; Secretary of Commerce Henry Wallace; Secretary of Labor Lewis Schwellenbach; and Secretary of Agriculture Clinton Anderson. This four-man committee was to meet frequently, figure out ways to maximize Executive pressure on Congress, and submit progress reports every two weeks to John Snyder. In actual fact, the burden of day-to-day concern about Executive pressures on S.380 rested on the shoulders of special assistants: Ansel Luxford, special assistant to Vinson, and Creekmore Fath and Thomas Emerson, respectively special assistant to Snyder and General Counsel of the O.W.M.R.

About the middle of October, 1945, it became abundantly clear to the Cabinet committee and to the O.W.M.R. staff that the Full Employment Bill was going to run into serious trouble in the House committee. Truman was informed that he would probably have to exert personal pressure on Manasco and Whittington and Joseph Mansfield of Texas, who were considered by Vinson and the O.W.M.R. staff to be key Democrats on the Expenditures Committee. To this Truman agreed, and on October 25 he talked with each of these three separately.[29] Mansfield was amenable to the pressure of "party loyalty," but Manasco and Whittington were stubborn. Finally, under advice from Vinson, Truman managed to extract a promise from Manasco and Whittington that some sort of bill would be reported out in return for his assurance that he would not insist on the original bill, the Senate-passed bill, or in fact even a bill with the words "full employment" in it. The strategy behind this was based upon a belief that unless the President went along with Manasco and Whittington, no bill at all would be reported out of committee, and that a weak House bill might well be strengthened in conference committee later on. This understanding between Truman and Manasco and Whittington was to have interesting repercussions when final action on the bill took place on the House floor.

[29] *PM*, Oct. 26, 1945.

*Executive Branch Testimony.*—Most of the administration witnesses testified late in the House committee proceedings. Harold
Smith of the Budget Bureau and Omar Bradley for the Veterans
Administration appeared early, but John Snyder, Lewis Schwellen-
back, Fred Vinson, Henry Wallace, and Clinton Anderson all appeared within the final week of hearings. With the exception of
Omar Bradley and John Snyder, all the officials came out strongly
for a liberal version of the bill—the Senate-passed version or better.
Omar Bradley was completely noncommittal; John Snyder was
caught between his desire to support the President and his cordial
dislike of full employment legislation. Snyder's testimony had been
prepared for him by the O.W.M.R. staff and was down-the-line for
a strong bill, but when the Congressmen started to question him,
Snyder wriggled and perspired. What happened has been enter-
tainingly reported by Bill Davidson in *Collier's:*

The published Full Employment Bill hearings before the Committee
on Expenditures in the Executive Departments, House of Representatives show that eight times Snyder had to admit that he didn't have the
answers to questions at hand, that he would have to "reread the bill," or
that he would "have to look into that."

He ended up by being pilloried by Representative Clare Hoffman of
Michigan, who asked him, "Did someone else prepare this statement for
you?"; kidded Snyder into admitting he knew all about electric razors,
washing machines and "the general over-all situation as to reconversion"; tripped him on some unemployment figures which Snyder had
just read but didn't seem to know anything about; and finally forced
an admission from Snyder that government spending in the depression
years "was not as productive as it should have been."

In other words, Snyder came to testify in favor of the government's
Full Employment Bill and was maneuvered into a position where he
was talking *against* it. He was saved on this occasion by a page boy coming in and announcing that Mr. Snyder had been called to the White
House. Later this got to be standard procedure nearly every time Snyder
testified—only with improved timing. It got so that he was called to go
to the White House immediately after he finished reading his prepared
report—and before the questions began.[30]

This hostility of Snyder's to the principles of a liberal bill was
a major breach in the phalanx of Executive pressures.[31]

[30] *Collier's,* Dec. 7, 1946, p. 63. Reprinted by permission of the publishers.

[31] This is the type of circumstance over which the institutional mechanisms of the
President's Executive Office have no control. The Legislative Reference Division of
the Bureau of the Budget can endorse in advance the prepared testimony of govern-

*Truman Goes to the People.*—By the end of October, the Congressional sponsors of the bill felt that Truman had not taken a strong enough stand on what they considered to be the delaying tactics of the Expenditures Committee. After liberal pressures had been exerted, the President sent a letter to Representative McCormack, House Majority leader, reaffirming the administration's support of the bill, emphasizing the urgency of the legislation, and stating his hope that the bill would be reported out by the committee at an early date, preferably in time for passage by Thanksgiving. The next evening, October 30, with no advance warning to Fred Vinson, the President went on the air and publicly castigated the Expenditures Committee for delaying action on the Full Employment Bill. Vinson, who had to testify the following day, was put on a nasty spot and had to spend a number of minutes in the hearing trying to smooth the ruffled feathers of Manasco and other committee members.[32] In defense of their delay, Manasco pointed out that the Cabinet members had not been able to appear earlier.

Truman's appeal to McCormack and the people seems, at first glance, to have had some weight. A week after his speech, formal committee hearings were closed. It was not until a month later, however, that a bill was finally reported out by the Expenditures Committee.

With the exception of pressures exerted by Vinson on Whittington during the redrafting process in the House subcommittee, no Executive pressures to speak of were mobilized between the end of the House hearings and the beginning of the floor debate in December.

### THE HOUSE SUBCOMMITTEE

Hearings had been held before the full Expenditures Committee, although many of the committee members had had a poor attendance record. After the hearings were finished on November 7, the committee met in executive session and promptly voted against H.R.2202, 17–3.[33] Actually, the sentiment of the committee majority was bitterly opposed to any of the three bills under considera-

ment officials as being "in accord with the program of the President," but there is no way of stopping a facial expression or a tone of voice which conveys a meaning quite opposite to that of the written statement.

[32] *House Hearings on H.R.2202*, pp. 932–933.
[33] *Congressional Record*, 79th Cong., 1st Sess., Dec. 13, 1945, p. 12204.

tion. Representative John Cochran, a friend of the original bill but a realistic politician, therefore moved that a subcommittee be appointed by Manasco to draft an acceptable House substitute.[34] This was carried. On this drafting subcommittee were Manasco, Whittington, Bender, Cochran, and Hoffman. In way of rough delineation, Manasco and Hoffman represented the extreme conservative position, Whittington the moderate conservative, and Bender and Cochran the liberal. The balance of forces played into the hands of Will Whittington who assumed major responsibility for drafting the House substitute bill.

A careful analysis of Whittington's reactions to various witnesses during the committee hearings reveals that he was striving for a bill which would exclude the last remnants of what he considered to be dangerous federal commitments and assurances (including the wording of the title), but would provide for an economic planning mechanism of some sort in the Executive and legislative branches, and for a moderate program of public works. This was essentially the position taken by the Committee for Economic Development,[35] the National Grange,[36] Dr. George Terborgh of the Machinery and Allied Products Institute,[37] and later, as we have seen, the U.S. Chamber of Commerce.[38] Terborgh made a particularly strong impression on Whittington. Terborgh had concluded his formal statement before the committee with the following words:

The Bill should be purged of its remaining vestiges of the right-to-a-job idea, its qualified but still persistent reliance on Government spending as a panacea, and the surviving remnants of its mandate for long-range (fiscal-year) forecasting. Relieved of these incongruous carry-overs from earlier drafts, the bill would boil down, save for its statement of objectives, to four essential features:

1. It is declared to be the responsibility of the Federal Government to foster private enterprise and to promote by means consistent with this and other obligations and objectives, a high and stable level of employment.

2. In the light of this responsibility, the Government is admonished to develop, and to pursue consistently, an appropriate economic program.

3. The task of evolving such a program is laid in the first instance

34 *Ibid.*, p. 12157.   35 *House Hearings on H.R.2202*, pp. 591–598.
36 *Ibid.*, especially pp. 1000–1003.   37 *Ibid.*, especially p. 614.
38 See U.S. Chamber of Commerce, "A Program for Sustaining Employment," *Report of Committee on Economic Policy* (Washington, 1945).

upon the President, who is instructed to submit to Congress quarterly his analysis of economic conditions and trends and his recommendations for policy.

4. There is created a special congressional joint committee to review the President's proposals and report to both Houses thereon.

To these four features we have proposed a fifth, a national economic commission appointed by the President and confirmed by the Senate, whose responsibility it should be to make continuous study of the art of business stabilization through Federal action.[39]

After careful questioning, Congressman Whittington said to Terborgh, "I think you have been very helpful, sir. You have been to me, and I want to say that I value such statements as men like you submit to us, because you are a fair witness, a reasonable witness, and if you don't know it, you say so." [40] Even Clare Hoffman was sufficiently impressed with Terborgh's ideas to ask him if he would be willing to submit to the committee a draft, "taking the Senate bill as a base, of your ideas of what a bill should be." [41] This Terborgh agreed to do.

Later on, in subcommittee, Whittington solicited additional drafts from the U.S. Chamber of Commerce, the Committee for Economic Development, and Secretary of the Treasury Fred Vinson.[42] With the aid of these drafts, Whittington pieced together a substitute bill which was finally submitted to the full committee for consideration.

The redrafting process in the subcommittee took almost the entire month of November, a period of time which seemed to many supporters of the original bill to indicate intentional delay.[43] President Truman, as we have seen, tried to exert direct and indirect pressures to hurry the Expenditures Committee along. But they would not be rushed, and it was not until December 5, after six weeks of hearings, nearly a month of redrafting, and four days of full committee debate, that a substitute bill was reported out.

THE HOUSE SUBSTITUTE

The substitute bill, retitled the "Employment and Production Act of 1946," rejected the fundamental principles of the Senate

[39] *House Hearings on H.R.2202*, p. 613.    [40] *Ibid.*, p. 624.
[41] *Ibid.*, p. 620.
[42] Representative Will Whittington, in an interview, Washington, D.C., June 1, 1946.
[43] In this connection, see the remarks of Representative John Cochran, *Congressional Record*, 79th Cong., 1st Sess., Dec. 13, 1945, p. 12157.

bill. It eliminated the declaration of the right to employment opportunity, of federal responsibility for full employment, the pledge of all the federal resources, including financial means to that end, and the safeguard against international economic warfare.

For these it substituted a policy of aiming for a "high" level of employment, production, and purchasing power, and of trying to prevent economic fluctuations by expanding and contracting public works and loans, and avoiding competition of government with private business enterprise.

The national budget was rejected with its goals, appraisal of economic trends, full employment program, and investigation into monopoly, and the distribution of national income. In its place was substituted an economic report on general economic conditions, causes underlying threats of inflation or deflation, and recommendations for further legislation of the kind indicated above.

The substitute bill provided for a Council of Economic Advisers, composed of three members at $15,000 a year, whose duties were to submit recommendations to the President whenever inflation or unemployment threatened, to consult with economic groups, and to submit annual and quarterly reports on economic trends. All these reports, studies, and recommendations to the President were to be made directly available to the joint committee.

The provision for a joint Congressional committee specified that eight members should be from the Appropriations and Ways and Means Committees of the House and parallel committees in the Senate, and reduced the total membership to 14.

The emasculation, or as some wit put it, the "Manasco-lation," of the policy commitments and the economic program of the original bill needs no further elucidation here. This was in line with the insistence of all the conservative pressures in and out of Congress. A few words should be said, however, about the new idea of a Council of Economic Advisers.

*The Council of Economic Advisers.*—In the various discussions which the original drafters and redrafters of S.380 carried on about the preparation of the National Employment and Production Budget, considerable attention was given to the problem of the institutionalization of the planning function in the Executive branch. It will be remembered that in the earliest preliminary drafts of the bill, the Bureau of the Budget was to be charged with the responsibility of preparing the National Employment and Production Budget under the general direction of the President. Then, the drafters, fearing the jealousy of other departments, deleted that section and the bill as introduced provided for the preparation of the National Budget "in the Executive Office of the President under the general direction and supervision of the President, and in consultation with the members of the Cabinet and other heads of departments and establishments." [44] The original bill also provided for Presidential discretion in establishing "such advisory boards or committees composed of representatives of industry, agriculture, labor, and State and local governments, and others, as he may deem advisable for the purpose of advising and consulting on methods of achieving the objectives of this Act." [45]

During the executive sessions of the Senate committee, the minority tried to press for an "Office of Director of the National Budget"—the director to be appointed by the President and confirmed by the Senate. The argument used by the minority was that "Planning of this economic program is extremely complicated and cannot possibly be done by the President himself. It should be done by an identifiable group, responsible to the Congress and the people, as well as to the President, and not by an anonymous group of economic planners." [46] The Senate sponsors of the bill responded to this suggestion as follows:

An amendment of this type would . . . impair the bill. Before there has been any experience in the development of a national production and employment budget, there can be no sound basis for establishing a specific administrative framework, within which the President should operate. The wiser course is to allow the President to work out this problem in consultation with his Cabinet. [47]

The Senate bill as passed made no change in the section dealing with the President's responsibility for directing and supervising the preparation of the National Budget, although it made mandatory the President's consultation with outside groups. [48]

[44] S.380, 79th Cong., 1st Sess., Jan. 22, 1945, Sec. 4(2).    [45] *Ibid.*, Sec. 4(c).
[46] U.S. Senate, "Assuring Full Employment in a Free Competitive Economy," *Minority Views from the Committee on Banking and Currency,* Senate Report No. 583, part 2, 79th Cong., 1st Sess., Sept. 24 (legislative day, Sept. 10), 1945 (Washington, 1945), p. 2.
[47] U.S. Senate, "Assuring Full Employment in a Free Competitive Economy," *Report from the Committee on Banking and Currency,* Senate Report No. 583, 79th Cong., 1st Sess., Sept. 22, 1945 (Washington, 1945), p. 36.
[48] S.380, 79th Cong., 1st Sess., Oct. 1, 1945, Sec. 4(b).

During the House hearings, Congressman Whittington's interest in a separate economic commission seems to have been initially aroused by George Terborgh.[49] Terborgh expressed fears that:

both the economic analysis and the economic policy may be prepared and promoted by men unknown to the public, whose appointment has not been confirmed by Congress, and who have no formal public responsibility. This set-up invites behind-the-scenes manipulation by Presidential advisers of the moment, possessed, it may be, both by a passion for anonymity and a passion for controlling national economic policy. However able and big-minded these advisers may be, the arrangement is bad. If the Federal Government is really serious about developing and implementing a full-employment policy—as it should be—it ought to make better organizational provision than is made in this bill.[50]

Some time between October 23 and October 31, Whittington had made up his mind to push for a permanent agency. In his colloquy with Secretary Vinson on October 31, Whittington said:

I think we ought to provide, in a constructive employment bill for the establishment of a permanent agency devoted to one thing and one thing alone, and that is to the implementing of the legislation that we pass to prevent unemployment, and that is to the studying of trends, with a staff at their command to furnish the President adequate information, that you, as Secretary of the Treasury, and other Secretaries in the Cabinet, are not able to furnish him because of the limited time at your disposal, and I want to supplement the joint congressional committee, in any legislation that is reported, if my suggestion is worth considering, by the establishment of a permanent board, agency, or commission, to give to the President of the United States the best available expert advice of the leading economists, the leading thinkers, the soundest planners of the country, that will enable them to make sound recommendations to the Executive and then to Congress.[51]

This suggestion caught Vinson by surprise,[52] and later on the Secretary of the Treasury, after criticizing this idea in a letter to Whittington, drew up a bill for a Cabinet committee (under his

[49] Four days earlier on October 19, Ralph Flanders of the C.E.D. had recommended to the committee a "President's Commission on Full Employment" (House Hearings, p. 594) and although Whittington was absent during Flanders' testimony, he received a copy of a C.E.D. policy statement called "Towards More Jobs and More Freedom" which spelled out this proposal. He also had access to the testimony of C.E.D.'s Paul Hoffman, who had advanced this suggestion during the Senate hearings in August (Senate Hearings, pp. 612–613). The dialogue between Terborgh and Whittington on p. 620 of the House hearings seems to indicate however, that the idea of a commission or committee had not previously occurred to Whittington.

[50] *House Hearings on H.R.2202*, pp. 612–613.

[51] *House Hearings on H.R.2202*, p. 959.     [52] *Ibid.*, pp. 959–960.

direction) with staff assistance, to perform the functions of the proposed economic commission or council. In opposition to both Vinson's plan and Whittington's plan, the staff of the Office of War
Mobilization and Reconversion drew up tentative blueprints for
a permanent coordinating and planning staff along the lines of the
O.W.M.R. in a reorganized Executive Office of the President.

Many of the sponsors of the bill believed that the attempt of the
House committee to establish a separate economic council was in
part motivated by a desire on the part of the conservatives to "divide
and conquer." Late in November, Whittington sent an early draft
of the subcommittee's substitute bill to Fred Vinson for comment.
This early draft included provisions which in substance would have
made the Council of Economic Advisers a completely independent
agency in the Executive branch. Vinson's comment is instructive:

The members of the Council, while appointed by the President, require
Senate confirmation. Their terms of office are fixed at five years, with
one member's term expiring each year. This technique is altogether too
rigid to succeed. It fails to give the President that degree of flexibility
and adaptibility which will be necessary if we are to constantly improve
our reporting and forecasting techniques and allow for speedy modifications if these prove essential. Moreover you confront a newly elected
President, bearing a direct mandate from the electorate, with the virtual
necesssity of having the National Budget or Economic Report prepared
by a body of men not elected by the people and not appointed by him. I
am confident that this certainly was not the intention of your subcommittee, but unfortunately it seems to be the case.[53]

Although substantial modifications were made in this section of
the House substitute, the bill as reported by the Expenditures
Committee still contained provisions which bothered the sponsors
of the original bill. The "give-away," according to the sponsors, was
the clause in the House substitute bill which read: "The President
is requested to make available to the Joint Committee on the
Economic Report, if it desires, the various studies, reports, and
recommendations of the Council which have been submitted to
the President." [54] This, the sponsors claimed, would enable the
joint committee to embarrass the President in case the Council's
recommendations did not jibe with the Chief Executive's. It would
enable the joint committee to split Executive planning into two

[53] Letter dated Nov. 24, 1945.
[54] S.380, 79th Cong., 1st Sess., Dec. 15, 1945, Sec. 4(c).

factions and play one off against the other. In conference, this particular clause was dropped.

*Whittington's Report.*—On December 5, 1945, Mr. Whittington
issued a report for the majority of the Expenditures Committee
"recommending that the bill, as amended, do pass." [55] The report
gives a clear indication of the majority's interest and worries. In
view of the various statements made over a period of years by the
N.A.M., the Chambers of Commerce, the Farm Bureau, the Committee for Constitutional Government, and other conservative pressure organizations, the following majority statement is significant:

The Committee substitute recognizes that the way in which to achieve
and maintain high levels of employment is to preserve and encourage
the American system of free competitive enterprise, to aid in the development and maintenance of conditions favorable to stimulating new
business, to encourage individual initiative and individual self-reliance,
to avoid Government competition with private business, and above all
to adopt sound fiscal practices and maintain the credit of the United
States.[56]

The report goes on to say:

The Senate and House bills declare a policy, but the declaration is perfunctory inasmuch as the assurance, guaranty, or right of employment
is, under those bills, really based upon Federal investments and expenditures. The provision in the Senate bill against deficit spending is nul-
lified by the concluding limitation that the goal of full employment will
not be interfered with. Private enterprise would thus be prevented not
only by uncertainty, but by the Government guaranty of jobs for all,
from maintaining the production necessary to high levels of employment. It has been said that neither the Senate nor the House Bill provides for a single job. The fact is, however, that they commit the Government to a policy of Federal expenditure and investment that will lead
to unbalanced budgets in guaranteeing employment. Citizens will be
misled. The vice in the bills is a committal to Federal expenditures to
guarantee or assure employment.[57]

The climax of the report is written in the same vein: "It is time
for a reaffirmance. It is time for a declaration that really means something. It is either private enterprise or stateism. A declaration at this
time is imperative if private enterprise is to function. The declara-

[55] House of Representatives, "Employment-Production Act," *Report from the Committee on Expenditures in the Executive Departments,* House Report No. 1334, 79th
Cong., 1st Sess., Dec. 5, 1945, p. 1.
[56] *Ibid.,* p. 6.          [57] *Ibid.*

tion must be sound. It must not be hampered with guaranties or assurances that would destroy." [58]

*The Minority Report.*—Strangely enough, even the emasculated House bill was too much for four of the most extreme conservatives on the committee: Clare Hoffman, Ralph Church, John Gibson, and Robert Rich.

The minority report made a scurrilous attack on the original bill, referring to "fraudulent propaganda" and claiming that "the public generally, and in particular members of labor organizations, believed that, if it was adopted and put into effect, each and every individual who for any reason was unemployed would be provided with a job." [59] The report then charged correctly that "Those advocating H.R.2202, realizing that the committee was not disposed to report that bill out, centered their efforts upon the reporting of *a* bill." [60] Commenting on this fact, the minority report continued: "Evidently following the New Deal theory, that, as always, we were now confronted by a crisis, and something—good or bad—requiring the expenditure of public funds should be done, the committee finally gave its support and has ordered reported the committee's substitute for—S.380." [61]

The minority attack on the substitute bill was limited to the charge that "the bill can only be construed as a planning measure, a new version of the National Resources Planning Board"; [62] that public works planning was already provided for in the federal government, and that the Economic Council and the joint committee represented extravagant duplication of existing and adequate governmental machinery. [63]

*Separate Views.*— Charles LaFollette, William Dawson, Edward Hart, and Alexander Resa filed a brief statement of opposition to the emasculated House substitute, but agreed "to vote to report legislation out of the committee so that the full membership of the House could have the opportunity to pass upon the subject matter involved." [64] They concluded their statement with the words, "Be-

[58] *Ibid.*, p. 7.    [59] *Ibid.*, p. 16.
[60] *Ibid.*, p. 17. The minority report, in order to substantiate this charge, quotes from an Associated Press interview with Representative Wright Patman. The AP quoted Patman as saying, "We are not concerned too much with just what kind of legislation the committee drafts, just so it doesn't keep the measure bottled up any longer. We have 116 co-sponsors in the House of my bill and all we need to do is get something to the floor so we have a target to shoot at."
[61] *Ibid.*    [62] *Ibid.*    [63] *Ibid.*    [64] *Ibid.*, p. 19.

cause the proposed legislation fails to give to the obligations of the Government adequate recognition and expression, we find it impossible to agree in full respect with the committee report." [65]

THE FLOOR FIGHT

Off and on during the year, a substantial amount of material for and against S.380 had been introduced into the *Congressional Record* in the form of brief speeches or extensions of remarks. It was part of the strategy of the sponsors in the Senate and the steering committee in the House to "keep it alive in the *Record*," and of course the opponents of the bill made efforts to counteract the effect of this strategy by introducing opposition material. Between October 1 and December 13, 1945, for instance, approximately fifty full employment items, floor speeches, newspaper editorials, magazine articles, statements by government officials, letters, and pressure group material, were placed in the *Record*. In addition, sizable premature debates developed on the House floor on November 6 and 8.[66]

The full and final debate on H.R.2202, however, did not come until December 13 and 14.

*Background of the Floor Fight.*—Before proceeding to an analysis of the final debate, it may be helpful to review certain factors which formed the political climate surrounding that debate. After eight months, S.380 had been passed in modified form by a Senate vote of 71 to 10. There was little agreement about the importance of the Senate modifications, even among the sponsors. Both the Senate bill and H.R. 2202 had been mauled by the House committee, the original bill having been rejected in executive session of the Expenditures Committee by a vote of 17 to 3. President Truman, under the advice of Fred Vinson, had pressured the leaders of the House committee to report out *a* bill, although he did not try to insist on the bill as introduced or the Senate bill as passed. By the first week in December, a subcommittee under the leadership of Manasco, Whittington, and Cochran had written a House substitute which was acceptable neither to the sponsors of the original bill, nor to a committee minority made up of Hoffman, Church,

[65] *Ibid.*
[66] *Congressional Record*, 79th Cong., 1st Sess.. Nov. 6, 1945, pp. 10450–10468; and Nov. 8, 1945, pp. 10549–10563.

Gibson, and Rich. In the meantime, the prognostications of economists about widespread postwar unemployment had failed to
materialize, and the first wave of postwar strikes had developed
throughout the nation. Finally, the conservative pressure groups
had mobilized their resources for an all-out attack on the bill during the period of the House consideration. All these things contributed to the setting in which the House debate on the Full Employment Bill took place.

*The Rule.*—It is a well-known fact that the Rules Committee
of the House has had, in the past, an inordinate amount of power.[67]
By controlling the time allotted for debate, by assigning the disposition of that time to certain Congressmen, by limiting the
number and type of amendments which can be offered on the floor,
and sometimes by rewriting bills or introducing them *de novo*, the
Rules Committee has exerted powerful influence on substantive
policy. In the 79th Congress, the balance of power in the Rules
Committee was on the side of Southern conservative Democrats and
Northern Republicans.[68] The chairman was Congressman Sabath
of Illinois, a venerable liberal, but he was virtually at the mercy of
his conservative majority.

The rule handed down for the Full Employment Bill was exactly
as requested by the chairman of the Expenditures Committee,
Carter Manasco.[69] It provided for one full day of general debate
on the bill, "to be equally divided and controlled by the chairman
and ranking minority member [Hoffman] of the Committee on Expenditures in the Executive Departments," [70] and, at the conclusion
of the general debate, for the reading of the bill for amendment
under the five-minute rule. Time, in other words, was to be controlled by Manasco and Hoffman, neither of whom had the slightest
interest in the original bill, except to kill it.

But the rule did not stop there. After authorizing control over the
debate, the Rules Committee provided:

It shall be in order to consider without the intervention of any point of
order the substitute amendment recommended by the Committee on

---

[67] See George B. Galloway, *Congress at the Crossroads* (New York, 1946), pp. 110–114.
By action of the 81st Congress, this power has been sharply curtailed.

[68] Of the eight Democrats on the Rules Committee, five came from south of the
Mason-Dixon line.

[69] Representative Carter Manasco, in an interview, Washington, D.C., Feb. 20,
1946.

[70] *Congressional Record,* 79th Cong., 1st Sess., Dec. 13, 1945, p. 12146.

Expenditures in the Executive Departments now in the bill, and such substitute for the purpose of amendment shall be considered under the 5-minute rule as an original bill. At the conclusion of such consideration the committee [of the whole] shall rise and report the bill to the House with such amendments as may have been adopted and the previous question shall be considered as ordered on the bill and the amendments thereto to final passage *without intervening motion except one motion to recommit.* (Italics supplied.) [71]

For reasons we shall note presently, this rule helped to make it virtually certain that if the House substitute were not adopted, nothing would be adopted. The rule (with the help of Speaker Rayburn) also made it impossible to get a roll-call vote on either the Senate bill as passed or H.R.2202 as originally introduced. The public will never know how the individual members of the House stood on the original bill or the modified Senate version. Carter Manasco, the Rules Committee, and perhaps the administration. planned it that way.

*Strategy and Denouement.*—The steering committee on H.R. 2202, under the leadership of Outland, Biemiller, and Patman, had met almost immediately after the substitute bill had been reported out by the Expenditures Committee. Finally agreeing that the Senate-passed bill was a good bill, and impressed with what they considered the "weakness" of the House substitute, they were determined to oppose the latter and to make a clear issue of the substitute vs. the Senate version of S.380. They planned to suggest no amendments to the substitute, to vote against it, and if their vote carried, to offer the Senate bill for a roll-call vote.[72] They recognized that H.R.2202 as introduced would have no chance of passing, but they were counting on a carry-over from the bipartisan support in the Senate, for the Senate version. If the Senate bill were rejected by the House on a roll-call vote, at least the issue could be taken to the people in the 1946 election.

This strategy was cut to pieces by the sponsors' enemies in the House and by the sponsors' friends in the administration. Here is the story.

The House debate was a three-cornered fight. Patman and Outland were struggling for a clear vote on the Senate bill, and consequently condemned the House substitute. Hoffman, Gibson,

[71] *Ibid.*
[72] See Patman's statement in the *Congressional Record*, 79th Cong., 1st Sess.. Dec. 13, 1945, pp. 12170–12171.

Church, and Rich wanted no bill, and condemned the House substitute, the original bill, and the Senate version. Whittington and Manasco wanted their modified version or nothing, and consequently reserved their venom for the sponsors of the original bill. The House as a whole, therefore, found itself confronted with a double pressure against both the original bill and the Senate-passed bill.

During the debate in the Committee of the Whole, every amendment to Whittington's House substitute was defeated, including the Dirksen amendment which was in substance a new bill designed to create a National Inventory Commission consisting of 30 members to make "a national inventory of the facilities and conditions affecting the national economy." [73] Things seemed to be ripe for a showdown on the House substitute—with the original sponsors of H.R.2202 and the conservative committee minority ready to lead the vote against it.

But on the morning of December 14, before the House debate began for the second and final day, the administration went to work. Convinced that if the House substitute were defeated, no bill at all would come out of the House, and believing that a weak House bill, which might be strengthened in conference, was better than no bill at all, Secretary Vinson attempted to put pressure on Speaker Rayburn, John McCormack (the majority leader), Wright Patman, and George Outland. Vinson explained the administration's position and asked the House sponsors to go along—to vote for the House substitute.[74] Outland and other members of the steering committee were furious, and refused to listen. After minutes of fruitless argument, Vinson gave up, called Henry Wallace and asked him to apply pressure on the sponsors.[75] Wallace reluctantly agreed, telephoned Congressman Neely of West Virginia,[76] repeated the administration's strategy and asked Neely to ask the rest of the sponsors to go along. Speaker Rayburn and Majority Leader McCormack had worked for almost two hours to get agreement on the administration's strategy, but it was Wallace's call that succeeded in breaking the morale of the sponsors. Finally, by a vote of 7–4,[77]

73 *Congressional Record*, 79th Cong., 1st Sess., Dec. 13, 1945, p. 12150.
74 U.D.A. *Congressional Newsletter*, Dec. 15, 1945.
75 Henry A. Wallace, in an interview, New York City, Feb. 10, 1947.
76 Andrew Biemiller, in an interview, Washington, D.C., July 22, 1947.
77 U.D.A. *Congressional Newsletter*, Dec. 15, 1945, p. 2.

the executive committee succumbed. Some of the sponsors emerged from the Rules Committee room "with tears in their eyes." [78]

What happened then on the floor of the House is bitterly related in a U.D.A. *Congressional Newsletter:*

With their backs broken by the morning conference, the liberals attempted a minor test by moving to substitute the original bill for the substitute. Since this was in the Committee of the Whole, no roll-call vote was possible, according to House Rules. With neither Majority Leader McCormack nor the new Whip Sparkman speaking for the Administration's own bill a 185–95 teller vote defeat was the best that could be accomplished. There followed, in such rapid-fire succession that many members hardly realized what was happening, a series of voice votes and two meaningless roll-calls that resulted in House passage of the Manasco-Whittington substitute bill.

*The Pay-Off:* In the final voting it became apparent that the Administration had agreed not only not to oppose the substitute, but also to prevent a roll-call on the straight issue of full employment, thus protecting the "Southern Gentlemen" from wrath of unemployed voters next November and in '48. It became clear that a *roll-call vote on the Senate Bill was possible and, in the event of defeat, the substitute could still have been saved.* This was how it happened: Hoffman, as expected, used his right as ranking minority committee member to move to recommit the legislation to the Manasco Committee. Liberal Republican LaFollette of Indiana immediately rose to amend Hoffman's motion to recommit *with instructions to report out the Senate bill.* (See Cong. Rec., December 14, pages 12259 and 12271.) As if by pre-arrangement, Manasco grabbed the floor microphone and moved the previous question which was hastily carried. *Had Rayburn recognized LaFollette first, or had the Administration floor leaders even supported a roll-call on Manasco's motion, a real test would have been obtained.*[79]

The final vote on the House substitute was a meaningless 255 to 126.[80] The House had passed the committee bill after witnessing a bitter game of opposing strategies. When the chips were down, the House sponsors of the bill did not have the cards. Manasco and Whittington, with the aid of Hoffman, the Rules Committee, a conservative House majority, and the administration, held a royal flush.

[78] *Ibid.* [79] *Ibid.*

[80] The vote was meaningless in the sense that there was no way of telling whether those who voted against the substitute bill did so because they wanted no bill at all, or because they believed the substitute did not go far enough. The party division was as follows: Yeas, 195 Democrats and 58 Republicans; Nays, 21 Democrats and 105 Republicans.

SUMMARY

Out of this confusing picture of the fate of the Full Employment Bill in the House, what factors emerge as dominant? They can be summarized even if, again, they cannot be accurately weighed.

1) referral of the bill to the conservatively-manned Expenditures Committee;
2) the lack of adequate staff assistance for the House sponsors and their inexperienced leaders;
3) the protracted indecision of the sponsors regarding the real meaning of the Senate-passed version of the bill;
4) weak executive pressures, conciliatory to Manasco and Whittington;
5) the timing of pressure activities by conservative interest groups;
6) the failure of dire economic predictions about unemployment to materialize, and the development of postwar strikes;
7) Whittington's intellectual leadership in drafting the House substitute with the aid of conservative business economists;
8) Manasco's floor strategy, conducted with the aid of Clare Hoffman, the Rules Committee, and the administration;
9) The overwhelming conservatism of the House of Representatives.

The last is not least. It was the underlying condition of the rest.

CHAPTER NINE

# *Public Opinion*

Public opinion has no easy vehicle for
its judgments, no quick channels for its
action. Nothing about the system is direct and simple.—Wilson, *Congressional
Government*, p. 331.

"IT IS CHARACTERISTIC of public opinion that it cannot generate a
proposal or series of proposals serving to satisfy its needs. Public
opinion can indicate very powerfully the general area of its needs,
but it remains for an individual or group of individuals to come
forward with specific proposals towards which opinion can display
approval or disapproval." [1] This is one of the conclusions reached
by Frank V. Cantwell in his study "Public Opinion and the Legislative Process." Another of Cantwell's conclusions is that "Public
opinion in a democracy responds to leadership and needs the
stimulus of leadership in order to crystallize one way or the other
on specific proposals." [2]

These conclusions are supported by the history of the Full Employment Bill. In 1944, public opinion "indicated . . . the general
area of its needs" on the subject of anticipated postwar unemployment by registering 67.7 percent in favor of the proposition that
the federal government should, if necessary, assure jobs for all.[3]
Both political parties during the 1944 campaign were, as we have

[1] Frank V. Cantwell, "Public Opinion and the Legislative Process," *American Political Science Review*, Vol. XL, No. 5, October, 1946, p. 933.
[2] *Ibid.*, p. 935.
[3] *Fortune* Poll, quoted in Washington *Evening Star*, Oct 30, 1944.

seen, responsive to this demonstration of public concern. So were Senator Murray and his staff.

A year later, just following V-J Day, the widespread concern of labor about transitional unemployment unquestionably had an effect upon the fate of the Full Employment Bill in the Senate. On the other hand, the dire predictions of government economists about continuing unemployment failed to materialize, and during the period of House consideration Clare Hoffman of Michigan took delight in quoting letters and newspapers on the subject of the prevailing shortage of labor.[4] Widespread articulate public concern about the full employment issue was not apparent during the House fight—at least in those rural and small-town districts from which a majority of our Congressmen come.[5]

This lack of general public concern was due both to the almost immediate absorption of war labor by peacetime industry, and to the failure of the President or anyone else to dramatize sufficiently the long-term need for full employment legislation. This lack of dramatic leadership meant, in fact, that at no time during the entire history of S.380, with the possible exception of the few weeks immediately following V-J Day, was there any indication that, apart from pressure groups, the public felt strongly about, or even knew about, the Full Employment Bill. No nation-wide polls were taken on S.380, but an extremely interesting local poll was taken of the 2d Congressional district in Illinois during July, 1945, seven months after the bill had been introduced.[6] The question was asked, "Have you heard of any bill before Congress that will plan for enough jobs for everyone after the war?" [7] The response, in percent, was as follows:

| | |
|---|---|
| No, have not heard | 69 |
| Have heard, but have no idea what it is | 19 |

[4] *Hearings before the Committee on Expenditures in the Executive Departments, on H.R.2202,* 79th Cong., 1st Sess., (Washington, 1945), pp. 376–378.

[5] Representatives Manasco and Whittington told me they received almost no mail on the full employment issue from their own constituents. Even after the Southern Conference for Human Welfare had put on a newspaper ad campaign in the heavily unionized city of Jasper, Alabama, Manasco's home town, the Congressman received only three letters of protest about his action on S.380. Whittington claims that during the entire fight over S.380, he received fewer than 25 letters from his district on the full employment issue.

[6] *What the People Think about Full Employment,* Citizens Research Bureau, sponsored by the Independent Voters of Illinois (Chicago, 1945).

[7] *Ibid.,* p. 1.

> Have heard, but have wrong idea what it is 4
> Have heard, and have right idea what it is 8

Next, the question was asked,

> What would you think of a bill like this?
> First, the President would find out each year how many jobs there are going to be for the coming year. Then, if there are not enough jobs for everyone, Congress would give financial help to private business so that it could provide more jobs. Then, if there were still too few jobs, the government would give contracts to private business to build public works to make up the balance of jobs needed.[8]

The response, in percent, was: For, 83; Against, 12; Doubtful, 5.

The next question named the bill: "Have you heard of the Murray Full Employment Bill?"[9] The percentage of replies was: Yes, 17; No, 81; Doubtful, 2.

It is, of course, impossible to generalize from the study of one Congressional district, but it is fair to hazard that if 81 percent of the people in a Congressional district in the heart of Chicago knew nothing about a Murray Full Employment Bill in July, 1945, the non-urban population was at least equally ignorant. In spite of the attempts of the sponsors of S.380, the staff, the Lib-Lab lobby, and President Truman to develop public support for the Full Employment Bill, the fact remains that their leadership was only partly effective. It was the force of economic circumstances as much as the work of the Lib-Lab lobby, which created intense urban-worker interest in the bill during the Senate fight, and the intensity of that interest dropped when circumstances changed. President Truman's radio appeal to the public in late November in which he accused the Expenditures Committee of sitting on the Full Employment Bill, brought almost no response.[10] The fact that any bill at all was finally passed is, of course, a tribute to the Lib-Lab lobby and the liberals in Congress who managed to create enough sustained noise so that a majority of legislators were at least semiconscious of a possible voter reaction in case nothing at all were done.

Because of the lack of sustained, intense, and widespread public interest in the Full Employment Bill, S.380 was shaped in the House by the more immediate and penetrating demands of those pressure groups which controlled or shared the personal opinions of the

8 *Ibid.*, p. 2.     9 *Ibid.*
10 Representative Carter Manasco, in an interview, Washington, D.C., Feb. 20, 1946

majority of representatives. Pressure groups are important in our national life because they are articulate about legislative detail, and when no voice is capable of bringing overwhelming public attention to bear on the specifics of law-making, the "public opinion" which tends to be dominant in the minds of most Congressmen is the articulate and effective expression of political and economic interests in their home constituencies which have made possible their election or which menace their chance of reelection. In many cases, the impact of this constituent opinion is extremely subtle. Usually, Congressmen share the value judgments of these dominant constituent interests, so that regardless of geographical source, the "public opinion" which finds its mark is composed of proposals, arguments, amendments, or interpretations which square with the presuppositions of the Congressmen themselves.

For a number of reasons, some of which have been suggested in an earlier chapter, Senators are more likely to take a broader view of "public opinion" than Representatives. Longer terms of office give Senators a degree of detachment from immediate constituent pressures which cannot be enjoyed by most Representatives. A state is likely to reflect a more complicated amalgam of opinions than is a Congressional district, thereby permitting Senators relatively more independence of thought and action. And closely tied in with this last, most states have at least one sizable urban area, the problems of which cannot be ignored by a Senator even if they can be by the Congressman from an adjoining small-town or rural district.

If the above analysis is correct, the relationship of public opinion to the legislative history of the Full Employment Bill can be summarized as follows

1. The widespread public concern about the possibility of postwar unemployment served as a favorable climate for the introduction of a full employment bill—particularly in the Senate.

2. The particular sensitivity of the Senate to conditions in urban areas helped to insure the passage of S.380 without serious modification soon after the end of the war when urban populations were especially conscious of transitional unemployment.

3. The relative immunity of most Congressmen to urban pressures, the failure of widespread unemployment to materialize, and the lack of dramatic political leadership left the way open during the period of House consideration for a drastic modification of the bill by small-town and rural Representatives.

We must examine the third factor a little more thoroughly.

A. N. Holcombe, in his study of *The Middle Class in American Politics,* divides Congressional districts into three categories: Metropolitan, Other Urban, and Rural. Holcombe explains this breakdown in the following words:

The voting strength of the urban population in the lower branch of the Congress cannot be . . . easily estimated. It is a fair assumption, however, that all congressional districts which are situated wholly within a metropolitan area, or which contain a metropolitan area of at least a quarter of a million population, are predominantly urban in politics. Other congressional districts, containing a smaller metropolitan area, may often, though not necessarily always, be dominated by the urban population. Congressional districts, which neither lie wholly or partly within a metropolitan area of any size within their own limits, will generally, though certainly not always be subject to domination by the rural population.[11]

On the basis of these assumptions, Holcombe finds that there are 123 Metropolitan districts, 87 Other Urban districts, and 225 Rural districts.[12] Let us look at some of the implications of these figures from the standpoint of voting records.

On August 18, 1946, the Washington *Post* published a C.I.O. evaluation of the 79th Congress's votes on 12 "key" issues. Votes were tabulated as "For C.I.O." and "Against C.I.O." In the House, only 137 out of the 435 Congressmen voted "for" the C.I.O. more times than they voted "against" it. Of these 137 only ten came from Southern states which, of course, are overwhelmingly rural. On the other hand, the ten states in the Union with the highest percentage of population living in urban areas provided 86 of the 137 liberal Congressmen. In twenty states more than 50 percent of the population lives in urban areas.[13] These twenty states accounted for 104 of the 137 liberals.

There is of course no complete correlation between urbanism and liberalism. George Outland and Charles LaFollette, two of the most aggressive liberals in the 79th Congress, represented nonurban areas.[14] Clarence Hancock, a rock-bound conservative,

11 A. N. Holcombe, *The Middle Class in American Politics* (Cambridge, Mass., Harvard University Press, 1940), p. 103. Reprinted by permission of the publishers.
12 *Ibid.*
13 U.S. Department of Commerce, *Statistical Abstract of the United States 1944-45* (Washington, 1945), p. 14, Table 11.
14 California 11th and Indiana 8th, respectively.

represented Onondaga County which is virtually coextensive with the city of Syracuse, New York.[15] No one can doubt, however, that the heavily populated urban areas tend by and large to reflect the needs and fears of the urban worker; the small-town and rural districts, the needs and fears of small business and of agriculture. If one is to understand the conservatism of the House of Representatives in relation to S.380, therefore, he must attempt to analyze the dominant opinions of small-town and agricultural America, the ways in which that opinion is shaped and the ways in which it manifests itself. Some of these problems will be discussed in this, some in the following chapter.

### SMALL-TOWN AND RURAL CONSERVATISM

When Robert Lynd revisited "Middletown" in 1935–36, he reported an "increasing pervasiveness of the power" of a wealthy family of manufacturers. Commenting on the control of the "X family," Lynd says:

Middletown has . . . at present what amounts to a reigning royal family. The power of this family has become so great as to differentiate the city today somewhat from cities with a more diffuse type of control. If, however, one views the Middletown pattern as simply concentrating and personalizing the type of control which control of capital gives to the business group in our culture, the Middletown situation may be viewed as epitomizing the American business-class control system. It may even foreshadow a pattern which may become increasingly prevalent in the future as the American propertied class strives to preserve its control.[16]

And to quote Lynd once more:

It is the impression of the investigator:
That the lines of leadership and the related controls are highly concentrated today in Middletown.
That this control net has tightened decidedly since 1925 and notably with the depression.
That the control is at very many points unconscious and, where conscious, well-meaning and "public spirited," as businessmen interpret that concept.
That the control system operates at many points to identify public welfare with business-class welfare.

15 New York 36th.
16 Robert S. Lynd and Helen M. Lynd, *Middletown in Transition* (New York, Harcourt, Brace and Company, Inc., 1937), p. 77. This and the following quotation are reprinted by permission of the publishers.

That there is little deliberate effort from above to organize local bankers, businessmen, and leaders of opinion into a self-conscious "we" pressure group; but that this sharply centripetal tendency of Middletown's businessmen is normal behavior in a capitalist, credit-controlled culture where there is a potential control center in the form of vast personal resources of demonstrated willingness to lend a friendly hand.[17]

The first hypothesis about the conservatism of the majority of Congressmen in the 79th Congress who came from predominantly small-town and rural districts is that the business-class control system to which Lynd refers has been extended and intensified during the past twelve years, and that this development is in part a result of the improved economic status of these areas since the middle thirties, in part the result of an increasingly cohesive business hostility to the New Deal and its implications. A corollary of this hypothesis is that the small independent farmer tends to be conservative, or indifferent to issues, unless he himself is in economic straits, and consequently, that the business-class control system tends increasingly not only to dominate small-town opinion, but through an identity of interest with big commercial farmers, articulate agricultural opinion as well.

The second hypothesis is that the legal and business backgrounds of three-quarters of the 435 representatives in the 79th Congress [18] was a reflection of, or at least played into the hands of, the business-class control system in those districts where urban or mine workers were not a serious political factor. Many of the lawyers in the 79th Congress received their legal training during the twenties or before, with all that this implies from the standpoint of economic and political philosophy. Most of them have been dependent for economic and professional success upon their local business communities. As the strength of the business-class control system has increased in the last twelve years, lawyer-politicians have found it increasingly expedient not to antagonize what Professor Hollingshead at Yale has called the Class I and II groups in the small towns.[19] Actually, most of the small-town lawyers by the time they get to Congress have assumed all the basic sentiments and attitudes of the business leaders in their respective communities, so that on many issues di-

[17] *Ibid.*, p. 99.
[18] George B. Galloway, *Congress at the Crossroads* (New York, 1946), p. 349.
[19] August B. Hollingshead, "Selected Characteristics of Classes in a Middle Western Community." *American Sociological Review*, XII, No. 4, August, 1947, 385–395.

rect pressures from back home are superfluous. In this connection, organizations like Rotary, Kiwanis, local chambers of commerce, and other similar groups which facilitate the exchange of business ideas, must not be underestimated.

The third hypothesis is that an important instrument of the business-class control system is the small-town and rural press. In Senator Murray's press-clipping folders on the Full Employment Bill for the year 1945, I counted 72 editorial comments in 50 small-town dailies and weeklies. Of these 72 editorial comments, all except five were hostile. Note some of the following "coincidences":

On February 20, 1945, without credit lines, editorials attacking the bill appeared in the Zanesville (Ohio) *Times-Recorder* and the Cheyenne *Wyoming State Tribune*. These editorials were identical.

On September 7, 1945, the Clarksburg (West Virginia) *Exponent* published an editorial against the bill. On September 10, 1945, the identical editorial appeared in the Lima (Ohio) *News*.

On September 7, 1945, identical editorials quoting anti-Full Employment Bill material prepared by the Committee for Constitutional Government, appeared in the Macon (Georgia) *Telegraph* and the Cumberland (Maryland) *Times*.

And note the authorities quoted in the following anti-Full Employment Bill editorials:

On February 12, 1945, the Columbia (South Carolina) *Record* quoted Rufus Tucker of the N.A.M.

On March 7, 1945, the Jackson (Michigan) *Citizen and Patriot* quoted Ira Mosher of the N.A.M.

On March 6, 1945, the Ft. Dodge (Iowa) *Messenger and Chronicle* quoted from an anti-deficit spending statement put out by a small group of New York businessmen called *Committee for Americans*.

On May 6, 1945, the Bluefield (West Virginia) *Telegraph* quoted Dr. Virgil Jordan, President of the National Industrial Conference Board.

On May 16, 1945, the Rapid City (South Dakota) *Journal* quoted H. W. Prentiss, Jr., of the N.A.M.

On September 6, 1945, the Woonsocket (Rhode Island) *Call* quoted Ira Mosher.

Since the editors and publishers of small-town papers are generally important members of the local business community, and since Congressmen pay a good deal of attention to the home-town press, editorial decisions to select for publication handouts from the national opinion machines of big business have a dual significance.

The fourth and final hypothesis is that the prior conditioning of Congressmen representing areas easily subjected to the business-class control system makes them unusually amenable to statements of conservative opinion regardless of where these statements originate. The real importance of the anti-Full Employment Bill editorials in the big metropolitan dailies, the syndicated columns of Paul Mallon,[20] Raymond Moley,[21] Walter Lippmann,[22] the Ralph Robey columns in *Newsweek*,[23] and scores of other hostile statements, was not that they created a widespread public opinion against the bill, but that they served as ammunition for a group of small-town and rural Congressmen who were ideologically receptive to these ideas.

[20] Oct. 2, 1945.    [21] Dec. 27, 1944.    [22] Sept. 26, 1945.
[23] July 9, 1945, p. 72; Sept. 10, 1945, p. 74; Oct. 8, 1945, p. 78; and Oct. 15, 1945, p. 78.

# CHAPTER TEN

# Personalities:

# Interpretations and Inferences

> Possibly the members from his own state
> know him, and receive him into full fel-
> lowship; but no one else knows him, ex-
> cept as an adherent of this or that party,
> or as a newcomer from this or that State.
> —Wilson, *Congressional Government*,
> p. 62.

BEFORE PROCEEDING to a study of the final phases of the legislative history of the Full Employment Bill, it is important to take a brief look at the backgrounds of the twelve legislators who composed the Joint Conference Committee. These twelve were not equally influential in determining the final shape of S.380. Actually, as we shall see, the issues before the Conference were largely determined by a struggle between Representatives Cochran and Whittington.

But in our search for a broad understanding of the forces which shaped the Employment Act of 1946, the members of the Joint Conference Committee assume a significance far beyond their individual contributions to the revision of the Full Employment Bill. The twelve conferees represented an ideological cross-section of the 79th Congress, and a study of these men may give us an insight into the factors of inheritance and environment which are omnipresent forces in legislative policy-making.

Why do legislators think the way they do about social issues? Why are they amenable to certain pressures and not to others? What influences in the past have molded the attitudes which they bring with them to Congress? These are questions of cardinal importance to an understanding of the policy-making process.

The very size of Congress tends to devitalize our appreciation of the individuality of its members, yet it is as individuals that Congressmen vote. It is true, of course, that many Congressmen follow the leader on many issues, but this fact simply poses the further question, why do some Congressmen accept the leadership of a Will Whittington while others accept the leadership of a John Cochran? Back of every Congressman's vote is a complex of subtle and overt influences, presuppositions, and value judgments.

### CONGRESSMEN ARE PEOPLE

The fate of any piece of legislation cannot be understood without an appreciation of the fact that Congressmen are people, with all that that banality implies. Like the rest of us they become bored by tedious debates, angered by personal affronts, inspired by the words of leaders they respect, irritated by the weather, confused by technical problems, upset by domestic misunderstandings or the illness of loved ones. Like any cross-section of the American public, they have been molded in their thinking by scores of influences: parents, teachers, friends, enemies, social status, occupation or profession, personal successes and failures, adult associates, regional interests, local opinions, party loyalties, and the general social, economic, moral, and intellectual milieu of their generation and culture.

The process of personal growth and change continues, of course, after a Congressman is elected to the national legislature. There he is subject to a series of new pressures and experiences, and a new perspective is virtually forced upon him if he remains for any length of time. The interests of Podunk come to be seen in relation to the interests of a thousand Podunks and a hundred Metropols; the Congressman meets men of experience and knowledge greater than his; he finds reinforcement for some of the ideas he holds and lack of reinforcement for others; he notes consciously or unconsciously the colleagues with whom he feels at ease and whose judgments he respects; he reevaluates his own capacity for leadership; he becomes acutely aware of the frustrations of the legislative process and the few moments in each session when *his* decisions may mean the success or failure of a policy which will affect millions of people. If at times he tends to overestimate his own importance in the scheme of things, there are scores of reminders, official and personal, that he is like the drunken poet who wandered into the zoo congratulating himself on being the highest product of evolution until finally he became sober enough to recognize that after all he was just "a little man in trousers slightly jagged." [1] Congressional service is a form of higher education.

But by and large, the basic social philosophy of a legislator is set before he comes to Congress. It is for this reason that the study of a legislator from the Washington perspective alone is bound to be one-dimensional. The behavior of an animal is shaped by his native habitat, and the Congressional animal is no exception. Of central importance to an understanding of the fate of S.380, therefore, is some appreciation of the types of background influences which helped to shape the social philosophies of the members of the 79th Congress.

### LIBERALS VERSUS CONSERVATIVES

By way of rough delineation, the social philosophies of the twelve members of the Joint Conference Committee may be diagrammed as follows:

#### SENATE CONFEREES

VERY LIB-ERAL     (Liberal)        (Conservative)     VERY CONSERV-ATIVE

Taylor Barkley Murdock Tobey    Taft Radcliffe Buck

#### HOUSE CONFEREES

VERY LIB-ERAL     (Liberal)        (Conservative)     VERY CONSERV-ATIVE

Cochran Bender    Whittington Manasco Hoffman

The following interpretations and inferences are based upon a personal interview with ten of the twelve conferees, and upon brief field studies of the home-towns and districts or states of all twelve. In each case, the question posed for investigation was, "Why did this particular legislator hold the ideas and values about social issues which caused him to look at the Full Employment Bill as he did?" The findings which are summarized below are cursory. Politi-

[1] Walter Lippmann, *The Good Society* (London, 1937), p. 25.

cal science has desperate need of the insights and techniques of the psychologists and sociologists if the motivations and behavior patterns of political leaders are to be adequately understood.[2]

## THE SIX CONSERVATIVES

### SENATOR CLAYTON DOUGLASS BUCK (REPUBLICAN), DELAWARE

Born, Buenavista, Md. (the family estate eight miles south of Wilmington), March 21, 1890; great-uncle, John M. Clayton, one-time Senator, Secretary of State, and co-author of the famous Clayton-Bulwer treaty with Great Britain; father, Francis N. Buck, an aristocratic farmer and active Democrat.

Attended Wilmington Friends School, graduating with honors in 1908; six months with Standard Arms Co.; few months at Beacom College; attended Univ. of Pennsylvania, Dept. of Chemical Engineering, 1909–11; left University suddenly in 1911, and the next day was working on the Du Pont road which was then being constructed in Delaware.

Became Asst. Engineer (1919) and Chief Engineer (1922) of State Highway Dept.; in service World War I at M.I.T. and at Princeton Aviation Ground School; married daughter of T. Coleman Du Pont in 1921; Governor of Delaware, 1929–37; member of Republican National Committee, 1930–37; elected U.S. Senate, 1942. Defeated for reelection, 1948.

Business interests: Board of Managers, the Wilmington Savings Fund Society; director, Continental Life Insurance Company; Board of Managers, Farmers Mutual Fire Insurance Company; director, J. A. Montgomery, Inc. (insurance brokers); president, Equitable Trust Company (later chairman of Board).

The tiny State of Delaware, which is considerably smaller than many Congressional districts, is in no small measure the personal preserve of the Du Pont family. It is true that the Du Pont control has been shaken on occasion, and that a large vote can sometimes disrupt the neat domination of the family over the organizations of

[2] The field studies have been undertaken on a highly unsystematic basis. In general, I have attempted to get at the values and motives of a legislator by talking with those people in his home town who would have had an opportunity to know both the subject and the predominant characteristics of his constituency. I have also tried to digest as much written material about each subject as time and resources have allowed. But no one is more conscious than I of the tentative character of my findings, and the unscientific intuitions on which some of these findings are based. It is my belief that further and more comprehensive studies of this nature are necessary if political scientists are to develop any real grasp of the forces at work in our national legislature.

Except for direct quotations documented in the footnotes, I have relied for information about all twelve of the following legislators upon the sources listed for each sketch and upon conversations with newspapermen; business, labor, and farm leaders; and other key citizens in each locality.

both political parties. But as one Wilmington editor put it, "One billion dollars piled up, even if the pile remains immobile, casts a long shadow." [3]

At the age of twenty-one, C. Douglass Buck came under the wing of politically minded T. Coleman Du Pont in connection with an enterprise which was to shape both their political futures. The Du Pont Highway, which runs the entire length of the state from Wilmington to Dalmar, was a major landmark in the history of Delaware politics. The highway was the brain child and gift of T. Coleman Du Pont. *Fortune Magazine* commented in 1935,

> Whether Coleman built his road for political purposes or whether its political possibilities became clear while he was building it, no one can say. But one result was to make it easier for Wilmington to dominate the State politically, to remove the barrier between the traditionally Democratic lower counties and Republican Wilmington, so that Wilmington with nearly half the voters in the State and with nearly all the money, could elect whom it pleased to whatever office.[4]

For Coleman, the road led to eventual domination of the state Republican machine and to the Senate. For Buck, the road led to business prominence and to the governorship and the Senate via the office of Chief Engineer of the Highway Department. Buck's fortunes were of course tied intimately to the career of Coleman Du Pont, a relationship which was abetted by Buck's marriage in 1921 to Alice Du Pont, Coleman's daughter.

To suggest that Buck as a Senator was a "tool" of the Du Ponts is to misinterpret the nature of what Lynd has called "the business-class control system." It was not the pressure of Du Pont *on* Buck but the pressure of Du Pont *in* Buck which was at work. In his first gubernatorial inaugural in 1929, Buck stated, "I have assumed the head of a great business—a business in many respects like that of a large corporation—in which the State officials are the officers and the people are the stockholders." [5] That such an analogy came trippingly to his mind is not strange.

    [3] Joseph Martin, editor and owner of the Wilmington *Sunday Star*, in an interview, Wilmington, Delaware, July 23, 1946.

    Other sources for the material on Senator Buck are: an interview with his Secretary, Frank Schroeder, Washington, July 16, 1946; *Fortune*, November, 1934, and January, 1935; George Kennan, "Holding up a State," *Outlook*, Feb. 7–21, 1903; William J. Robertson, "The Du Ponts," Philadelphia *Record*, Jan. 30, 1933; Wilmington *News Journal* library; Wilmington Public Library, file on "Delaware Politics and Government"; Wilmington *Sunday Star*, Jan. 13, 1929 and Jan. 17, 1937.

    [4] January, 1935, pp. 122, 125.        [5] Wilmington *News Journal*, Jan. 15, 1929.

Senator Buck is no "man of the people," and except for an occasional play for the Polish vote in Wilmington, he seldom if ever has talked like one. He is a member of one of the ruling families in the American economy; he is at home in the luxurious estates of Newcastle county; he shares the fears of the economic and social class epitomized by the Du Pont name—the fears of any aristocracy in a revolutionary world.

Buck was one of ten Senators to vote against the Full Employment Bill in the Senate. In trying to justify his stand against S.380, he issued a statement in which he characterized the bill as a "hoax" on labor and as "not in the interest of the farmer." The statement concluded with an honest résumé of Buck's own philosophy: "The remedy for unemployment is to balance the federal budget, reduce taxes on industry, remove government restrictions on business, and provide credit for small business, when venture capital will come out of hiding and full employment will become a reality instead of a political issue." [6] It was perhaps Buck's own realization that he was not representative of a large segment of the American population which made him write in this same statement, "To oppose legislation that is supposed to provide wide employment is to commit political hara kiri, but I would rather leave public office than support a bill in which I do not have faith."

Buck has been loyal to his background, his family, and his class, and in 1948 he paid the political price.

## SENATOR GEORGE RADCLIFFE (DEMOCRAT), MARYLAND

Born, Lloyds, Md., August 22, 1877; father, John Anthony LeCompte Radcliffe, a shipbuilder and farmer; graduated from Cambridge Seminary (Md.) in 1893; received B.A., Johns Hopkins, 1897; Ph.D., Johns Hopkins, 1900.

Principal, Cambridge Seminary, 1900–1901; history teacher, Baltimore City College, 1902–3; Bachelor of Law, Univ. Maryland Law College, 1903; admitted to state bar same year.

Employed as attorney, American Bonding Co., Baltimore, until 1904; vice president, 1906; president, 1914–1930, becoming one of nation's outstanding authorities in the casualty business.

From 1916 to 1919, a member of Baltimore Board of Liquor License Commissioners; 1919–21, Maryland Secretary of State; 1932–33, chairman, Maryland State Democratic Campaign Committee; early 1934, appointed by Roosevelt to be Regional Administrator of P.W.A.; elected

6 Wilmington *Morning News*, Sept. 30, 1945.

U.S. Senate, 1934; reelected 1940; defeated in Democratic primaries, 1946.

Business connections: Board of Directors, American Bonding Co., the Fidelity Trust Co., the Title Guarantee and Trust Co., and the Baltimore Trust Co.; first vice president, director, and member of Executive Committee of the Fidelity and Deposit Co.

When George Radcliffe was nominated for the Senate in 1934, his political opponents claimed he would become a "rubber stamp" for President Roosevelt. This was perhaps a natural deduction from Radcliffe's long friendship with Roosevelt which had begun in the early 1920's when F.D.R. became a New York vice president of the Fidelity and Deposit Company. Radcliffe was at that time Roosevelt's boss. The opposition attack in 1934 also stemmed from Radcliffe's ringing endorsement of the President's emergency program and from the fact that the social aspects of the New Deal were singled out by Radcliffe for special praise. If his Republican opponents had wanted to press their case even further, they could have searched the record and discovered that Radcliffe had taken graduate work in history at Johns Hopkins back in 1899 when Woodrow Wilson was on the faculty.

What his opponents failed to appreciate was that this erudite scholar and public servant had for thirty years prior to his election to the Senate been one of the most successful financial leaders of one of the most conservative business communities in America. For years, the banking and business leaders of Baltimore have constituted one of the most forceful groups in Maryland politics—Democratic as well as Republican. The effectiveness of this business control can be appreciated when one recognizes that Maryland has had, during the past fourteen years, one of the most consistently conservative Democratic delegations in Congress.

Radcliffe's apparent liberalism in 1934 was shared by a large bloc of the business community. They had been badly scared by the banking crisis in 1932–33, they were appreciative of Roosevelt's will to act, and they sincerely endorsed some of the early New Deal legislation like Depositor's Insurance. But the honeymoon was short. By 1937, Radcliffe had split with the President on the Supreme Court packing plan; in 1938 he became campaign manager for conservative Senator Millard Tydings who was on the President's purge list; and as the years went by, Radcliffe found himself more and more out of sympathy with the New Deal economic program.

His variegated business responsibilities in Baltimore and his growing hostility to the Roosevelt domestic program meant that Radcliffe came increasingly to treat his Senatorial duties as a side line. The *Congressional Record* shows that between the 76th and 79th Congress, Radcliffe was absent on 87 roll calls. His colleagues came to joke about "Radcliffe Thursdays" because the Senator used to spend that day of the week in business board meetings in Baltimore.

Radcliffe is a true conservative. His speeches abound with phrases like "sound policies" and "careful procedures"—phrases which cautious and successful members of the banking profession use and follow. The new, the untried, the experimental are suspect in the field of national policy just as they are in banking policy. The Full Employment Bill worried the Maryland Senator as few other proposed policies ever had. He was "amazed at the one-sidedness of the bill with its 'guarantee' to labor"; he was disturbed by the "unsound" spending program.[7] He worked in the closest possible relationship with Taft (whom he greatly admired) on "needed" amendments to the bill. He fought the liberal wing of his own party and joined forces with the conservative wing of the opposition party in order to modify a piece of legislation which he felt was aimed straight at the American way of life.

George Radcliffe, as a Senator, was a representative of a well-knit and influential class of citizens in America; the business and financial leaders who have built their success out of personal honesty and cautious decisions. Radcliffe tries, by his own admission, to face life "objectively." But his associations and experiences have limited the scope of his objectivity. Like sincere labor leaders and liberal legislators on the other side, Radcliffe is in part a prisoner of his long personal and occupational associations. "So much a long communion tends to make us what we are."

## SENATOR ROBERT A. TAFT (REPUBLICAN) OF OHIO

Born, Cincinnati, Ohio, September 8, 1889; son of William Howard Taft; educated in Cincinnati public schools, and Taft School (Conn.);

7 Senator George Radcliffe, in an interview, Baltimore, Maryland, Aug. 21, 1946. Other sources for this material are: an interview with Senator Radcliffe in Washington, July 17, 1946; Kumner and Latrobe, *The Free State of Maryland,* IV (Baltimore, 1942), 1457–1458; *Tercentenary History of Maryland,* III (Chicago and Baltimore, 1925), 750–752; Baltimore Public Library, "Maryland Vertical File"; Baltimore *Sun,* June 15, Aug. 1, 1943, Feb. 21 and June 17, 1946; George S. Perry, "Baltimore." *Saturday Evening Post,* May 11, 1946; *Washington Post,* Nov. 9, 1934.

received B.A., Yale, 1910; LL.B., Harvard Law School, 1913; married Martha Wheaton Bowers, 1914; four children.

Assistant Counsel, U.S. Food Administration during World War I; accompanied Hoover abroad on relief administration work, 1919. Member of Ohio House of Representatives, 1921–26 (Speaker, 1926); Ohio Senate, 1931–32; elected U.S. Senate, 1938; reelected 1944.

Corporation law practice in Cincinnati since 1915; Maxwell and Ramsey, 1915–19; Taft and Taft, 1920–1938; Taft, Stettinius, and Hollister, 1938–.

Taft is one of the best-known public figures in America. A man of astounding intellectual vitality, he has won his way to a position of leadership in the Senate and the Republican Party by hard work, moral courage, and mental ability. Often tactless and "old Betty-ish," he is perhaps the leading conservative spokesman in America. In trying to sum up the influences in his life which had been most instrumental in shaping his social and economic philosophy, Taft in 1946 noted two outstanding factors: his father, and twenty-five years of corporation law practice in Cincinnati. Then, as an after-thought, Taft added, "But I have been interested in social problems. I have always been active in charity work in Cincinnati." [8]

Born into a socially prominent Cincinnati family, the son of the 26th President of the United States; educated at an exclusive private school, Yale, and Harvard; married to an able, ambitious, and conservative wife; Taft's early environment made a heavy impression on him. These early factors were reinforced by his successful corporate law practice. After graduating from Harvard Law School at the top of his class, Taft made an easy entrance into the business community in his home town of Cincinnati. His first clients were his aunt and uncle, who held equity in such important city institutions as the *Times-Star* and the Cincinnati Street Railway System. Uncle Charles turned to Bob for a complete reorganization of the Street Railway System, a task which took the young lawyer eleven years.

[8] Senator Robert A. Taft, in an interview, Washington, D.C., July 17, 1946.

Other sources are Joseph and Stewart Alsop, "Taft and Vandenburg," *Life*, Oct. 7, 1946; Cincinnati Public Library, file on "Senator Robert A. Taft"; Charles Dexter, "The Tafts of Ohio," *Reader's Scope*, February, 1946; Morris D. Ervin, "The White House Lures Another Taft," *Christian Science Monitor*, Jan. 13, 1940; "Taft as a 'Liberal,'" *New Republic*, May 27, 1946; *Newsweek*, July 15, 1946, pp. 287–288; George S. Perry, "Cincinnati," *Saturday Evening Post*, April 20, 1946; Robert A. Taft, "No Substitute for Freedom," *Collier's*, Feb. 1, 1947, and "Shall the Government Guarantee Employment," address to the National Industrial Conference Board at New York, Jan. 18, 1945 (mimeograph); *Time*, April 15, 1946, p. 20; "The Age of Taft," *Time*, Jan. 20, 1947; Washington *Post*, March 17, 1940.

Taft's law practice has always been "clean"—no criminal or marital cases. His clients have been firms like the Gruen Watch Company, Globe-Wernike, and the Cincinnati Milling Machine Company. He has had a large estate and trust business. It is fair to say that almost all his professional relationships have been with wealthy and successful persons and corporations. One disgruntled competitor once made the remark, "We lawyers never got along with Bob too well. His clients were too powerful for us and he was too cold." [9] Taft himself, partly through inheritance, partly through personal financial successes, has managed to acquire a considerable stake in a variety of Cincinnati enterprises—from toll bridges to newspapers to brewery warehouses to real estate.

Taft's political associations have also contributed to his conservatism. Starting early at the precinct level, Taft has long been associated with one of the tightest and most conservative Republican county machines in America. Hamilton county has for years been organized down to the last doorbell, and even the success of the city charter movement, which precipitated a friendly feud between Bob and reformer brother Charlie, has not shaken the Republican County machine in state and national elections. It was through this machine that Taft first entered state politics, and it has been a major factor in his political success ever since. The conservative businessmen of Cincinnati contribute both time and money to the Hamilton County Republican machine, and Taft has always been an organization man.

Granted this sort of background, the question may well be asked why Taft was willing to accept the Senate version of the Full Employment Bill against the protests of the major spokesmen for the business community in America. Cynical political observers would probably point to Taft's narrow margin of victory in 1944 when because of labor opposition he gained a plurality of only 18,000 out of almost 3,000,000 votes cast in the Ohio Senatorial contest. Others might suggest that Taft wanted to be President and felt the need for broadening the base of his political support. Who is to say that in the recesses of the mind where motives are manufactured, experiences or aspirations of this sort may not have had some influence?

But there is another way of interpreting the various liberal

9 Charles Dexter, "The Tafts of Ohio," *Reader's Scope*, February, 1946, p. 5.

gestures which Taft has made in the past few years in such areas as employment policy, housing, and health. For all Taft's coldness and frequent tactlessness, he does have a profound sense of public responsibility and he is impressed by facts. A reasonable man has the capacity for growth and adaptation, and although Taft's sympathies may be limited by his conservative background, he is not a slave to consistency or blind passions. Still conservative, still paternalistic, the Ohio Senator continues to be a spokesman for the class in society he knows and understands. But not before his death will anyone be able to speak with complete authority about the "education" of Robert A. Taft.

## REPRESENTATIVE CLARE HOFFMAN (REPUBLICAN), 4TH CONGRESSIONAL DISTRICT, MICHIGAN

Born, Vicksburg, Pa., September 10, 1875; father, Samuel D. Hoffman, a carriage-maker and farmer; family moved to Constantine, Michigan, when Clare was a year old; graduated Constantine High School; took law degree Northwestern Law School after one and a half years, 1896; married, 1899; law practice in Allegan, Michigan, until 1934, when elected to Congress; County Prosecutor, Allegan County, late twenties and early thirties; head of county Republican Committee for many years; reelected to Congress, 1936, 1938, 1940, 1942, 1944, 1946.
Owner: Allegan *Gazette*, real estate, large fruit farm.

Curmudgeons are difficult to analyze. No matter how many environmental factors a biographer may discover, he is forced to pay tribute to the perverse genes which produced the superfluity of vitriol in the curmudgeon's mind. Clare Hoffman of Michigan is a conservative curmudgeon. One of the cleverest courtroom lawyers in the history of Michigan legal practice, Hoffman has many admirers, but few close friends. He is anti-union, anti-liberal, and zenophobic. One of his closest friends in Congress is Representative John Rankin of Mississippi.

Hoffman is the product of a Pennsylvania Dutch ancestry and a rural Anglo-Saxon upbringing in the southwest corner of Michigan. The area which now constitutes the 4th Congressional district was originally settled by New Englanders and Genesee Valley New Yorkers in the 1830's. By and large, the present inhabitants of the district have roots in the land going back three generations, with all that that implies from the standpoint of political continuity and economic conservatism. (The population of Hoffman's home county, Allegan, has remained almost stationary since 1910, although the state population has doubled.)

One Allegan lawyer who has followed Hoffman's career with considerable interest for a number of years explains the Congressman entirely on the basis of the people in his district. The people, according to this lawyer, are "litigous [sic], provincial, and reactionary"—a description which leads the lawyer to conclude that Allegan is "a lawyer's paradise. Everyone hates everyone else, and people would rather cut off their right hand than settle out of court." [10]

This picture may be overdrawn, but there is just enough truth in it to warrant its inclusion in a pen portrait of this type. The fruit and truck farmers who constitute the largest economic bloc in the district are rabidly independent and singularly humorless. Their chief contact with labor is with the migratory fruit-pickers: Mexicans, "Okies," and Jamaicans, who follow the fruit belt and who are often tempted away from the Michigan orchards by high wages in Chicago and Detroit. Ingrown intellectually as well as genealogically, the farmers take their cue on national issues from the ubiquitous Chicago *Tribune*, two other Republican dailies, the Kalamazoo *Gazette* and the Grand Rapids *Press*, and a set of weekly papers which feature N.A.M. cartoons and editorals and/or a weekly Washington column written by Clare Hoffman. Hoffman owns the Allegan *Gazette* and owns the building in which the Allegan *News* is published.

Hoffman's conservatism is a reflection of the environment in which he was raised: the provincialism and bigotry of undiluted Anglo-Saxon stock; the rugged individualism of the small, independent farmers; the hard and frugal life of those whose security rests upon long hours and the rigid discipline of the elements. Isolated from and suspicious of the forces which have shaped urban

10 In an interview in Allegan, Michigan, June 5, 1947.
Other sources for this sketch are: an interview with Representative Hoffman, Washington, June 1, 1946; Pioneer Society of the State of Michigan, *Pioneer Collections*, III (Lansing, 1881), 270; Milo M. Quaife, *Michigan's County Flags and Histories* (limited 1st ed., Detroit, 1940); *Who's Who in Michigan*, I (1947), 719; Allegan *Gazette*, 1944–1946; Ann Arbor *News*, Feb. 9 and March 16, 1946; Will Chasan and Esther Jack, "Clare E. Hoffman of Michigan," *Nation*, Aug. 15, 1942; Volta Torrey, "How Clare Hoffman Stays in Congress," *PM*, Sept. 12, 1943; University of Michigan Library (Ann Arbor), file on "Michigan Politicians"; Washington *Post*, April 18, May 28, and May 29, 1942.

America, Hoffman and his constituents are fighting the rear-guard action of an isolated society.

The Full Employment Bill to Hoffman was a direct challenge to his way of life—to the benefits of the rugged, Spartan existence which produced the self-made men of his generation. Hoffman is something of an anachronism in American life, just as his district is. Perhaps the Congressman's bitterness towards S.380 was in part the result of his realization that Allegan county was powerless to stop the restless political tide of interdependent, insecure, polyglot, urban America.

REPRESENTATIVE CARTER MANASCO (DEMOCRAT), 7TH CONGRESSIONAL DISTRICT, ALABAMA

Born Townley, Ala., January 3, 1902; son of tenant farmer; educated public schools (three and a half months a year); 1920, entered Howard College in Birmingham for two years; 1927, received law degree from University of Alabama (through which he had earned his way by coal mining); tried to set up law practice in Jasper, Alabama, 1927–29; ran for and elected to state legislature, 1930; 1933, came to Washington to work in legal division of Justice Dept.; same year, became clerk to Speaker Will Bankhead; continued as clerk until 1940 when Speaker died; continued for short time as clerk to Walter Will Bankhead; elected to 77th Congress on June 24, 1941, to fill vacancy caused by resignation of Walter Will Bankhead; reelected to 78th, 79th, and 80th Congresses; defeated in 1948 primaries; married; Baptist and Mason.

When Carter Manasco is asked about his conservatism, he replies that he wants to perpetuate the type of society which permits the son of a tenant farmer to become a Congressman. He also states that America is a republic, not a democracy, and that it should stay a republic.[11] These two explanations suggest a lot about Manasco and his district.

Manasco's father died of pellagra. The Manasco homestead in Townley is situated near the railroad tracks in a dismally dirty coal region. Although superior to the shanties of the poor whites, the

[11] Sources for this sketch are: interviews with Representative Manasco in Washington on Feb. 20, 1946, and in Jasper, Alabama, on July 31, 1947; Birmingham *News-Age-Herald*, March 3, 1946; *Franklin County Times* (Russelville, Ala.), May 4, 1944; Helen Fuller, "Manasco, One-Man Bottleneck," *New Republic*, Dec. 10, 1945; *Mountain Eagle* (Jasper), April 27, June 29, Sept. 28, and Nov. 9, 1944, March 1, Nov. 8, and Nov. 15, 1945, and Feb. 21, 1946; *Union News* (Jasper), June 1, 1944, and Nov. 22, 1945.

house reflects the poverty of the section. Near by are the warped and wobbly shacks of the miners and the rural slum dwellers.

Carter Manasco grew up in this type of environment, and although his grandfather had been a figure of some importance in state politics, young Carter had to struggle with the poverty resulting from his own father's illness. Even when he reached maturity, Carter had to work in Alabama and Illinois coal mines for seven years in order to pay for his education. He was not successful as a lawyer in Jasper, and the state legislature and later Washington were the first experiences of success and prestige that Carter knew. Perhaps the memory of his politician grandfather, perhaps the simple necessity of economic security, drove Manasco into politics; but he has been kept in public life by love for the occupation which has given him security and prestige. His slight tendency toward pomposity in committee sessions was an understandable compensation for the years of hard and depressing work in the mines and the failures of his early struggles for professional status in law.

Manasco's conservatism seems at first glance to be incompatible with his background. Experiences in the mines made men like Senators Murray and Murdock sensitive to the needs of union labor. Manasco, with a much longer exposure to mining, has been an almost consistent enemy of organized labor—at least from organized labor's point of view. The explanation lies in the nature of the seventh district in Alabama, and Manasco's perhaps unconscious realization that his prestige and security were dependent upon not antagonizing those forces which control the political life of that district.

The Alabama Seventh is one of the poorest Congressional districts in America. The percentage of Negroes is extremely small, but the poor whites of the hills are ignorant, depressed, and isolated. Political life in the Seventh District is largely dominated by the more prosperous farmers in Cullman, Blount, and Pickens counties, and by the small businessmen in the towns and the big businessmen who exert absentee control from Birmingham. Mine workers are largely confined to Walker county, and tend to be apathetic politically, although their opposition was certainly a factor in Manasco's defeat in the 1948 primaries.

The dominant organization in the district is the Farm Bureau, which has state-wide political power and which is associated in subtle ways with powerful business groups like the Alabama Power Company, the banks, the Illinois Central Railroad, the Northern Alabama Lumber Company, and other business giants of the state which constitute the so-called "Big Mules" and which frequently help to pay the campaign expenses of *all* contestants. A light vote is more easily controlled than a heavy vote, and in a big year the Seventh District is not likely to bring out more than 10 percent of its population to the polls. In off-year, uncontested elections, those voting drop to 4 percent of the population. Those who do vote, by and large, are those with property, those with status, those who have a specific economic interest in seeing to it that the right people represent them. Manasco was talking from observation when he stated that his America is a republic rather than a democracy.

Manasco would deny fiercely and in one sense accurately that his vote was ever controlled by anyone. He has not made money from his position, and the chances are that he would have resisted crass lobbying, regardless of source. But Manasco's "independent" vote has pleased both the Farm Bureau and the Big Mules in his state, and it is they who, generally speaking, constitute the effective sources of political power in Manasco's district, political fortunes in the primaries to the contrary notwithstanding. It was to a representative of the General Motors Corporation, rather than to the United Mine Workers, that Manasco turned for aid during the House hearings on the Full Employment Bill; it was Manasco who challenged S.380 on the grounds that it might drain farm labor off the farms. It was Manasco who told me, apropos of Luther Patrick's liberal voting record, "If I represented the city of Birmingham, I'd probably vote that way too."

REPRESENTATIVE WILLIAM WHITTINGTON (DEMOCRAT), 3RD CONGRESSIONAL DISTRICT, MISSISSIPPI

Born Little Springs, Miss., May 4, 1878; father, small farmer, and reasonably prosperous merchant (sent 8 children to college); attended public schools in Franklin and Amito counties; graduated with first honors from Mississippi College, 1898; law degree, University of Mississippi, 1899; principal and teacher in Roxie, Miss. school for six months; law practice in Franklin County until 1903; moved to Greenwood, Miss., 1904, where he practiced law and built up holdings in cotton; state Senator, 1916–20, and 1924; elected 69th Congress; reelected to each succeeding Congress, including 80th; prominent Baptist; owns ten thousand acres of cotton and considerable real estate in and around Greenwood; married; three children; Elk, Kiwanian, Scottish Rite, Delta Council.

The third Congressional district of Mississippi is roughly co-extensive with the so-called Mississippi Delta—a flat, bow-shaped area which stretches along the river from historic Vicksburg on the south to the Tennessee border on the north, and inland to a maximum depth of one hundred miles. Seventy-three percent Negro in population, one of the wealthiest cotton areas in the world, the Delta is dominated politically and economically by an aristocratic junta called the Delta Council, which is made up of the leading cotton growers, bankers, lawyers, and businessmen in the area. Representative Will Whittington is a member of the Delta Council.

Whittington started his legal career in Greenwood in the prosperous law office of McClurd and Gardner, which specialized in railroad and power company litigation. Within a few years, Whittington had established such a successful practice that he was able to invest his savings in cotton plantations. Over a period of time he developed, with the assistance of his brother Charles, a tremendous stake in cotton which he has been able to maintain to this day.

Whittington has done a great deal for Delta Cotton. The Delta area, in fact the whole lower Mississippi basin, owes him a lasting debt of gratitude for his expert flood control efforts. Like any good representative from a one-crop district, Whittington has done his best to safeguard the basis of the economic life of his area. Like any good Delta citizen he has tried to keep "cotton up and the river down." But Whittington is more than a spokesman for cotton; he is the Washington representative of a way of life—of a patriarchal and paternalistic class society in which the economic leaders are the philosopher-kings. It would be hard to discover an area in America where a sense of *noblesse oblige* is more pervasive.

Whittington and the other leaders of the Delta Council have no use for the corrupt demagoguery of the Bilbo element in Mississippi. Almost without exception, the leaders of the Council are public-spirited, successful, gracious, and honest men, who are interested in what they consider to be the economic welfare and the social stability of their little world. While believing in segregation and "keeping the Negro in his place," they take an interest in the health and education of the colored population, and although that interest is in part motivated by economic factors, it is not without humanitarian overtones. While holding to extremely conservative social and economic views themselves, the Council leaders take pride in the fact that one of the great fighting liberals in American journalism, Hodding Carter, publishes his newspaper in the heart of the Delta region.

Apart from the narrow interests of cotton, the Delta leaders are identified with big business and big agriculture on a national scale. W. T. Wynn, one of the founders of the Delta Council, has been on the board of directors of Electric Bond and Share in New York. Oscar Johnston, a Council elder-statesman, and a past president of the National Cotton Council, has been on the board of the Illinois Central Railroad. The Council itself was originally an offshoot of the Chamber of Commerce in the area, and works in close cooperation with the Mississippi Farm Bureau. Through a remarkable educational campaign, and through a tight control over the political life of the Delta, the Council has managed to spread the economic philosophy of conservative business interests.

In the last Congressional election, Whittington, unopposed, received 4,000 votes. There are over 435,000 people in the Third District, which means that less than one percent of the population took pains to, or were allowed to, vote. But as W. T. Wynn once remarked, "We don't *elect* our political representatives, we *draft* them." [12] This type of political behavior is "justified" by the fact that half the adult population has had less than five years of schooling, and only 10 percent have completed high school.

Such is the society which has shaped Will Whittington's philosophy. The remarkable thing is that Whittington has been a moderate or what he himself has called "a conservative liberal." Perhaps his strong sense of party loyalty has forced him to seek for ways of accommodating the goals of the liberal Democrats without doing too much violence to his own economic presuppositions; perhaps a sense of public service and responsibility, common to most of the Delta Council leaders, has led Whittington to view national issues

[12] In an interview, Greenville, Mississippi, Aug. 3, 1947.

Other sources for this sketch: an interview with Representative Whittington in Washington, June 1, 1946; Delta Council (Stoneville, Miss.) *Annual Reports*, 1941–1946, and *Delta Council History, 1938–1943; Delta Democrat-Times* (Greenville, Miss.), 1946–1947; Peter F. Drucker, "Exit King Cotton." *Harper's Magazine*, May, 1946; and the *Official Biography* of Whittington (mimeograph; Washington, 1946).

with an uncommon breadth of perspective. Unlike Carter Manasco and Clare Hoffman, Whittington seemed genuinely interested in producing an Employment Act, and if his backgrounds led him to turn for advice to the Chamber of Commerce and the C.E.D., the fact still remains that he was eager to produce some sort of meaningful legislation. Without him, the Employment Act of 1946 might never have been passed.

## LIBERALS

### SENATOR GLEN H. TAYLOR (DEMOCRAT), IDAHO

Born Portland, Ore., April 12, 1904; large family; son of Reverend Pleasant John Taylor, a former Texas Ranger who became an itinerant preacher in the Northwest; raised on family homestead near Kooskia, Idaho, in Idaho County; father became ill when Glen was in eighth grade; Glen had to leave school to earn a living; joined older brother in traveling show business; married in late twenties; in middle thirties, after brief stay in Texas, Taylor returned to Idaho, got job on radio station in Pocatello; ran for Congress in 1938 Democratic primaries; defeated; ran for Senate in 1940; nominated, but defeated in general election; ran for Senate in 1942, after working in war plant in California; won nomination again, but defeated in general election; returned to war plant work in California; returned to Idaho, 1944; ran for, and was elected to the Senate. In 1948, ran for Vice President on Wallace ticket.

Senator Glen Taylor claims he had no social philosophy until the depression of the early thirties. When the depression of 1929 hit Idaho, Taylor and his wife, Dora, were playing in an itinerant dramatic stock company. The depression and the competition of the "talkies" forced the stock company into desperate straits. As Taylor has put it, "People brought chickens and vegetables and traded them for tickets. . . . Some nights we'd take in only two or three dollars, and that's when I started thinking about economics." [13]

Perhaps the turning point in Taylor's life was his happening

[13] Kyle Crichton, "Idaho's Hot Potato," *Collier's*, June 30, 1945, p. 21.
Other sources are: an interview with Senator Taylor in Washington, July 15, 1946; Lawrence H. Chamberlain, "Idaho: State of Sectional Schisms," in Thomas C. Donnelly, *Rocky Mountain Politics* (Albuquerque, 1940), pp. 150–188; Byron Defenbach, *Idaho, the Place and Its People* (Chicago and New York, 1933), p. 559; *The Idaho Encyclopedia* (Federal Writers Project of the W.P.A., Washington, 1938); *Idaho Daily Statesman*, May 31, 1946; *Idaho State Journal*, Aug. 15, 20, 23, 28, 1940; *PM*, Sept. 7, 1945; Pocatello *Tribune*, Nov. 2, 1942; Washington *Post*, Jan. 6, July 12, 1946; Washington *Star*, Dec. 10, 1944.

upon a book by King C. Gillette called *The People's Corporation.* Untutored in economics, Taylor found in Gillette's book what was to him a convincing explanation of the evils of capitalism and a possible way out. Not satisfied with one answer, however, Taylor began to read every book on economics he could understand. Stuart Chase particularly made a heavy impression on him. Oftentimes, Taylor would read until sun-up, searching for an understanding of the social and economic disaster which he saw all about him.

In 1935, the drought made continuance of a newly formed musical "ranch gang" impossible, and Taylor and his wife went to Texas for a year, living on what fish he was able to catch in the Gulf of Mexico. While in Texas, Taylor read a book which contained the phrase "The only purpose of knowledge is action," which phrase he credits with starting him thinking about the possibility of getting into politics. He soon returned to Idaho, settled in Pocatello, and decided to run for Congress in 1938.

To earn a living, prior to and during his campaign, Taylor started up his "ranch gang" once again and managed to win a spot on Station KSEI, where he featured the singing voice of his four-year-old son Arod (Dora spelled backwards). The show was an instantaneous hit, and was a major factor in Taylor's political build-up.

His campaign for Congress in the 1938 primaries was conducted without the support of the Democratic Party organization. To the surprise of almost everyone, he ran fourth in a field of nine. In his campaigns for the Senate in 1940 and 1942, Taylor used his showmanship to the hilt. In 1940, he toured the state with his family, sang songs, attracted crowds, and gave them political talks. In 1942, he rode a white horse the entire length of the state. Finally, in 1944, he campaigned in a business suit, received the backing of the Democratic State Committee, and won the election. All his campaign speeches were variations on the same theme: "I can represent the common man because I am one."

Taylor has been accused of demagoguery, clowning, and cheapness. He has been and still is fought by all the major business pressure groups in his state. His great political asset has been his ability to convince the unorganized poor of his state that he is their friend.

Out of a bitter personal experience and a sensitive and undisciplined social conscience has come a strange product of American politics. Part showman, part martyr, Taylor has a flare for public life, a passionate interest in the "forgotten man," a misanthropic contempt for the prosperous, and more recently, a firm belief in the conspiratorial designs of what he believes is a business-military coalition in America set on war.

Taylor's attitude towards S.380 has already been suggested in his comment about the Senate changes in the bill (see pp. 122–123). He was representative of a handful of legislators in both Houses who supported the Full Employment Bill out of deep personal conviction, and who looked with dismay on every change which appeared to weaken the symbolism of the pending legislation.

### Senator Alben W. Barkley (Democrat), Kentucky

Born in a log cabin in Graves County, Ky., November 24, 1877; son of a tenant-farmer; educated in the county schools and in Marvin College, Clinton, Ky., graduating there in 1897, receiving A.B. degree, afterward attending Emory College at Oxford, Ga., and the University of Virginia Law School at Charlottesville, Va.; admitted to the bar at Paducah, Ky., in 1901; was married June 23, 1903, and had three children; elected prosecuting attorney for McCracken County in 1905 for a term of four years; at expiration of term was elected judge of the McCracken County Court and served until elected to Congress; was elected to 63d and all succeeding Congresses; was chairman State Democratic Conventions at Louisville, 1919, and Lexington, 1924; was delegate-at-large to Democratic National Conventions at San Francisco in 1920, at New York in 1924, at Houston in 1928, at Chicago in 1932, at Philadelphia in 1936, at Chicago in 1940 and 1944, and Philadelphia, 1948; served as permanent chairman at Democratic National Convention of 1940; elected to U.S. Senate from Kentucky for term beginning March 4, 1927; reelected for term beginning March 4, 1933; reelected for term beginning January 3, 1939; and reelected for term beginning January 3, 1945; was elected Majority Leader of the Senate in 1937 which position he held until January, 1947, when he became Minority Leader; 1948 Vice Presidential nominee on Democratic ticket; elected Vice President, 1948.

Few men in American public life have understood the anatomy of Congressional government more fully than Alben Barkley. His uninterrupted tenure on Capitol Hill since 1912, his personal energy, and his broad personal sympathies have combined to make him one of the most distinguished and popular politician-statesmen of the twentieth century. Coming from a border state, Barkley has been the great mediator between the Northern and Southern wings of the Democratic Party, a fact which led to his Vice Presidential nomination in the divided Democratic convention of 1948.

Barkley was born and raised in the Jackson Purchase area of Western Kentucky. "The last frontier of the state, it formed a core of Jacksonian democracy, the most intensely Southern and Democratic of all sections of the state." [14] Barkley's early years were spent in poverty and hard farm labor. He worked his way through college and law school and has never been affluent. Even today his Paducah property consists of a modest farm on the outskirts of the city.

Barkley has always been a "New Dealer." His family was passionately devoted to William Jennings Bryan, and Alben's first election to Congress came in 1912, the year of the triumph of Woodrow Wilson. Barkley gives Wilson major credit for shaping his social philosophy, but it is probably true that the agrarian liberalism of his early environment made him unusually receptive to the ideas implicit in Wilson's "New Freedom."

Barkley has spent almost all his adult life in Congress, and although he has fought for his liberal beliefs both before, during, and after the Roosevelt era, his chief genius has not been in the field of legislative draftsmanship. The Kentucky Senator has cultivated an almost uncanny sense of the possible in the legislative process, and as Majority Leader from 1937 to 1947 he won the respect of all factions in both parties by his fairness, humor, and patience. Party loyalty has been one of his dominating passions. His temporary break with Roosevelt over the tax vote in 1944 was newsworthy for this very reason.

Barkley has taken pains not to antagonize the main economic interests of his state. He voted for a tariff on coal in 1931, he has fought legislation opposed by the racing people, he has attempted to appease strong tobacco interests like the Burley Tobacco Cooperative, he has dispensed his share of patronage, he has paid close attention to the needs of the railroad workers and United Mine Workers. But on broad national issues his first loyalty has been to his party and to his own liberal philosophy.

Barkley's social philosophy was molded by his early environment

14 J. B. Shannon, "Alben W. Barkley," in J. T. Salter, ed., *Public Men* (Chapel Hill, N.C., 1946), p. 242.

Other sources are: an interview with Senator Barkley in Paducah, Aug. 5, 1947; *Christian Science Monitor*, July 21, 22, 1937; Drew Pearson, "Washington Merry-Go-Round," Washington *Post*, June 7, 1946; Amy Porter, "Weep No More Kentucky," *Collier's*, March 30, 1946; Paul A. Porter, "Washington Merry-Go-Round," Boston *Traveler*, Aug. 29, 1946; "Who's Who in the Government," *U.S. News*, Aug. 19, 1935; Washington *Post*, July 22, 1937; Washington *Star*, July 16, 21, Aug. 8, Oct. 20, 1937.

and by his admiration for Woodrow Wilson. He has grown through long experience into an efficient political broker. But he is more than a liberal and a politician. Perhaps the uniqueness of Barkley stems from something else—a quality of personality which political scientists can describe but cannot explain. Woodrow Wilson once wrote a sketch of Henry Clay which included the words:

In Henry Clay we have an American of a most authentic pattern. There was no man of his generation who represented more of America than he did. The singular, almost irresistible attraction he had for men of every class and every temperament came, not from the arts of the politician, but from the instant sympathy established between him and every fellow countryman of his.[15]

As Paul Porter has said, "Some future historian cannot but apply Wilson's description of Clay to Senator Barkley. The characterization is too strikingly similar to go unnoticed." [16]

SENATOR ABE MURDOCK (DEMOCRAT) OF UTAH

Born Austin, Nev., July 18, 1893; grandfather John Murdock, one of early Mormon pioneers, first Bishop of Beaver Stake, Utah; father, Orrice Abram Murdock, graduate of Michigan Law School, a local lawyer and county politician in Beaver, Utah, where Abe grew up; attended University of Utah law course but did not finish; maternal uncles interested in mining; worked intermittently as miner from age 16 to 29, spending much of his free time prospecting; passed bar in 1922; elected county attorney in same year, which office he held for three terms; city attorney for Beaver for several terms and attorney for Board of Education several years; elected to Congress in 1932; reelected 1934, 1936, 1938; elected to Senate, 1940; defeated for reelection in 1946; appointed by President Truman to the N.L.R.B. in 1947.

Senator Abe Murdock comes by his liberalism honestly. He remembers with pride that his father fought local interests for years in an attempt to have a telephone system installed in Beaver, Utah. Abe, himself, worked in the mines as a young man and came to appreciate the worker's point of view. But probably more important in determining his social philosophy than these early experiences, were the circumstances by which Murdock was catapulted from a small-town law office into the halls of Congress.

A deadlock in the Democratic State Convention of 1932 got Murdock the nomination for the first Congressional district. Sur-

15 "Washington Merry-Go-Round." Boston *Traveler*, Aug. 29, 1946.    16 *Ibid.*

prised by this sudden piece of luck, but thoroughly pessimistic about the chances of beating the incumbent Republican opponent who had held office for twelve years, Murdock campaigned on the issue of the depression. He now recalls that he was unable to pay the taxes on his farm in 1931, and when challenged about this in a political meeting during the 1932 campaign, he asked all those who had been unable to pay their taxes to stand. The great majority of the audience responded, and Murdock indicated that this was one reason he was running for Congress.

Murdock rode into Congress on Roosevelt's coattails, a fact which he never forgot. He tried to repay his political chief by voting "regular," and this seems to be the main explanation for his liberal voting record. Referring to Murdock and J. W. Robinson back in 1940, one careful student of Utah politics observed,

Abe Murdock and J. W. Robinson, Utah's representatives in the House, are country lawyers and more or less conservative politicians, who follow the winds of party fortunes. They are pro-labor and New Deal, although the A.F.L. may not support Murdock in 1940. These men trail along with party and economic leaders and have little influence in shaping party and governmental policies.[17]

Murdock's record in Congress during the thirties and early forties lends weight to this appraisal. He voted with the President, but he became the servant of every major pressure group in his state. Even after he was elected Senator in 1940, he concentrated his efforts on the needs of constituent economic interests almost without discrimination: silver, gold, salt cake, livestock, lead, zinc, copper, beet sugar—to name but a few.

Murdock's philosophy of politics was summed up in a statement which he made in announcing his candidacy for reelection as a Senator in 1946:

I have always believed that the primary function of a Senator from Utah is to work for the development of our resources in the best interests of

17 F. H. Jones, "Utah: Sagebrush Democracy," in T. C. Donnelly (ed.), *Rocky Mountain Politics* (Albuquerque, 1940), pp. 32–33.

Other sources for this sketch are: an interview with Senator Murdock in Washington, July 18, 1946; Albert E. Bowen, *The Church Welfare Plan* (Salt Lake City, Deseret Sunday School Union, 1946); Milton I. Hunter, *Utah in Her Western Setting* (Salt Lake City, 1944); Charles P. Schleicher and G. Homer Durham, *Utah, the State and Its Government* (New York, 1943); G. Homer Durham, "A Political Interpretation of Mormon History," *Pacific Historical Review*, XIII, No. 2 (June, 1944); Salt Lake *Tribune-Telegram* library, file on "Murdock"; Washington *Star*, March 4, 1933.

all of the people. A Senator from Utah, if he functions properly, must be a worker. At all times he must be at the disposal of his state and his people to accomplish the work that will increase their prosperity and security. He must thoroughly know Utah and its resources. He must have vision to see how these resources can best be developed and utilized in the public interest.[18]

Murdock typified a group of liberal legislators in the 79th Congress who made no real contribution to the policy development of S.380, but who were willing in a passive way to accept whatever the sponsors of the original bill were able to get through. With varying degrees of personal conviction, their keen sense of past political favors tended to dominate their voting behavior. A large number of Congressmen from overwhelmingly urban districts fell into this class. They were readily distinguishable from men like Senators Murray and Taylor, and Representatives George Outland, Andrew Biemiller, Jerry Voorhis, and Charles LaFollette, whose basic motivations seemed to stem almost solely from a passionate social philosophy.

### SENATOR CHARLES TOBEY (REPUBLICAN), NEW HAMPSHIRE

Born Roxbury, Mass., July 22, 1880; father, William A. Tobey, an accountant with Parker Wilder & Co., Boston, for 53 years; graduated from Roxbury Latin High School (in those years, one of best in Boston area); proceeded to work for a Boston bank; 1903, Tobey established home in Temple, N.H., where he and his wife engaged in raising chickens; soon settled down in business with the F. M. Hoyt Shoe Company (New Hampshire) of which he later became president; made start in politics as head of the Temple Board of Selectmen; elected to New Hampshire House of Representatives, 1915–16, and again in 1919–20; in second term served as Speaker; after one more term as a state Representative in 1923–24, elected to state Senate; senators elected him their president and N.H. Lt. Governor; Governor of N.H., 1929–30; elected U.S. Congress in 1932 from N.H.'s 2d district; reelected 1934 and 1936; elected U.S. Senator in 1938; reelected by close margin in 1944; U.S. delegate to the Bretton Woods Monetary Conference, July, 1944.

Senator Charles W. Tobey is a complicated character. His social philosophy is the result of the impact of a changing economic and political world upon a stern and rockbound New England conscience. Brought up in the militant independence and isolation of agricultural and small-town New England, Tobey's religious ethics

[18] Salt Lake *Tribune*, May 19, 1946.

and almost crabbed integrity have forced him through a series of intellectual realignments under the pressure of economic transformations within his state, and political upheavals the world over.

Tobey considers his "progressivism" as going back to his Bull Moose days in 1912, but as recently as 1940, he introduced a resolution to strike out the income questions in the census questionnaire on the grounds that such questions were an invasion of privacy. He asked people to start "anti-snooping" clubs, and was openly rebuked by President Roosevelt for advising Americans to violate the law. As one commentator put it, "This fast-talking, old fashioned, nightshirt wearing, God-fearing New Hampshire gent . . . has done more to advertise this year's census than if Harry Hopkins had hired Billy Rose to do it." [19]

This side of Tobey's character cannot be understood without an appreciation of the physical isolation of his farm in Temple, New Hampshire—a farm which he once called "the original Garden of Eden without the original sin." Tobey's farm is some distance from the center of Temple, and the town of Temple itself is so small that a motorist must drive with extreme caution in order not to miss it entirely. Long communion with nature, coupled with the ingrown habits which come with isolated and reasonably self-sufficient living, must inevitably make a mark on a man's outlook. Tobey's business and early political associations in Concord, Manchester, and Nashua simply reinforced this pattern of thinking. The men he dealt with were, by and large, products of the same type of isolation and ingrown habits. Northern New England until quite recently has been the stronghold of an almost homogeneous culture. Moral rectitude, religious conformity, Republicanism, regional independence, and economic conservatism have been its watchwords. Tobey grew up in, and is partly a product of, this environment.

But to leave Tobey at that would be to ignore half the story. The

[19] Quoted in Maxine Block, ed., *Current Biography* (New York, 1941), p. 863.

Other sources are: an interview with Senator Tobey in Washington, May 16, 1946; H. H. Metcalf, ed., *One Thousand New Hampshire Notables* (Concord, 1919), p. 440; New Hampshire Planning and Development Commission, *Made in New Hampshire, a Directory of Manufactured Products* (Concord, 1947); Hobart Pillsbury, *New Hampshire: a History* (New York, 1927), p. 176; Concord *Daily Monitor* and *New Hampshire Patriot*, May–November, 1944; Frank Gervasi, "Yankee Gad-Fly," *Collier's*, Aug. 2, 1947; Drew Pearson, "Washington Merry-Go-Round," Washington *Post*, May 6, 1946; St. Louis *Post-Dispatch*, March 24, 1946; *Time*, June 23, 1941, p. 54.

New Hampshire Senator had two experiences comparatively late
in his career which shook him deeply. The first was Pearl Harbor.
Although Tobey had backed the League of Nations following
World War I, he was a pre-World War II isolationist of the most
rabid variety. The broad and complex world of hatreds and strife
on the other side of the earth had seemed a long way from Temple,
New Hampshire. Like many other sincere isolationists, Tobey
hated war, felt that the European struggle was none of our affair,
that we had no business "pulling England's chestnuts out of the
fire," that Roosevelt was a warmonger, and that America had an
obligation to stay out of the conflict and become an oasis of freedom
and sanity. The Japanese attack in 1941 destroyed the foundations
of Tobey's thinking. During the next three years, he struggled
towards a new orientation. In 1944 he was asked to become a United
States delegate to the Bretton Woods Monetary Conference, and
this experience for Tobey resulted in a climactic break with the
past. He became one of the champions of international cooperation in the Senate, and has remained one to this day. This has meant
frequent fights with the Taft branch of the Republican Party, a
fact which has bothered Tobey not a bit. His Republicanism has
never been allowed to interfere with his conscience, and since 1944
with increasing frequency Tobey has found himself in opposition
to the titular leaders of his party in the Senate.

Tobey's second "Road to Damascus" came in the 1944 elections
when he was nearly defeated for reelection by the labor vote in
his state. There has been a marked change in his attitude towards
domestic issues since that election.

Tobey represents an extremely limited classification of legislators: the independent, conscience-bound mavericks, who do constant battle with their limited pasts, who struggle to adapt themselves to a new age, and who see themselves, in a slightly messianic
way, as the guardians of moral rectitude in a naughty world of
compromise and chicanery.

Tobey was, as we have seen, one of the Republican sponsors of
the Full Employment Bill; he made a few significant additions to
the content of the bill in the Conference Committee. He backed the
bill not because of any party pressure, or because of any constituent
pressure narrowly conceived, but because he thought the bill was
right. That he failed to see in the bill the dangers which his more

conservative colleagues saw, was a reflection both of his independence and of his political education.

REPRESENTATIVE JOHN J. COCHRAN (DEMOCRAT), 13TH CONGRESSIONAL DISTRICT, MISSOURI

Born Webster Grove, Mo., August 11, 1880; father, an accountant in St. Louis; left school after 8th grade and worked as copy boy and later as sports reporter for St. Louis *Post-Dispatch* and other newspapers; studied law, and passed bar but never practiced; 1912, became secretary to Congressman William Igoe of St. Louis; spent 14 years on Capitol Hill as secretary and clerk in both House and Senate; elected to Congress 1926, reelected every year until 1946 when he resigned because of ill health; ran for Senate in 1944, but defeated by Harry S. Truman; died, July, 1946.

Back in 1878, J. A. Dacus and J. W. Buel, in a book called *A Tour of St. Louis,* had this to say about the children who lived in the notorious Kerry Patch region of the city: "On their pathway never a stray sunbeam falls. Parents are very poor, and often dissipated and vicious. Their homes are grimy, filthy abodes, which must necessarily extinguish lofty aspirations. Commencing bad, the children of such homes continue bad all through their careers." [20]

Sixty-six years later, the St. Louis *Post-Dispatch* carried an editorial about one of these Kerry Patch children: "It is no risk of extravagant statement, we think, to say that John J. Cochran, who withdrew yesterday from the primary, is just about the finest public servant Missouri has ever sent to Washington." [21]

Jack Cochran was a remarkable man. Brought up in a shantytown region of central St. Louis, forced because of his father's ill health to go to work before he could so much as attend high school, Cochran came up the hard way. Politics intrigued him, even as a

[20] (St. Louis, 1878), p. 408.
Other sources for this sketch are: William Hyde and Howard L. Conrad, *Encyclopedia of the History of St. Louis,* II (1899), 1172; J. Thomas Scharf, *History of St. Louis City and County,* II (Philadelphia, 1883), 1017; F. C. Shoemaker, *Missouri and Missourians,* II (Chicago, 1946), 400–406; Board of Election Commissioners, *Map of St. Louis 1946: Congressional Districts;* John J. Cochran, "Statement on Employment Act of 1946," press release, Washington, Feb. 6, 1946; St. Louis *Globe-Democrat,* July 26, Aug. 3, 1934; St. Louis *Post-Dispatch,* May 24, 1935, Oct. 21, 1937, March 9, June 2, Oct. 23, 27, 1942, Sept. 14, 1943, April 7, 15, 1944, July 17, 31, 1946; St. Louis Social Planning Council, *Selected Indicators of Social Conditions in St. Louis City and County* (1946); St. Louis *Star-Times,* July 18, 1934, April 3, 1944; Washington *Star,* Nov. 16, 1941.
[21] July 17, 1946.

youth. When he was sixteen he carried a banner in a torchlight parade for William Jennings Bryan, and by the time he was in his middle twenties he worked as a clerk in the office of the Board of Election Commissioners and for three years as a Street Department employee. His great political idol at that time was William Igoe, a young and successful lawyer, who was just beginning to make his name in city politics. In 1912, Igoe was elected to Congress and took Cochran along to Washington as his secretary.

From Igoe, Cochran learned to pay attention to constituent mail. When Cochran became a Congressman in 1926, he saw to it that every letter from his district received a personal reply. If letters came in opposition to a position taken by Cochran, the Congressman wrote careful notes of explanation. Thus his political success was partly a reflection of a personal interest in the problems of his constituents. As he himself once said, "I learned soon after coming to Washington that it was just as important to get a certain document for somebody back home as for some European diplomat—hell, *more* important, because that little guy back home votes." [22] So devoted was Cochran to the interests of St. Louis that the *Globe-Democrat* reported back in 1934, "He has been practically the Washington representative of the St. Louis Chamber of Commerce since his early days as a congressional secretary." [23]

But Cochran was more than an astute "errand boy." The letters he received from his 13th district, the North end of St. Louis, told him the problems of the urban poor and middle class—of the Negroes, the Jews, the Italians, the Irish—the folks with whom he had grown up and whose troubles he especially could appreciate. Once commenting on pressure groups, Cochran said, "When you stop to look at it, it's very clear. The little people are stockholders in the Government, just like the big shots. Who are you going to listen to, the employer of 500 people or the 500 people?" [24]

Cochran, until the early years of World War II, had one of the most remarkable attendance records on the floor of the House of any legislator. During his first eight years as a Congressman, he didn't miss a single roll call. His record failed only when a serious circulatory illness in 1942 necessitated the amputation of both legs

[22] St. Louis *Post-Dispatch*, Aug. 22, 1943.
[23] St. Louis *Globe-Democrat*, Aug. 5, 1934.
[24] St. Louis *Post-Dispatch*, Aug. 22, 1943.

above the knees. But even after his operations, while experiencing acute physical suffering and confined to a wheel chair, he turned out more work than most of his colleagues. Andrew Biemiller commented apropos of the Full Employment Bill struggle, "It used to make us younger fellows feel like two cents. We'd get fed up or exhausted in committee discussions or hearings, but Jack Cochran kept fighting the battle for all of us until the last word was spoken." [25]

Cochran voted the straight New Deal line, but it was from conviction as well as party loyalty. When the Hannegan–Dickman Democratic machine in St. Louis pulled a shady political trick and tried to "steal" the governorship in 1940, Cochran was almost the sole voice in the party to make a public protest. His liberal convictions grew out of his background and his concern for the welfare of his constituents. He never forgot his own early struggles. But he lived according to principle rather than political expediency. As he said towards the end of his life about the people of his city, "They've treated me mighty swell. I've tried to do everything I could for them. Sometimes I've had to say 'no,' but when I did I explained why. And in such cases they've taken it all right." [26] When his health finally broke, soon after the passage of the Employment Act of 1946 which he did so much to promote, he announced his retirement in characteristic language: "I am not willing to render part-time service to my country as a member of Congress in this critical period, nor am I willing to let my present illness interfere with full and complete service to my district." [27]

John J. Cochran represented the best in urban politics. He will not soon be forgotten by the people of St. Louis.

REPRESENTATIVE-AT-LARGE GEORGE BENDER (REPUBLICAN), OHIO

Born Cleveland, Ohio, September 29, 1896; father, a butcher; educated in Cleveland public schools and West Commerce High School; at 24, youngest state senator ever elected; reelected, five consecutive terms; elected 76th Congress; reelected to each succeeding Congress including 80th; defeated 1948; president, G. H. Bender Insurance Co.; chairman, Cuyahoga County Republican General Committee; president, Cuyahoga County League of Republican Clubs; president, Ohio Federation

25 In an interview, Washington, D.C., July 23, 1947.
26 St. Louis *Post-Dispatch*, Aug. 22, 1943.
27 St. Louis *Globe-Democrat*, July 17, 1946.

of Republican Clubs; editor and publisher, *The Ohio Republican* and *The National Republican;* formerly Religious Editor of the Cleveland *Plain Dealer,* reporter on Cleveland *Press* and Cleveland *News,* and advertising manager of Cleveland department stores; author: *The Challenge of 1940;* married; two children.

George Bender's boyhood hero was Theodore Roosevelt. In 1912, at the age of sixteen, Bender stumped the old 18th Ward of Cleveland's east side to drum up votes for the Bull Moose leader, "and jumped into political fame a few days later when the vote showed his to be the only ward the great man carried in Cleveland." [28] This victory made a deep impression on Bender, and he vowed then and there to make a career out of politics.

Bender's youth was spent in hard work. At the age of twelve he was at work as an assistant in his father's meat market; he earned pin money by selling newspapers on the corner of East 55th Street and Woodland. When he finished high school, he tried his hand at newspaper work and advertising, but his real love was politics.

At the age of twenty-four, he ran for and was elected to the state senate, becoming the youngest man ever to have held such a position. Almost at once he set out to "liberalize" the Republican party in his state. In the state senate he was the leader of the fight for a child labor amendment, and for a minimum wage bill for women. Almost single-handedly, he fought the Anti-Saloon League to a standstill over the issue of the liquor-raiding activities of justices of the peace. In December, 1933, when Bender was elected President of the League of Republican Clubs in Ohio, he called for the nomination of a state ticket composed of "progressive, earnest, anti-Wall Street Republicans." [29] During most of his political career he had the backing of the Railroad Brotherhoods, the Ohio State Federation of Labor, the Ohio State Building Trades Council, and the United Mine Workers. In 1940, he was a strong Willkie supporter, and in 1944, when he ran ahead of Taft, he tried to convince his colleagues that the size of his plurality indicated the direction in

[28] Cleveland *Press,* Oct. 8, 1930.

Other sources for this sketch are: an interview with Representative Bender in Washington, July 12, 1946; his *Challenge of 1940* (New York, 1940) and election pamphlet, 1944; Cleveland *News,* Oct. 27, 1938, Oct. 11, 1941; Cleveland *Plain-Dealer,* May 15, June 20, 1931, April 11, 1944; Cleveland *Press,* June 7, 1943, June 22, 1944; Washington *Post,* Jan. 19, 1939.

[29] Cleveland *Plain Dealer,* Dec. 29, 1933.

which Republicans would have to move if they wanted political success.

Bender's liberalism is not a simple thing, however. All his life, his liberal social philosophy has been inextricably entwined with penny-ante ward politics. Bender, as a Congressman-at-Large, stuck to the Republican Party and thereby pulled in the heavy downstate Republican vote. He also voted as a liberal on many domestic issues and paid attention to patronage and organization in Ohio's industrial northeast, where the labor vote is important.

Bender's power in Cleveland Republican circles was not an easy thing to maintain. His hold over Cuyahoga County was made possible in part by a shift in the nature of Republican leadership. Fifty years ago, Republican precinct chairmen throughout the county were businessmen, lawyers, and important public office holders. Today, the locus of power has shifted, except in down-town Cleveland, to small shopkeepers and patronage politicians—groups which Bender understands and which formed the basis of his political power. Bender used his tremendous energy and advertising abilities to keep the organization under his control, but he has long been at odds with the down-town Republican leaders who tried for more than ten years to dislodge him.

Bender has consistently attacked what he believed to be the incompetence and dishonesty of the New Deal Democrats, and he has spread his ideas through his own Republican newspapers, *The Ohio Republican* and *The National Republican*. His book, *The Challenge of 1940,* was an anti-New Deal, pro-Willkie statement which added up to a declaration that true liberalism and good government could be achieved only through the vehicle of the Republican Party.

Bender was one of the original sponsors of the Full Employment Bill in the House. He attacked the Employment Act of 1946 as an almost meaningless compromise, and charged the responsibility to the Southern Democrats and to Truman's inability to lead his own party. His reaction to the Employment Act was, perhaps, indicative of the liberalism and political opportunism which have characterized his career.

In a study of policy-making it is not enough that we understand influences external to the policy-maker. Constitutions and statutes, public opinion and pressures, facts and arguments, parties and patronage—these are factors which are important only as they reach and are interpreted and accepted by men's minds and prejudices. Like the action of light on variegated surfaces, external factors are absorbed, refracted, or reflected, according to the peculiar qualities of the minds they reach. The Full Employment Bill was in no small measure shaped by forces and culture symbols in Greenwood, Mississippi; Allegan, Michigan; Pocatello, Idaho; Wilmington, Delaware; and Temple, New Hampshire. If Congressional policy-making is complex it is in part because America is a vast and complex continent and because our political and our constitutional systems give more than permissive support to semi-anarchic behavior on the part of our chosen legislative representatives.

# CHAPTER ELEVEN

# Conference and Compromise

> . . . the Conference Committee strikes a deficient compromise balance according to time-honored custom.—Wilson, *Congressional Government,* p. 164.

THE INSTITUTION of the conference committee is one of long standing. By the middle of the nineteenth century, according to Ada McCown,

the custom of presenting identical reports from the committees of conference in both houses, of granting high privilege to these conference reports, of voting upon the conference report as a whole and permitting no amendment of it, of keeping secret the discussions carried on in the meetings of the conference committee, had become established in American parliamentary practice.[1]

After the House of Representatives had passed its version of H.R.2202 on December 14, 1945, the next step in the policy-making process was the appointment, in both Houses, of conference managers to whom was given the task of attempting to work out some compromise between the Senate-passed bill and the House substitute. Technically, the task of naming managers is the responsibility of the presiding officer in each house. Actually, the respective standing committee chairmen usually make recommendations which are automatically followed.[2] As we have noted, the Senate managers were Barkley, Murdock, Taylor, and Radcliffe, Democrats; and

---

[1] Ada C. McCown, *The Congressional Conference Committee* (1927), pp. 254–255, quoted in George Galloway, *Congress at the Crossroads* (New York, 1946), p. 98.
[2] See J. P. Chamberlain, *Legislative Processes* (New York, 1936), pp. 244–245.

Tobey, Taft, and Buck, Republicans. The House managers were Manasco, Cochran, and Whittington, Democrats; and Bender and Hoffman, Republicans. Senator Wagner was initially appointed to chair the conference, but he was taken sick early in January, and Senator Barkley was prevailed upon to take the New York Senator's place.

PRE-CONFERENCE MANEUVERS

The Joint Conference Committee meetings began on January 22, 1946, just a year after the introduction of the Senate bill. Between December 14, 1945, and the Conference sessions, however, the issue of the fate of S.380 was by no means dormant. Immediately after the House vote, the liberal House sponsors went to Robert Hannegan with a passionate plea for the Democratic Party chairman to put pressure on President Truman. The feeling of the sponsors was that Truman had let them down in the House struggle, that the party had lost popular prestige among its liberal supporters as a result, and that the only way the President could recoup his lost prestige would be for him to insist that the Conference Committee report out a strong and progressive full employment bill.

Simultaneously, the Continuations Group of the Lib-Lab lobby submitted to Truman a statement signed by all its members, memorializing the President to veto any Conference bill which did not measure up to liberal standards.[3]

As a result of these pressures, Truman on December 20, 1945, sent identical letters to Wagner and Manasco stating, ". . . no bill which provides substantially less than the Senate version can efficiently accomplish the purposes intended." [4] On January 3, 1946, Truman followed this up with a radio speech in which he made a "blunt request for real full employment legislation . . . urging voters to let their representatives know their sentiments." [5] Finally in his Message to Congress of January 21, 1946, Truman restated his desire that "a satisfactory Full Employment Bill such as the Senate bill now in conference between the Senate and the House" be passed.[6] The Message to Congress, which had been prepared in

[3] Union for Democratic Action, "News Flash on Full Employment," No. 7 (Washington, Jan. 8, 1946).

[4] *Congressional Record*, 79th Cong., 2d Sess., Feb. 6, 1946, p. 1000.

[5] U.D.A., "News Flash."

[6] *Message of the President on the State of the Union and Transmitting the Budget for 1947* (Washington, 1946), p. xxii.

part by the Budget Bureau, had a number of references to the need for strong full employment legislation,[7] and altogether represented the strongest Presidential pressure for a liberal bill which came from the White House during the entire course of the struggle over S.380.

These general pressures, however, were not supported by any concrete proposals to the conferees from the Executive branch— and thereby hangs a tale. It was the intention of Secretary of the Treasury Fred Vinson to work out a compromise version of the Full Employment Bill which might, with the weight of the President behind it, be accepted in part or as a whole by the Congressional conferees. Vinson and his assistants produced such a draft which provided, among other things, for a Cabinet committee under the directorship of the Secretary of the Treasury to replace the House-proposed Council of Economic Advisers. Vinson submitted his draft to Truman, who, in turn, referred it to John Snyder for comment. Snyder, for reasons best known to himself, pigeonholed the Vinson draft, with the result that the Conference Committee had to proceed without the benefit of an administration-endorsed substitute. It is impossible to say whether or not an administration draft would have had much influence on the conferees, but the friction between Snyder and Vinson was certainly no help to the liberal cause. For a solid month, unified administration pressures were precluded by an internecine feud between two of the President's most powerful subordinates.

In the meantime, the key Congressional sponsors of the original Full Employment Bill were not idle. They recognized the fight ahead in the conference, and they attempted to develop a flexible strategy. Roughly speaking, they were bent on preserving as much of the language and substance of the Senate bill as possible, but in line with their decision about the Hatch amendment back in September, they were also concerned with establishing a series of positions to which they might retreat without losing the major battle. What these positions were will become apparent when we proceed to the story of the Conference Committee in action.

### THE CONFERENCE COMMITTEE IN ACTION

Conference action began on January 22 and ended on February 2. The sessions were held in Senator Barkley's office in the Capitol,

[7] *Ibid.*, see pp. vi, x, xxii, xxiv, xxvii, xxxvii, and lvi.

and were fairly well attended. Barkley, Taft, Murdock, Tobey, Cochran, Whittington, and Manasco were the most faithful members, although Buck and Hoffman appeared often enough to let their colleagues know that, in the words of an early Marx brothers song, "whatever it is, we're against it."

The struggle in the conference was between Barkley and Cochran on the one hand, and Congressman Will Whittington, author of the House bill, on the other. Bertram Gross, as Wagner's special representative, was present at every meeting, as were Middleton Beaman of the House Office of Legislative Counsel and Charles Boots of the Senate Office of Legislative Counsel. A few minutes before each conference session, Gross buttonholed Barkley or Cochran or both, discussed with them the strategy of the day, gave them draft proposals—some purely for bargaining purposes—and in the case of Barkley, filled in the gaps in the busy Majority Leader's knowledge about the history and meaning of the various sections of the bill.

Beaman and Boots tried to keep track of the various agreements and disagreements in order that they might be of maximum assistance in preparing, with the aid of the respective managers, working drafts for each new conference session.

*Stalemate.*—During the first two conference sessions, the possibility of any agreement between the House managers and the Senate managers seemed remote. Whittington outlined in detail the House objections to the Senate version of S.380, and made it quite clear that the House managers would not accept any compromise bill which contained the words "full employment" or "the right to work," or which suggested any government guarantee of employment, or which placed the ultimate emphasis upon federal spending. Barkley, for the Senate managers, on the other hand, issued a blast against the House substitute and reminded the conferees of the President's warning that only something close to the Senate version would be acceptable to him. Basing his remarks on an analysis of the House substitute prepared by Gross, Barkley outlined both the omissions and the "weaknesses" of each section of the House bill. Granted the adamant attitude of both sides, it was obvious that someone would have to retreat if the conference was to proceed.

*The Struggle over the Declaration of Policy.*—The deadlock was broken on the third and fourth days of the conference when Gross worked out for Barkley a series of alternative policy declarations, none of which contained the term "full employment," but all of which contained the phrase "conditions under which there will be afforded useful and remunerative employment opportunities, including self-employment, for all Americans who are willing to work and are seeking work." The nature of the first concession on the part of the Senate sponsors is important, for it illustrates the technique used by Gross all the way through the conference debate. If the House managers objected to a particular phrase, Gross went to a thesaurus and juggled words around until he hit on a verbal equivalent. The fact that both sides were ultimately satisfied with most of the compromises made during the conference struggle cannot be understood without an appreciation of this technique. The House managers believed that real Senate concessions were being made with every change in language; the Senate sponsors were satisfied that a rose by any other name smells as sweet.

Perhaps the crowning example of this battle of the thesauruses was the fate of the "spending" provisions. S. 380 as passed by the Senate had included the following words in the declaration of policy:

Sec. 2 (d) . . . the Federal Government shall . . . develop and pursue a consistent and carefully planned economic program. . . . Such program shall among other things . . .

(4) to the extent that continuing full employment cannot otherwise be attained, provide, consistent with the needs and obligations of the Federal Government and other essential considerations of national policy, such volume of Federal investment and expenditure as may be needed . . . to achieve the objective of continuing full employment.[8]

This provision had been attacked by almost every conservative spokesman, and it was one of the sections of the bill which the House managers in the conference insisted would have to come out. By the time the Conference Committee met, Gross and the leading Congressional sponsors of the bill had already come to the conclusion that special reliance on spending was both disadvantageous politically and naive programmatically. Although for bargaining purposes, they opposed Whittington's insistence that the spending provisions would have to come out, it is interesting to note that on January 18, three days *before* the conference, Gross had drafted a

8 S.380, 79th Cong., 1st Sess., Oct. 1, 1945.

substitute policy statement which made no reference to government spending. What finally emerged in place of the spending clauses was a broad statement, part of which Gross had lifted from President Roosevelt's declaration of war against Germany in 1941:

> Sec. 2. The Congress hereby declares that it is the continuing policy and responsibility of the Federal Government to use all practicable means . . . *to coordinate and utilize all its plans, functions, and resources* for the purpose of maintaining conditions under which . . . [Emphasis supplied.] [9]

Since part of the "resources" of the federal government are its instrumentalities for spending and investment, and since the phrase finally accepted read "all . . . resources," the Senate sponsors felt, not without reason, that the conference phraseology was stronger than that in the original bill or in the Senate version. The House managers felt equally certain that dropping any specific mention of federal spending was a victory for their side. Conceivably they were both right.

The debate on the opening declaration of policy consumed the better part of five conference sessions. Every attempt by Whittington to dilute the policy declaration beyond a point acceptable to the Senate managers was countered by an attempt on the part of the latter to reintroduce the phrase "full employment." "Full employment" had been a point of contention from the very beginning of the bill's long history. Almost impossible of unambiguous definition, the phrase had been challenged by Taft and Radcliffe in the Senate, and had been completely deleted from the House substitute. In conference, Whittington made it clear that under no circumstances would the phrase be admitted, and although the Senate managers had made an initial concession by deleting the phrase, they attempted for bargaining purposes to reintroduce it. At long last, Senator Tobey came through with "maximum" to replace "full," and everyone seemed satisfied. Tobey was also responsible for adding the phrase "and the general welfare" after "free competitive enterprise" in the statement of the government's obligation to "foster and promote."

*The Abortive Strategy.*—Mention of Tobey's contributions to the conference brings to mind a carefully conceived strategy which

[9] Public Law 304, 79th Cong., 2d Sess., approved Feb. 20, 1946.

was developed by certain people in the Executive branch. Towards the end of the conference, Tobey was approached by an administration friend of the original bill and was given the following sales talk. The original bill, of which Tobey was a co-sponsor, was being cut to pieces, not by Republicans but by Southern Democrats. The year 1946 was an election year. If Tobey in conference could press for a liberal version of S.380, the Republican Party could take the credit for saving the Full Employment Bill. Tobey was impressed, and agreed to present a strong bill to the conference on February 2. The strategist then went to Whittington and informed him that a rumor was abroad to the effect that Tobey was going to put the Democratic Party on the spot, and that unless the Democrats in the conference succeeded on their own initiative in bringing out a liberal bill, the Republicans could make a successful campaign issue out of the situation. Whether or not this news impressed Whittington will never be known, for on February 2, the Edwin Pauley affair broke,[10] Tobey raced off to the new fray, and failed to appear at the conference session on S.380.

*The Final Agreement.*—Once agreement had been reached on the Declaration of Policy, the rest of the discussion went rapidly. The section dealing with the Economic Report of the President was a condensation and clarification of the House substitute on this issue. Written by Gross and introduced by Cochran, this revised section was adopted with almost no opposition.

The provisions for the Council of Economic Advisers as outlined in the House substitute were taken over almost intact, although certain important modifications were made, and at one point Whittington startled the conferees by introducing a brand new proposal. The big issue, of course, was the relationship of the Council to the President and to Congress. The Senate managers insisted that any provision which in any way served to make ambiguous the relation of the Council to the President would be unacceptable. The House bill, it will be remembered, carried the statement, "The President is requested to make available to the Joint Committee on the Economic Report, if it desires, the various studies, reports, and recommendations of the Council which have been submitted to the

---

[10] Truman submitted Pauley's name for confirmation to the post of Undersecretary of the Navy. Pauley's background in oil and Democratic Party politics turned many Senators against him and his name was finally withdrawn.

President." [11] The Senate managers forced the House managers to delete this section, but just when agreement seemed to be reached, Whittington came up with a completely new proposal, authored by the U.S. Chamber of Commerce and calling for the establishment of an "independent agency, an Economic Commission." After a hot debate on January 31, Whittington finally backed down, and agreement was reached.

With the general sanction of all concerned, the membership on the proposed Joint Committee on the Economic Report was cut to seven representatives from each House. Any larger number was felt to be unwieldy. Little debate developed on the issue of appropriations for the Council and for the Joint Committee.

A rapid survey of the work of the conference gives no real indication of the human side of the proceedings. Major credit for keeping the discussion moving must go to Senator Alben Barkley. Whenever discussions became tense and acrimonious, Barkley, as chairman, relieved the tension with a joke or a gentle whim. He performed what John Chamberlain has called the function of the "master broker" [12]—the classic job of the statesman-politician: the discovery of areas of agreement. This was not always easy in the Full Employment conference. Ideological conflicts were mixed up with personality conflicts. Senator Taylor was angry with Senator Taft when the latter dismissed the old-age pension provisions of the Senate bill as "window dressing"; Senator Tobey took such a personal dislike to Representative Carter Manasco that he had to force himself to sit in the same room with him; on the rare occasions when Clare Hoffman appeared, tempers rose noticeably; Whittington had to exercise considerable tact in getting Manasco to agree to a number of the compromises.

But on February 2, 1946, the job was done. The long legislative battle was all but completed.

## THE EMPLOYMENT ACT OF 1946

Before turning to the ratification of the conference bill by the House and Senate, it may be of interest to analyze the Employment Act of 1946 [13] as a composite product. The conference bill had in it parts of S.380 as introduced, as passed by the Senate, as passed by

11 S.380, 79th Cong., 1st Sess., Dec. 5, 1945, p. 19.
12 *The American Stakes* (New York, 1940).       13 Public Law 304.

the House, and as modified by the conferees. It is here presented in such a way as to indicate the contributions of each phase of draftsmanship. Portions of the Act taken from the original bill are in ordinary text type; the contributions of the Senate version are in *lower case italics;* contributions of the House substitute are in SMALL CAPITALS; and the changes and additions of the conferees are written in *SMALL ITALIC CAPITALS.*

## EMPLOYMENT ACT OF 1946

### An ACT

To DECLARE a national policy ON EMPLOYMENT, PRODUCTION, AND PURCHASING POWER *AND FOR OTHER PURPOSES.*

Be it enacted by the Senate and House of Representatives of the United States of America in Congress assembled.

SEC. 1. This Act may be cited as the *"EMPLOYMENT ACT OF 1946."*

### Declaration of Policy

SEC. 2. The Congress hereby declares that it is the CONTINUING policy *AND responsibility of the Federal Government TO USE ALL PRACTICABLE MEANS consistent with its needs and obligations and other essential considerations of national policy WITH THE ASSIST-ANCE AND COOPERATION OF* industry, agriculture, labor, and State and local governments, *TO COORDINATE AND UTILIZE ALL ITS PLANS, FUNCTIONS, AND RESOURCES FOR THE PURPOSE OF CREATING AND MAINTAINING, IN A MANNER CALCULATED* to foster AND PROMOTE free competitive enterprise and the general welfare, *CONDITIONS UNDER WHICH* THERE WILL BE AFFORDED *useful employment, FOR THOSE* able, *WILLING,* and seeking to work, *AND* TO PROMOTE *MAXIMUM* EMPLOYMENT, PRODUCTION, AND PURCHASING POWER.

### ECONOMIC REPORT OF THE PRESIDENT

SEC. 3(a) The President shall transmit to the Congress WITHIN SIXTY DAYS AFTER THE BEGINNING OF EACH REGULAR SESSION (COM-MENCING WITH THE YEAR 1947) AN ECONOMIC REPORT (HEREINAFTER CALLED THE "ECONOMIC REPORT") *SETTING FORTH (1) THE LEVELS* OF EMPLOYMENT, PRODUCTION, AND PURCHASING POWER *OBTAINING IN THE UNITED STATES AND SUCH LEVELS NEEDED TO CARRY OUT*

*THE POLICY DECLARED IN SECTION 2;* (2) current *and foreseeable trends in the levels of* EMPLOYMENT, PRODUCTION, AND PURCHASING POWER; (3) *a review of the economic program of the Federal Government* AND A REVIEW OF ECONOMIC CONDITIONS AFFECTING EMPLOYMENT IN THE UNITED STATES OR ANY CONSIDERABLE PORTION THEREOF during the preceding year and of their effect upon EMPLOYMENT, PRODUCTION, AND PURCHASING POWER; AND (4) *A PROGRAM FOR CARRYING OUT THE POLICY DECLARED IN SECTION 2, TOGETHER WITH* such recommendations for legislation as he may deem necessary or desirable.

(b) The President may transmit from time to time to the Congress reports supplementary to THE ECONOMIC REPORT, *EACH OF WHICH SHALL INCLUDE SUCH SUPPLEMENTARY OR REVISED RECOMMENDATIONS AS HE MAY DEEM NECESSARY OR DESIRABLE TO ACHIEVE THE POLICY DECLARED IN SECTION 2.*

(c) THE ECONOMIC REPORT, AND *ALL* SUPPLEMENTARY REPORTS *TRANSMITTED UNDER SUBSECTION (B), SHALL, WHEN TRANSMITTED* TO CONGRESS, BE REFERRED TO the Joint Committee CREATED BY SECTION 5.

### COUNCIL OF ECONOMIC ADVISERS TO THE PRESIDENT

SEC. 4(a) THERE IS HEREBY CREATED IN THE EXECUTIVE OFFICE OF THE PRESIDENT A COUNCIL OF ECONOMIC ADVISERS (HEREINAFTER CALLED THE "COUNCIL"). THE COUNCIL SHALL BE COMPOSED OF THREE MEMBERS WHO SHALL BE APPOINTED BY THE PRESIDENT, BY AND WITH THE ADVICE AND CONSENT OF THE SENATE, AND EACH OF WHOM SHALL BE A PERSON WHO, AS A RESULT OF HIS TRAINING, EXPERIENCE, AND ATTAINMENTS, IS EXCEPTIONALLY QUALIFIED TO ANALYZE AND INTERPRET ECONOMIC DEVELOPMENTS, TO APPRAISE PROGRAMS AND ACTIVITIES OF THE GOVERNMENT IN THE LIGHT OF THE POLICY DECLARED IN SECTION 2, AND TO FORMULATE AND RECOMMEND NATIONAL ECONOMIC POLICY TO PROMOTE EMPLOYMENT, PRODUCTION, AND PURCHASING POWER UNDER FREE COMPETITIVE ENTERPRISE. EACH MEMBER OF THE COUNCIL SHALL RECEIVE COMPENSATION AT THE RATE OF $15,000 PER ANNUM. THE PRESIDENT SHALL DESIGNATE ONE OF THE MEMBERS OF THE COUNCIL AS CHAIRMAN AND ONE AS VICE CHAIRMAN, WHO SHALL ACT AS CHAIRMAN IN THE ABSENCE OF THE CHAIRMAN.

(b) THE COUNCIL IS AUTHORIZED TO EMPLOY, AND FIX THE COM-

PENSATION OF, SUCH SPECIALISTS AND OTHER EXPERTS AS MAY BE
NECESSARY FOR THE CARRYING OUT OF ITS FUNCTIONS UNDER THIS ACT,
WITHOUT REGARD TO THE CIVIL-SERVICE LAWS AND THE CLASSIFICA-
TION ACT OF 1923, AS AMENDED, AND IS AUTHORIZED, SUBJECT TO THE
CIVIL-SERVICE LAWS, TO EMPLOY SUCH OTHER OFFICERS AND EMPLOY-
EES AS MAY BE NECESSARY FOR CARRYING OUT ITS FUNCTIONS UNDER
THIS ACT, AND FIX THEIR COMPENSATION IN ACCORDANCE WITH THE
CLASSIFICATION ACT OF 1923, AS AMENDED.

(C) IT SHALL BE THE DUTY and function OF THE COUNCIL:

(1) TO ASSIST AND ADVISE THE PRESIDENT IN THE PREPARATION
OF THE ECONOMIC REPORT:

(2) TO GATHER TIMELY AND AUTHORITATIVE INFORMATION
CONCERNING ECONOMIC DEVELOPMENTS AND ECONOMIC
TRENDS, BOTH CURRENT AND PROSPECTIVE, TO ANALYZE
AND INTERPRET SUCH INFORMATION IN THE LIGHT OF THE
POLICY DECLARED IN SECTION 2 FOR THE PURPOSE OF DE-
TERMINING WHETHER SUCH DEVELOPMENTS AND TRENDS
ARE INTERFERING, OR ARE LIKELY TO INTERFERE, WITH THE
ACHIEVEMENT OF SUCH POLICY, AND TO COMPILE AND SUB-
MIT TO THE PRESIDENT STUDIES RELATING TO SUCH DEVEL-
OPMENTS AND TRENDS;

(3) TO APPRAISE THE VARIOUS PROGRAMS AND ACTIVITIES OF
THE FEDERAL GOVERNMENT IN THE LIGHT OF THE POLICY
DECLARED IN SECTION 2 FOR THE PURPOSE OF DETERMINING
THE EXTENT TO WHICH SUCH PROGRAMS AND ACTIVITIES
ARE CONTRIBUTING, AND THE EXTENT TO WHICH THEY ARE
NOT CONTRIBUTING, TO THE ACHIEVEMENT OF SUCH POLICY,
AND TO MAKE RECOMMENDATIONS TO THE PRESIDENT WITH
RESPECT THERETO;

(4) to develop AND RECOMMEND TO THE PRESIDENT NATIONAL
ECONOMIC POLICIES TO FOSTER AND PROMOTE FREE COM-
PETITIVE ENTERPRISE, TO AVOID ECONOMIC FLUCTUATIONS
OR TO DIMINISH THE EFFECTS THEREOF, AND TO MAINTAIN
EMPLOYMENT, PRODUCTION, AND PURCHASING POWER;

(5) TO MAKE AND FURNISH SUCH STUDIES, REPORTS THEREON,
AND RECOMMENDATIONS WITH RESPECT TO MATTERS OF
FEDERAL ECONOMIC POLICY and legislation AS THE PRESI-
DENT MAY REQUEST.

(d) THE COUNCIL SHALL MAKE AN ANNUAL REPORT TO THE PRESI-
DENT IN *DECEMBER OF EACH YEAR.*

(e) IN EXERCISING ITS POWERS, FUNCTIONS AND DUTIES UNDER THIS
ACT:

    (1) THE COUNCIL MAY CONSTITUTE SUCH ADVISORY COMMIT-
    TEES AND MAY CONSULT WITH SUCH REPRESENTATIVES OF
    INDUSTRY, AGRICULTURAL, LABOR, CONSUMERS, State and
    local governments, AND OTHER GROUPS, AS IT DEEMS ADVIS-
    ABLE;

    (2) THE COUNCIL SHALL, TO THE FULLEST EXTENT POSSIBLE,
    UTILIZE THE SERVICES, FACILITIES, AND INFORMATION (IN-
    CLUDING STATISTICAL INFORMATION) OF OTHER GOVERN-
    MENT AGENCIES AS WELL AS OF PRIVATE RESEARCH AGEN-
    CIES, IN ORDER THAT DUPLICATION OF EFFORT AND EXPENSE
    MAY BE AVOIDED.

(f) TO ENABLE THE COUNCIL TO EXERCISE ITS POWERS, FUNCTIONS,
AND DUTIES UNDER THIS ACT, THERE ARE AUTHORIZED TO BE APPRO-
PRIATED (EXCEPT FOR THE SALARIES OF THE MEMBERS AND THE SALA-
RIES OF OFFICERS AND EMPLOYEES OF THE COUNCIL) SUCH SUMS AS MAY
BE NECESSARY. FOR THE SALARIES OF THE MEMBERS AND THE SALARIES
OF OFFICERS AND EMPLOYEES OF THE COUNCIL, THERE IS AUTHOR-
IZED TO BE APPROPRIATED NOT EXCEEDING $345,000 IN THE AGGRE-
GATE FOR EACH FISCAL YEAR.

## Joint Committee on the ECONOMIC REPORT

SEC. 5. (a) There is hereby established a Joint Committee on
the ECONOMIC REPORT, to be composed of *SEVEN* Members of the
Senate, to be appointed by the President of the Senate, AND *SEVEN*
Members of the House of Representatives, to be appointed by the
Speaker of the House of Representatives. The party representation
on the joint committee shall as nearly as may be feasible reflect the
relative membership of the majority and minority parties in the
Senate and House of Representatives.

(b) It shall be the function of the joint committee—

    (1) to make a continuing study of matters related to the
    ECONOMIC REPORT;

    (2) TO STUDY MEANS OF COORDINATING PROGRAMS IN ORDER
    TO FURTHER THE POLICY OF THIS ACT: AND

(3) as a guide to the several committees of the Congress dealing with legislation relating to the ECONOMIC REPORT, not later than *MAY 1* of each year (BEGINNING WITH THE YEAR 1947) to file a report with the Senate and the House of Representatives containing its findings and recommendations with respect to each of the main recommendations made by the President in the ECONOMIC REPORT, AND FROM TIME TO TIME TO MAKE SUCH OTHER REPORTS AND RECOMMENDATIONS TO THE SENATE AND HOUSE OF REPRESENTATIVES AS IT DEEMS ADVISABLE.

(c). Vacancies in the membership of the joint committee shall not affect the power of the remaining members to execute the functions of the joint committee, and shall be filled in the same manner as in the case of the original selection. The joint committee shall select a chairman and a vice chairman from among its members.

(d) The joint committee, or any duly authorized subcommittee thereof, is authorized TO HOLD SUCH HEARINGS AS IT DEEMS ADVISABLE, AND, WITHIN THE LIMITATIONS OF ITS APPROPRIATIONS, the joint committee is empowered to appoint and fix the compensation of such experts, consultants, technicians and clerical and stenographic assistants, to procure such printing and binding, and to make such expenditures, as it deems necessary and advisable. The cost of stenographic services to report hearings of the joint committee, OR ANY SUBCOMMITTEE THEREOF, shall not exceed 25 cents per hundred words. The joint committee is authorized to utilize the departments and establishments of the Government, AND ALSO OF PRIVATE RESEARCH AGENCIES.[14]

(e) *THERE IS HEREBY AUTHORIZED TO BE APPROPRIATED FOR EACH FISCAL YEAR THE SUM OF $50,000, OR SO MUCH THEREOF AS MAY BE NECESSARY, TO CARRY OUT THE PROVISIONS OF THIS SECTION, TO BE DISBURSED BY THE SECRETARY OF THE SENATE ON VOUCHERS SIGNED BY THE CHAIRMAN OR VICE CHAIRMAN.*

Such was the eclectic product of the personalities and pressures which struggled for more than a year over the fate of S.380. But who had won? What did it all mean?

[14] Remember where Gross and Whittington respectively got most of their research assistance?

HOUSE AND SENATE APPROVAL

On February 6, 1946, the House listened to a number of schools of opinion about the meaning and value of the Employment Act of 1946.[15] Whittington and Manasco reported that the Act was acceptable to them, that the Senate managers had given in at every important point, and that the conference bill was, to all intents and purposes, the House substitute. Cochran and Patman backed the conference bill as one which the liberals could support with good conscience. Some of the strong phrases were missing, they admitted, but the meat of the original bill was still there. Bender claimed that the conference bill was a fake, that it was not a full employment bill, but that he would support it reluctantly as a move in the right direction. Hoffman and Church also called the bill a fake, but vehemently protested its passage on the grounds that it represented unnecessary duplication of existing powers, and would lead to nothing constructive. After outlining the steps provided for by the Act, Hoffman characterized the whole procedure as chasing "the devil of unemployment around the stump, never quite catching him." [16]

On one thing almost everyone was agreed: that the question of Presidential appointments to the Council was of vital importance. The conservatives wanted men "of business ability." [17] The liberals wanted men who were "wholeheartedly devoted to the principles of the bill." [18]

The Employment Act of 1946 was finally passed in the House by a vote of 320 to 84 (see Appendix C). Two days later, on February 8, with the endorsement of both Senator Murray and Senator Taft, the conference bill went through the Senate without opposition. It was signed by President Truman and became law on February 20, 1946.

And what of the reaction of the interested pressure groups and the press? The Continuations Group, after being assured by Senator Murray and Bertram Gross that the Act was a worthy result of their labors, dutifully submitted a memorandum to Truman asking that he sign the conference bill. Many liberals felt secretly, however, that the conference bill was a weak and meaningless wraith. Some

15 *Congressional Record,* 79th Cong., 2d Sess., pp. 999–1009.     16 *Ibid.,* p. 1001.
17 *Ibid.,* p. 1000.
18 *Congressional Record,* 79th Cong., 2d Sess., Feb. 8, 1946, p. 1170.

members of the C.I.O. were particularly bitter. Most conservatives rejoiced that the teeth had been removed from the original bill, and in general the press gave it short shrift as a watered-down version of S.380. A few, and as time went on, a growing number of people, felt that whatever the hopes and fears of those responsible for the final Act, S.380 as passed was an important step in the direction of coordinated and responsible economic planning in the federal government.

# Conclusion and Hypotheses

The Constitution is not honored by blind worship. The more open-eyed we become, as a nation, to its defects, and the prompter we grow in applying with the unhesitating courage of conviction all thoroughly-tested or well-considered expedients necessary to make self-government among us a straight-forward thing of simple method, single, unstinted power, and clear responsibility, the nearer will we approach to the sound sense and practical genius of the great and honorable statesmen of 1787.—Wilson, *Congressional Government*, pp. 332–333.

WITH THE President's approval of Public Law 304, we come to the end of our story, although by no means do we come to the end of the politics of the Employment Act of 1946. In the selection of top personnel for the Council of Economic Advisers, President Truman was subjected to a barrage of pressures; [1] the composition and activi-

[1] The choice of Edwin G. Nourse, former vice president of the Brookings Institution; John D. Clark, businessman and former dean of the College of Business Administration of the University of Nebraska; and Leon Keyserling, a New Deal lawyer and economist, indicates that the President wanted to antagonize as few interests as possible.

ties of the Joint Committee on the Economic Report have reflected political decisions; the attempt of the Economic Council during the past three years to establish itself in the Executive hierarchy, to define the scope of its responsibilities and to develop a working philosophy, can only be understood in the context of American political processes broadly conceived. Already the Employment Act has been amended by another piece of legislation: the Legislative Reorganization Act of 1946, which revised the time schedule for the submission and consideration of the Economic Report. As time goes on, it is inevitable that further changes will take place in the scope of responsibilities of the President's Council and of the Joint Committee on the Economic Report, and it is certain that America is experiencing one of the first, rather than one of the last, experiments in economic planning and coordination.

Whether the Employment Act of 1946 was a "good thing" or a "bad thing" is, in the context of this book, beside the point. The real question posed by the story of S.380 is what it suggests about the Congressional formulation of important social and economic policies in the middle of the twentieth century.

Certainly one generalization is that the process is almost unbelievably complex. Legislative policy-making appears to be the result of a confluence of factors streaming from an almost endless number of tributaries: national experience, the contributions of social theorists, the clash of powerful economic interests, the quality of Presidential leadership, other institutional and personal ambitions and administrative arrangements in the Executive Branch, the initiative, effort, and ambitions of individual legislators and their governmental and non-governmental staffs, the policy commitments of political parties, and the predominant culture symbols in the minds both of leaders and followers in the Congress.

Most of these forces appear to be involved at every important stage in the policy-making process, and they act only within the most general limits of popular concern about a specific issue.

In the absence of a widely recognized crisis, legislative policy-making tends to be fought out at the level of largely irresponsible personal and group stratagems and compromises based upon temporary power coalitions of political, administrative, and non-governmental interests.

This type of policy-making is in part responsible for, and is certainly aided and abetted by, the rules, structures, and procedures of the Congress, and by a widely shared folklore of American Constitutional theory which is uncritically accepted by the great majority of our national legislators—the sanctity of Congressional prerogatives and the desirability of competing power systems in the federal government.

Put in its baldest form, the story of S.380 adds up to the fact that majority sentiment expressed in popular elections for a particular economic policy can be, and frequently is, almost hopelessly splintered by the power struggles of competing political, administrative, and private interests, and is finally pieced together, if at all, only by the most laborious, complicated, and frequently covert coalition strategies.

Granted that basic to the drafting of a full employment bill in the United States was a public awareness that the recurrence of widespread unemployment was a frightening possibility in the postwar years, the fact remains that the American voter could not and cannot hold any recognizable group, interest, or individual responsible for the Employment Act of 1946.

Certainly President Truman cannot be held responsible. It is true that he attempted to provide political leadership through his messages to Congress, his radio appeals to the public, the testimony of members of his Cabinet before the Senate and House committees, his conversations with key Congressional leaders, and his appointment of a Cabinet committee under Fred Vinson to press for passage of a strong bill. It is true also that he signed the final compromise Act. But the forces which shaped and modified the legislation were far beyond his control, and it is almost certain that if he had vetoed the conference bill he would have got nothing in its place.

The political parties cannot be held responsible, except in the negative sense that their weakness made irresponsibility inevitable. Both the Democratic and Republican Party platforms in 1944 paid their respects to the issue of full or high level employment, and both Presidential candidates as party leaders endorsed the principle of federal responsibility for providing "jobs for all." But during the legislative struggle over S.380, with the exception of the division on the two Hickenlooper amendments in the Senate, there was little indication that party affiliation was an important determinant of voting behavior. Neither Republicans nor Democrats were able to present an even reasonably solid phalanx for or against the bill at the crucial stage of House consideration. Party lines were crossed with impunity. In short, so complicated were the interparty alignments that it is literally impossible for the voter to hold either party separately, or both parties together, responsible for the Employment Act of 1946.

Can responsibility be placed on the pressure groups? Not in any meaningful political sense. The National Farmers Union authored the proposal which in turn stimulated the drafting of S.380. The Lib-Lab lobby, under the leadership of the Continuations Group, worked diligently for a strong bill. But what of the Committee for Economic Development, the United States Chamber of Commerce, and the Machinery and Allied Products Institute which were of great importance in shaping the substance of the final bill? And what of the more uncompromising pressures from the "right" which opened the hole through which the more moderate conservative spokesmen ran? Even if there were mechanisms, which there are not, for identifying the various pressure-group influences and their respective impacts upon the policy-making process, how could the voting public hold them accountable?

Who remains? The individual Senators and Congressmen? But what control does a national popular majority have over a Will Whittington of Mississippi or a Clare Hoffman of Michigan or a John Cochran of St. Louis? These men were not representatives of national political parties based upon national programs. They were representatives of the dominant interests and culture symbols of tiny geographical areas which, even if taken in the aggregate, do not give a fair quantitative weighting to the sentiments and expectations of a national popular majority. Furthermore, the committee system in Congress means that key representatives may have an inordinate amount of individual power in the shaping of national destinies, even when those key representatives are effectively accountable only to a tiny economic and political junta in one Congressional District.

These are some of the facts of our political life. Their seriousness in terms of the future of American democracy are discounted both by those who fear majority rule and by those who have a sanguine faith that the American genius for unity in times of dire emergency will somehow continue to save "Pauline" as she dangles from the edge of the cliff.

The American democracy is built upon a number of unwritten propositions. One of the basic tenets is that political mechanisms are creatures of human intelligence and human will; that they are subject to change as human needs and expectations change. In an age when national problems require national answers and when democratic expectations have reached a point of no return in the direction of governmental responsibility for protecting citizens from the ravages of economic forces beyond their separate control, is it not time that intelligence was reapplied to our basic political institutions? Whether the American system can long endure depends upon a number of factors, but surely one of the most important ingredients of survival is a responsible political system which will reflect the will of the majority and which will enable the citizens to hold identifiable rulers accountable for policy decisions.

I fail to see how this can be done except by strengthening the only two instruments in our political life which have an inherent responsibility to the nation as nation: the President and the national political parties. This does not suggest a sudden adoption of the British system, a change which is out of the question. Nor does it imply the development of rigid class and ideological divisions in our society. In anything as huge as the American continent, economic and cultural diversity is as inevitable as it is desirable. The strengthening of Presidential leadership and party cohesion as rational instruments of majority rule would not mean that pressure groups and regional needs would suddenly be exorcised ruthlessly from any influence in decision-making at the national level. It would mean that after those forces had contributed their points of view and their respective energies in the formulation of national policies, the public could hold an identifiable institutional leadership responsible for final decisions.

Furthermore, the strengthening of party cohesion in Congress would unquestionably enhance the collective power and prestige of that vital institution. The present splintering of decision-making leads to inevitable confusion and frustration among our national legislators, and in some cases, such as in filibusters, to a travesty of democratic processes. Congress must have the continuing right of introducing, revising, and enacting legislation, but these functions should be carried on in such a way that the public can pin responsibility unequivocally.

In the absence of a responsible political system we run the grave risk of public cynicism and frustration, and of neglecting policies which could anticipate and to some extent preclude serious economic crises.

The story of the Employment Act of 1946 suggests a need for more responsible policy-making in our national legislature. It also suggests that until we move in that direction, national economic policies will continue to be formulated by a kaleidoscopic and largely irresponsible interplay of ideas, interests, institutions, and individuals.

*Appendices*

# Appendix A

## The Full Employment Bill as Originally Introduced
79th Congress, 1st Session
S.380

### IN THE SENATE OF THE UNITED STATES

January 22, 1945

Mr. Murray (for himself, Mr. Wagner, Mr. Thomas of Utah, Mr. O'Mahoney, Mr. Morse, Mr. Tobey, Mr. Aiken, and Mr. Langer) introduced the following bill; which was read twice and referred to the Committee on Banking and Currency

### A BILL

To establish a national policy and program for assuring continuing full employment in a free competitive economy, through the concerted efforts of industry, agriculture, labor, State and local governments, and the Federal Government.

Be it enacted by the Senate and House of Representatives of the United States of America in Congress assembled,

SECTION 1. This Act may be cited as the "Full Employment Act of 1945."

#### DECLARATION OF POLICY

SEC. 2. The Congress hereby declares that—

(a) It is the policy of the United States to foster free competitive enterprise and the investment of private capital in trade and commerce and in the development of the natural resources of the United States;

(b) All Americans able to work and seeking work have the right to useful, remunerative, regular, and full-time employment, and it is the policy of the United States to assure the existence at all times of sufficient employment opportunities to enable all Americans who have finished their schooling and who do not have full-time housekeeping responsibilities freely to exercise this right;

(c) In order to carry out the policies set forth in subsections (a) and (b) of this section, and in order to (1) promote the general welfare of the Nation; (2) foster and protect the American home and the American family as the foundation of the American way of life; (3) raise the standard of living of the American people; (4) provide adequate employment opportunities for returning veterans; (5) contribute to the full utilization of our national resources; (6) develop trade and commerce among the several States and with foreign nations; (7) preserve and strengthen competitive private enterprise, particularly small business enterprise; (8) strengthen the national defense and security; and (9) contribute to the establishment and maintenance of lasting peace among nations, it is essential that continuing full employment be maintained in the United States;

(d) In order to assist industry, agriculture, labor and State and local governments in achieving continuing full employment, it is the responsibility of the Federal Government to pursue such consistent and openly arrived at economic policies and programs as will stimulate and encourage the highest feasible levels of employment opportunities through private and other non-Federal investment and expenditure;

(e) To the extent that continuing full employment cannot otherwise be achieved, it is the further responsibility of the Federal Government to provide such volume of Federal investment and expenditure as may be needed to assure continuing full employment; and

(f) Such investment and expenditure by the Federal Government shall be designed to contribute to the national wealth and well-being, and to stimulate increased employment opportunities by private enterprise.

### THE NATIONAL PRODUCTION AND EMPLOYMENT BUDGET

SEC. 3. (a) The President shall transmit to Congress at the beginning of each regular session the National Production and Employment Budget (hereinafter referred to as the "National Budget"), which shall set forth in summary and detail, for the ensuing fiscal year or such longer period as the President may deem appropriate—

(1) the estimated size of the labor force, including the self-employed in industry and agriculture;

(2) the estimated aggregate volume of investment and expenditure by private enterprises, consumers, State and local governments, and the Federal Government, required to produce such volume of the gross national product, at the expected level of prices, as will be necessary to provide employment opportunities for such labor force (such dollar volume being hereinafter referred to as the "full employment volume of production"); and

(3) the estimated aggregate volume of prospective investment and expenditure by private enterprises, consumers, State and local governments, and the Federal Government (not taking into account any increased or decreased investment or expenditure which might be ex-

pected to result from the programs set forth in such Budget). The estimates and information herein called for shall take account of such foreign investments and expenditure for exports and imports as affect the volume of the gross national product.

(b) The extent, if any, by which the estimated aggregate volume of prospective investment and expenditure for any fiscal year or other period, as set forth in the National Budget in accordance with paragraph (a) (3) of this section, is less than the estimated aggregate volume of investment and expenditure required to assure a full employment volume of production, as set forth in the National Budget in accordance with paragraph (a) (2) of this section, shall for the purposes of this title be regarded as a prospective deficiency in the National Budget. When there is a prospective deficiency in the National Budget for any fiscal year or other period, the President shall set forth in such Budget a general program for encouraging such increased non-Federal investment and expenditure, particularly investment and expenditure which will promote increased employment opportunities by private enterprise, as will prevent such deficiency to the greatest possible extent. The President shall also include in such Budget such recommendations for legislation relating to such program as he may deem necessary or desirable. Such program may include, but need not be limited to, current and projected Federal policies and activities with reference to banking and currency, monopoly and competition, wages and working conditions, foreign trade and investment, agriculture, taxation, social security, the development of natural resources, and such other matters as may directly or indirectly affect the level of non-Federal investment and expenditure.

(c) To the extent, if any, that such increased non-Federal investment and expenditure as may be expected to result from actions taken under the program set forth in accordance with subsection (b) of this section are deemed insufficient to provide a full employment volume of production, the President shall transmit a general program for such Federal investment and expenditure as will be sufficient to bring the aggregate volume of investment and expenditure by private business, consumers, State and local government, and the Federal Government, up to the level required to assure a full employment volume of production. Such program shall be designed to contribute to the national wealth and well-being, and to stimulate additional non-Federal investment and expenditure. Any of such programs calling for the construction of public works by the Federal Government shall provide for the performance of the necessary construction work by private concerns under contracts awarded in accordance with applicable laws, except where the performance of such work by some other method is necessary by reason of special circumstances or is authorized by other provisions of law.

(d) If the estimated aggregate volume of prospective investment and expenditure for any fiscal year or other period, as set forth in the National Budget in accordance with paragraph (a) (3) of this section, is more than the estimated aggregate volume of investment and expenditure required to assure a full employment volume of production, as set forth in the National Budget in accordance with paragraph (a) (2) of this section, the President shall set forth in such Budget a general program for preventing inflationary economic dislocations, or diminishing the aggregate volume of investment and expenditure to the level required to assure a full employment volume of production, or both.

(e) The programs referred to in subsections (b), (c), and (d) of this section shall include such measures as may be necessary to assure that monopolistic practices with respect to prices, production, or distribution, or other monopolisitic practices, will not interfere with the achievement of the purposes of this Act.

(f) The National Budget shall include a report on the distribution of the national income during the preceding fiscal year, or such longer period as the President may deem appropriate, together with an evaluation of the effect upon the distribution of the national income of the programs set forth in such Budget.

(g) The President may from time to time transmit to Congress such supplemental or revised estimates, information, programs, or legislative recommendations as he may deem necessary or desirable in connection with the National Budget.

### PREPARATION OF NATIONAL BUDGET

SEC. 4. (a) The National Budget shall be prepared in the Executive Office of the President under the general direction and supervision of the President, and in consultation with the members of his Cabinet and other heads of departments and establishments.

(b) The President shall transmit to the several departments and establishments such preliminary estimates and other information as will enable them to prepare such plans and programs as may be needed during the ensuing or subsequent fiscal years to help achieve a full employment volume of production.

(c) The President may establish such advisory boards or committees composed of representatives of industry, agriculture, labor, and State and local governments, and others, as he may deem advisable for the purpose of advising and consulting on methods of achieving the objectives of this Act.

### JOINT COMMITTEE ON THE NATIONAL BUDGET

SEC. 5. (a) There is hereby established a Joint Committee on the National Budget, to be composed of the chairmen and ranking minority members of the Senate Committees on Appropriations, Banking and Currency, Education and Labor, and Finance, and seven additional Members of the Senate, to be appointed by the President of the Senate; and the chairmen and ranking minority members of the House Committees on Appropriations, Banking and Currency, Labor, and Ways and Means, and seven additional Members of the House of Representatives to be appointed by the Speaker of the House of Representatives. The party representation of the Joint Committee shall reflect the relative membership of the majority and minority parties in the Senate and the House of Representatives.

(b) It shall be the function of the Joint Committee—

(1) to make a study of the National Budget transmitted to Congress by the President in accordance with section 3 of this Act; and

(2) to report to the Senate and the House of Representatives, not later than March 1 of each year, its findings and recommendations with respect to the National Budget, together with a joint resolution setting forth for the ensuing fiscal year a general policy with respect to such National Budget to serve as a guide to the several committees of Congress dealing with legislation relating to such National Budget.

(c) Vacancies in the membership of the Joint Committee shall not affect the power of the remaining members to execute the functions of the committee, and shall be filled in the same manner as in the case of the original selection. The committee shall select a chairman and a vice chairman from among its members.

(d) The Joint Committee, or any duly authorized subcommittee thereof, is authorized to sit and act at such places and times, to require by subpena or otherwise the attendance of such witnesses and the production of such books, papers, and documents, to administer such oaths, to take such testimony, to procure such printing and binding, and to make such expenditures as it deems advisable. The cost of stenographic services to report such hearings shall not be in excess of 25 cents per hundred words. The provisions of sections 102 to 104, inclusive, of the Revised Statutes shall apply in case of any failure of any witness to comply with any subpena, or to testify when summoned, under authority of this section.

(e) The Joint Committee is empowered to appoint and fix the compensation of such experts, consultants, technicians, and clerical and stenographic assistance as it deems necessary and advisable, but the compensation so fixed shall not exceed the compensation prescribed under the Classification Act of 1923, as amended, for comparable duties. The committee may utilize such voluntary and uncompensated services as it deems necessary and is authorized to utilize the services, information, facilities, and personnel of the departments and establishments.

(f) The expenses of the Joint Committee shall be paid one-half from the contingent fund of the Senate and one-half from the contingent fund of the House of Representatives upon vouchers signed by the chairman or vice chairman.

## RATE OF EXPENDITURES

SEC. 6. (a) The President shall review quarterly all Federal investment and expenditure for the purpose of ascertaining the extent to which the current and anticipated level of non-Federal investment and expenditure warrants any change in the volume of such Federal investment and expenditure.

(b) Subject to such principles and standards as may be set forth in applicable appropriation Acts and other statutes, the rate of Federal investment and expenditure may be varied to whatever extent and in whatever manner the President may determine to be necessary for the purpose of assisting in assuring continuing full employment, with due consideration being given to current and anticipated variations in savings and in investment and expenditure by private business, consumers, State and local governments, and the Federal Government.

## AID TO COMMITTEES

SEC. 7. The heads of departments and establishments shall, at the request of any committee of either House of Congress, furnish such committee with such aid and information with regard to the National Budget as it may request.

## INTERPRETATION

SEC. 8. Nothing contained herein shall be construed as calling for or authorizing—

(a) the operation of plants, factories, or other productive facilities by the Federal Government;

(b) the use of compulsory measures of any type whatsoever in determining the allocation or distribution of manpower;

(c) any change in the existing procedures on appropriations; or

(d) the carrying out of, or any appropriation for, any program set forth in the National Budget, unless such program shall have been authorized by provisions of law other than this Act.

# Appendix B

## The 116 Co-Sponsors of H.R.2202 in the House of Representatives

| STATE<br>_Congressman_ | _Party_ | _District_ | _Type of District_ [1] |
|---|---|---|---|
| ALABAMA | | | |
| Luther Patrick | D | 9 | Birmingham |
| ARIZONA | | | |
| Richard Harless | D | A.L. | mixed |
| John R. Murdock | D | A.L. | mixed |
| CALIFORNIA | | | |
| Helen G. Douglas | D | 14 | Los Angeles |
| Clyde Doyle | D | 18 | Los Angeles |
| Frank R. Havenner | D | 4 | San Francisco |
| Ned R. Healy | D | 13 | Los Angeles |
| Chet Holifield | D | 19 | Los Angeles |
| Ed V. Izac | D | 23 | mixed |
| Clair Engle | D | 2 | rural |
| Cecil R. King | D | 17 | Los Angeles |
| Gordon McDonough | R | 15 | Los Angeles |
| George P. Miller | D | 6 | mixed |
| George E. Outland | D | 11 | rural |
| E. E. Patterson | D | 16 | Los Angeles |
| H. R. Sheppard | D | 21 | Los Angeles |
| J. H. Tolan | D | 7 | Oakland |
| Jerry Voorhis | D | 12 | Los Angeles |
| Richard J. Welch | R | 5 | San Francisco |

[1] "Rural" is arbitrarily defined as a Congressional District which has no urban concentration greater than 50,000 population; "mixed," as a district containing one or more urban concentrations greater than 50,000, but less than 250,000. For districts in or containing an urban concentration greater than 250,000, the name of the metropolitan area is given. It should be remembered in connection with many rural areas in states like West Virginia and Pennsylvania that the mine worker vote may be important.

This chart is based upon the _Congressional Directory_, 79th Cong., 1st Sess., August, 1944; the Rand-McNally Congressional District maps; and the _Cities Supplement_, Statistical Abstract of the U.S., September, 1944.

| STATE<br>*Congressman* | *Party* | *District* | *Type of<br>District* |
|---|---|---|---|
| CONNECTICUT | | | |
| James P. Geelan | D | 3 | mixed |
| H. P. Kopplemann | D | 1 | mixed |
| Clare Booth Luce | R | 4 | mixed |
| Joseph F. Ryter | D | A.L. | mixed |
| Chase Going Woodhouse | D | 2 | rural |
| DELAWARE | | | |
| Philip A. Traynor | D | A.L. | mixed |
| ILLINOIS | | | |
| Emily Taft Douglas | D | A.L. | mixed |
| William L. Dawson | D | 1 | Chicago |
| Thomas S. Gordon | D | 8 | Chicago |
| Martin Gorski | D | 4 | Chicago |
| Edward A. Kelly | D | 3 | Chicago |
| William A. Link | D | 7 | Chicago |
| Thomas J. O'Brien | D | 6 | Chicago |
| Melvin Price | D | 22 | mixed |
| Alexander J. Resa | D | 9 | Chicago |
| William A. Rowan | D | 2 | Chicago |
| Adolph J. Sabath | D | 5 | Chicago |
| INDIANA | | | |
| Ray J. Madden | D | 1 | mixed |
| KENTUCKY | | | |
| Joe B. Bates | D | 8 | rural |
| Earle C. Clements | D | 2 | rural |
| MASSACHUSETTS | | | |
| Thomas J. Lane | D | 7 | mixed |
| MICHIGAN | | | |
| John Lesinski | D | 16 | Detroit |
| John D. Dingell | D | 15 | Detroit |
| Frank E. Hook | D | 12 | rural |
| George D. O'Brien | D | 13 | Detroit |
| Louis C. Rabaut | D | 14 | Detroit |
| George G. Sadowski | D | 1 | Detroit |
| MINNESOTA | | | |
| William J. Gallagher | D | 3 | mixed |
| Frank T. Starkey | D | 4 | St. Paul |
| MISSOURI | | | |
| A. S. J. Carnahan | D | 8 | rural |
| John J. Cochran | D | 13 | St. Louis |
| John B. Sullivan | D | 11 | St. Louis |
| MONTANA | | | |
| Mike Mansfield | D | 1 | rural |
| NEVADA | | | |
| Berkeley L. Bunker | D | A.L. | rural |

| STATE<br>*Congressman* | *Party* | *District* | *Type of District* |
|---|---|---|---|
| NEW JERSEY | | | |
| Edward J. Hart | D | 14 | Jersey City |
| Mary T. Norton | D | 13 | Jersey City |
| Charles A. Wolverton | R | 1 | mixed |
| NEW YORK | | | |
| Joseph Clark Baldwin | R | 17 | New York |
| William B. Barry | D | 4 | New York |
| Charles A. Buckley | D | 25 | New York |
| William T. Byrne | D | 32 | mixed |
| Emanuel Cellar | D | 15 | New York |
| James J. Delaney | D | 6 | New York |
| Samuel Dickstein | D | 19 | New York |
| Walter A. Lynch | D | 23 | New York |
| Vito Marcantonio | ALP | 18 | New York |
| Joseph L. Pfeffer | D | 8 | New York |
| Adam C. Powell | D | 22 | New York |
| Peter A. Quinn | D | 26 | New York |
| Leo F. Rayfiel | D | 14 | New York |
| George F. Rogers | D | 40 | mixed |
| John J. Roomey | D | 12 | New York |
| James H. Torrens | D | 21 | New York |
| OHIO | | | |
| George H. Bender | R | A.L. | mixed |
| Walter E. Brehm | R | 11 | rural |
| Edward J. Gardner | D | 3 | mixed |
| Walter B. Huber | D | 14 | mixed |
| Michael Kirwan | D | 19 | mixed |
| Homer A. Ramey | R | 9 | Toledo |
| William R. Thom | D | 16 | mixed |
| Michael A. Feighan | D | 20 | Cleveland |
| OKLAHOMA | | | |
| William G. Stigler | D | 2 | rural |
| Victor Wickersham | D | 7 | rural |
| OREGON | | | |
| Homer D. Angell | R | 3 | Portland |
| PENNSYLVANIA | | | |
| William A. Barrett | D | 1 | Philadelphia |
| Michael J. Bradley | D | 3 | Philadelphia |
| Herman P. Eberharter | D | 32 | Pittsburgh |
| Daniel J. Flood | D | 11 | mixed |
| William T. Granahan | D | 2 | Philadelphia |
| William J. Green Jr. | D | 5 | Philadelphia |
| Daniel K. Hoch | D | 13 | mixed |
| Augustine B. Kelley | D | 27 | rural |
| Herbert J. McGlinchey | D | 6 | Philadelphia |
| Thomas E. Morgan | D | 24 | rural |
| John W. Murphy | D | 10 | mixed |
| Samuel A. Weiss | D | 33 | Pittsburgh |

| STATE<br>Congressman | Party | District | Type of<br>District |
|---|---|---|---|
| **RHODE ISLAND** | | | |
| John E. Fogarty | D | 2 | mixed |
| Aime J. Forand | D | 1 | mixed |
| **TENNESSEE** | | | |
| Albert Gore | D | 4 | rural |
| Estes Kefauver | D | 3 | mixed |
| J. Percy Priest | D | 6 | mixed |
| **TEXAS** | | | |
| J. M. Combs | D | 2 | mixed |
| Wright Patman | D | 1 | rural |
| **UTAH** | | | |
| Walter K. Granger | D | 1 | rural |
| J. W. Robinson | D | 2 | mixed |
| **VIRGINIA** | | | |
| John W. Flannagan | D | 9 | rural |
| **WASHINGTON** | | | |
| John M. Coffee | D | 6 | mixed |
| Hugh De Lacy | D | 1 | Seattle |
| Henry M. Jackson | D | 2 | rural |
| Charles R. Savage | D | 3 | rural |
| **WEST VIRGINIA** | | | |
| Cleveland M. Bailey | D | 3 | rural |
| E. H. Hedrick | D | 6 | mixed |
| John West Key | D | 5 | rural |
| Matthew M. Neeley | D | 1 | mixed |
| Jennings Randolph | R | 2 | rural |
| **WISCONSIN** | | | |
| Andrew J. Biemiller | D | 5 | Milwaukee |
| Alvin E. O'Konski | R | 10 | rural |

SUMMARY

| Type of District | Number | Percent of Total |
|---|---|---|
| Urban | 58 | 50 |
| Mixed | 34 | 29 |
| Rural | 34 | 21 |
| TOTAL | 116 | 100 |

| Party | Number | Percent of Total |
|---|---|---|
| Democratic | 105 | 91 |
| Republican | 10 | 8 |
| Other | 1 | 1 |
| TOTAL | 116 | 100 |

# *Appendix C*

## The 84 Nay Votes Cast against the Conference Bill (S.380) in the House of Representatives, February 6, 1946 [1]

| STATE<br>*Congressman* | *Party* | *District* | *Type of District* [2] |
|---|---|---|---|
| ARKANSAS | | | |
| E. C. Gathings | D | 1 | rural |
| W. F. Norrell | D | 6 | rural |
| | | | |
| CALIFORNIA | | | |
| John Phillips | R | 22 | rural |
| | | | |
| GEORGIA | | | |
| John S. Gibson | D | 8 | rural |
| John S. Wood | D | 9 | rural |
| | | | |
| ILLINOIS | | | |
| Leo E. Allen | R | 13 | rural |
| Leslie C. Arends | R | 17 | rural |
| C. W. Bishop | R | 25 | rural |
| Ralph E. Church | R | 10 | mixed |
| Noah M. Mason | R | 12 | mixed |
| Jessie Sumner | R | 18 | mixed |
| | | | |
| INDIANA | | | |
| Charles A. Hallech | R | 2 | rural |
| | | | |
| IOWA | | | |
| James I. Dolliver | R | 6 | rural |
| John W. Gwynne | R | 3 | mixed |
| Charles B. Hoeven | R | 8 | mixed |
| Ben F. Jensen | R | 7 | rural |
| Karl M. LeCompte | R | 4 | rural |
| Thomas E. Martin | R | 1 | mixed |
| Henry O. Talle | R | 2 | mixed |

[1] *Congressional Record*, 79th Cong., 2d Sess., Feb. 6, 1946, p. 1009.
[2] See footnote 1, Appendix B.

| STATE<br>*Congressman* | *Party* | *District* | *Type of District* |
|---|---|---|---|
| KANSAS | | | |
| Frank Carlson | R | 6 | rural |
| Clifford R. Hope | R | 5 | rural |
| Errett P. Scrivner | R | 2 | mixed |
| Thomas W. Winter | R | 3 | rural |
| KENTUCKY | | | |
| Andrew J. May | D | 7 | rural |
| LOUISIANA | | | |
| Paul H. Maloney | D | 2 | New Orleans |
| MAINE | | | |
| Frank Fellows | R | 3 | rural |
| Robert Hale | R | 1 | mixed |
| MARYLAND | | | |
| Dudley G. Roe | D | 1 | rural |
| MASSACHUSETTS | | | |
| Angier L. Goodwin | R | 8 | mixed |
| Pere C. Holmes | R | 4 | mixed |
| MICHIGAN | | | |
| Fred L. Crawford | R | 8 | mixed |
| George A. Dondero | R | 17 | mixed |
| Clare E. Hoffman | R | 4 | rural |
| Bartel J. Jonkman | R | 5 | mixed |
| Paul W. Shafer | R | 3 | mixed |
| Roy O. Woodruff | R | 10 | rural |
| MINNESOTA | | | |
| H. Carl Andresen | R | 7 | rural |
| Harold Knutsen | R | 6 | rural |
| MISSISSIPPI | | | |
| Thomas G. Abernethy | D | 4 | rural |
| Dan R. McGehee | D | 7 | mixed |
| John E. Rankin | D | 1 | rural |
| Jamie L. Whitten | D | 2 | rural |
| Arthur Winstead | D | 5 | rural |
| MISSOURI | | | |
| Walter C. Ploeser | R | 12 | St. Louis |
| Max Schwabe | R | 2 | rural |
| Dewey Short | R | 7 | rural |
| NEBRASKA | | | |
| Howard H. Buffett | R | 2 | mixed |
| Carl T. Curtis | R | 1 | mixed |
| A. L. Miller | R | 4 | rural |
| Karl Stefan | R | 3 | rural |

| STATE<br>Congressman | Party | District | Type of<br>District |
|---|---|---|---|
| **NEW YORK** | | | |
| Ralph W. Gwinn | R | 27 | mixed |
| Clarence E. Hancock | R | 36 | mixed |
| Jay LeFevre | R | 30 | rural |
| John Taber | R | 38 | rural |
| **OHIO** | | | |
| Clarence J. Brown | R | 7 | mixed |
| Cliff Clevenger | R | 5 | rural |
| Charles H. Elston | R | 1 | Cincinnati |
| Thomas A. Jenkins | R | 10 | rural |
| Robert F. Jones | R | 4 | rural |
| Frederick C. Smith | R | 8 | rural |
| **OKLAHOMA** | | | |
| Ross Rizley | R | 8 | rural |
| George B. Schwabe | R | 1 | mixed |
| **OREGON** | | | |
| Harris Ellsworth | R | 4 | rural |
| Lowell Stockman | R | 2 | rural |
| **PENNSYLVANIA** | | | |
| Leon H. Gavin | R | 19 | rural |
| William D. Gillette | R | 14 | rural |
| Louis E. Graham | R | 25 | rural |
| Chester H. Gross | R | 21 | mixed |
| J. Roland Kinzer | R | 9 | mixed |
| John C. Kunkel | R | 18 | mixed |
| Samuel K. McConnell Jr. | R | 16 | rural |
| Robert F. Rich | R | 15 | rural |
| Robert L. Rodgers | R | 28 | mixed |
| Richard M. Simpson | R | 17 | rural |
| **TENNESSEE** | | | |
| Clifford Davis | D | 10 | Memphis |
| John Jennings Jr. | R | 2 | mixed |
| B. Carroll Reece | R | 1 | rural |
| **TEXAS** | | | |
| Paul J. Kilday | D | 20 | San Antonio |
| Fritz G. Lanham | D | 12 | mixed |
| Tom Pickett | D | 7 | rural |
| Milton H. West | D | 15 | rural |
| **WEST VIRGINIA** | | | |
| Hubert S. Ellis | R | 4 | mixed |
| **WISCONSIN** | | | |
| John W. Byrnes | R | 8 | rural |
| Lawrence H. Smith | R | 1 | mixed |

SUMMARY

| Type of District | Number | Percent of Total |
|---|---|---|
| Urban | 5 | 6 |
| Mixed | 29 | 34 |
| Rural | 50 | 60 |
| TOTAL | 84 | 100 |

| Party | Number | Percent of Total |
|---|---|---|
| Democratic | 17 | 20 |
| Republican | 67 | 80 |
| Other | 0 | 0 |
| TOTAL | 84 | 100 |

# Appendix D

## Interviews

❦

| Name | Institution |
|---|---|
| Anderson, Dewey | Senate Small Business Committee |
| Bailey, Fred | National Grange |
| Barkley, Alben | U.S. Senator from Kentucky |
| Bean, Louis | Bureau of the Budget |
| Bender, George | Representative-at-large, Ohio |
| Benoit-Smullyan, Emile | Bureau of Labor Statistics |
| Biemiller, Andrew | Americans for Democratic Action |
| Burns, Arthur | George Washington University |
| Burns, James | Graduate Student, Harvard University |
| Colby, Mr. | Brookings Institution |
| Conal, Barney | Voters Research Institute |
| Costello, John | Los Angeles Chamber of Commerce |
| Crawford, Kenneth | *Newsweek* |
| Eberhardt, John | Social Science Research Council Fellow |
| Ezekiel, Mordecai | Bureau of Agricultural Economics |
| Fath, Creekmore | Office of War Mobilization and Reconversion |
| Fuller, Helen | *New Republic* |
| Galloway, George | Joint Committee on the Organization of Congress |
| Gauntlet, Helen | Senate Banking and Currency Committee staff |
| Goldwasser, Betti | Senate Banking and Currency Committee staff |
| Gordon, Kermit | Department of State |
| Gross, Bertram | Senate Banking and Currency Committee staff |
| Hauser, Philip | Department of Commerce |
| Henderson, Leon | Research Institute of America |
| Hoffman, Clare | Representative, 4th C.D., Michigan |
| Ingebretsen, James C. | Los Angeles Chamber of Commerce |
| Jackson, Gardner | National Farmers Union |
| Jaszi, George | Department of Commerce |
| Lamb, Robert | C.I.O. Steel Workers of America |
| Loeb, James, Jr. | Union for Democratic Action |
| Luxford, Ansel | Treasury Department |

| | |
|---|---|
| McCaffree, Floyd | Republican National Headquarters |
| McCune, Wesley | *Time* Inc. |
| Maddox, James | Bureau of Agricultural Economics |
| Manasco, Carter | Representative, 7th C.D., Alabama |
| Murdock, Abe | U.S. Senator from Utah |
| Murray, James E. | U.S. Senator from Montana |
| Outland, George | Representative, 11th C.D., California |
| Parel, James D. | American Farm Bureau Federation |
| Perry, John | New Council of American Business |
| Pierson, John H. C. | Bureau of Labor Statistics |
| Radcliffe, George | U.S. Senator from Maryland |
| Riddick, Floyd M. | U.S. Chamber of Commerce |
| Robertson, Nathan | *PM* |
| Schimmel, Herbert | Senate Military Affairs Committee staff |
| Schlesinger, Arthur Jr. | Author |
| Schmidt, Emerson P. | U.S. Chamber of Commerce |
| Schroeder, Frank | Secretary to Senator C. D. Buck of Delaware |
| Shishkin, Boris | American Federation of Labor |
| Siegrist, Mrs. | Independent Voters of Illinois |
| Sifton, Paul | Union for Democratic Action |
| Smith, Russell | National Farmers Union |
| Smithies, Arthur | Bureau of the Budget |
| Stettner, Leonora | Senate Banking and Currency Committee staff |
| Taft, Robert A. | U.S. Senator from Ohio |
| Taylor, Glen | U.S. Senator from Idaho |
| Terborgh, George | Machinery and Allied Products Institute |
| Thomerson, Harold | Secretary to Representative John Folger of North Carolina |
| Thompson, Sam | Department of Commerce |
| Tobey, Charles | U.S. Senator from New Hampshire |
| Ullman, Morris B. | Bureau of the Census |
| Vinson, Fred | Chief Justice of the U.S. Supreme Court |
| Ward, Paul | *Baltimore Sun* |
| Whittington, William | Representative, 3d C.D., Mississippi |
| Wickwar, Hardy | U.N.R.R.A. |
| Wright, Theodore | Civil Aeronautics Board |
| Young, William | Clerk of the House Committee on Expenditures in the Executive Departments |
| Zeller, Belle | Brooklyn College |

### Major New York Interviews

| *Name* | *Institution* |
|---|---|
| Backman, Jules | New York University School of Commerce |
| Bradley, Dwight | National Citizens Political Action Committee |
| Horsch, Miss | National Association of Manufacturers |
| McKane, Miss | National Association of Manufacturers |
| Spahr, Walter E. | New York University School of Commerce |
| Wallace, Henry A. | *New Republic* |
| Weber, Palmer | C.I.O. Political Action Committee |

# *Bibliography*

## GOVERNMENT SOURCES

Commissioner of Labor. First Annual Report. 1886.

Congressional Directory. 79th Cong., 1st Sess., 1945; 2d Sess., 1946.

Congressional Record. 78th and 79th Congresses.

Council of Economic Advisers. First Annual Report to the President 1946.

Department of Agriculture. Expansion of Foreign Trade. Miscellaneous Publication No. 582. 1945.

—— Maintenance of Full Employment. Miscellaneous Publication No. 570. 1945.

—— Post-War Agriculture and Employment. Miscellaneous Publication No. 562. 1945.

Department of Commerce. Statistical Abstract of the United States, 1944–45. 1945.

Department of Labor. Central Records. National Archives, 16/71.

—— Income from Wages and Salaries in the Post-War Period. Bulletin No. 845. 1945.

Library of Congress, Legislative Reference Service. Abstracts of Post-War Literature. Mimeograph. 1944–1945.

National Resources Planning Board. After Defense—What? 1941.

President of the United States. Economic Report. Transmitted to the congress, Jan. 8, 1947.

President's Commission on Unemployment, Report [to President Harding], Sept. 26 to Oct. 13, 1921. 1921.

### U.S. CONGRESS BILLS

A Bill to Establish a National Policy and Program for Assuring Continuing Full Employment: War Contracts Subcommittee Print No. 1 (78th Cong., 2d Sess., Dec. 18, 1944); War Contracts Subcommittee Prints (79th Cong., 1st Sess., Jan. 15, 16, 17, 18, 1945); War Contracts Subcommittee Preliminary Print (79th Cong., 1st Sess., Jan. 22, 1945).

S.380 (79th Cong., 1st Sess., Jan. 22, 1945): Committee Prints (79th Cong., 1st Sess., Aug. 19, 26, 28, 30, Sept. 7, 10, 11, 15, 1945); Report No. 583, Calendar No. 582 (79th Cong., 1st Sess., Sept. 22, 1945); in the House of Representatives (79th Cong., 1st Sess., Oct. 1, 1945); Union Calendar No. 403, Report No. 1334 (79th Cong., 1st Sess., Dec. 5, 1945); as Agreed to in Conference (79th Cong., 2d Sess., Feb. 2, 1946); Public Law 304 (79th Cong., 2d Sess.; approved Feb. 20, 1946.
S.2177: Report No. 1400, Calendar No. 1427. 79th Cong., 2d Sess., May 31, 1946.

HOUSE OF REPRESENTATIVES

Committee on Expenditures in the Executive Departments. Full Employment Act of 1945: Hearings on H.R.2202. 79th Cong., 1st Sess., 1945.
Conference Report: Declaring a National Policy on Employment, Production and Purchasing Power, and for Other Purposes. H. Report No. 1520. 79th Cong., 2d Sess., Feb. 5, 1946.
Select Committee on National Defense Migration. Final Report. H. Report No. 3. 77th Cong., 1st Sess., 1941.
Special Committee on Post-War Economic Policy and Planning. Economic Problems of the Reconversion Period. H. Report No. 1855. 78th Cong., 2d Sess., Sept. 8, 1944.
—— Post-War Public Works and Construction. H. Report No. 852. 79th Cong., 1st Sess., July 3, 1945.
—— Summary of Activities of the Special Committee. H. Report No. 2071. 78th Cong., 2d Sess., Dec. 14, 1944.
—— Final Report: Reconversion Experience and Current Economic Problems. H. Report No. 2729. 79th Cong., 2d Sess., Dec. 12, 1946.
Special Committee to Investigate Campaign Expenditures. Campaign Expenditures: Hearings on H. Res. 645. 79th Cong., 2d Sess., 1945.
Special Committee Relative to the Causes of the General Depression. The Causes of the General Depression. H. Misc. Doc. No. 29. 45th Cong., 3d Sess., 1879.
Special Joint Committee on the Organization of Congress. A Select, Annotated Bibliography on the Organization, Procedure, and Reorganization of Congress. Joint Committee Print. 79th Cong., 1st Sess., Oct. 20, 1945.
—— Symposium on Congress by Members of Congress and Others. Joint Committee Print. 79th Cong., 1st Sess., 1945.

SENATE

Committee on Banking and Currency. Full Employment Act of 1945: Hearings on S.380. 79th Cong., 1st Sess., 1945.
—— Major Issues on the Full Employment Bill. Mimeograph. June 30, 1945.

# Bibliography

—— Assuring Full Employment in a Free Competitive Economy: S. Subcommittee Print (79th Cong., 1st Sess., Sept. 18, 1945); S. Report No. 583 (79th Cong., 1st Sess., Sept. 22, 1945); Minority Views, S. Report No. 583, Part 2 (79th Cong., 1st Sess., Sept. 24, 1945).

—— Summary of Federal Agency Reports on Full Employment Bill. S. Committee Print No. 1. 79th Cong., 1st Sess., July 12, 1945.

—— Bibliography on Full Employment. S. Committee Print No. 2. 79th Cong., 1st Sess., June 25, 1945.

—— History of the Employment Stabilization Act of 1931. S. Committee Print No. 3. 79th Cong., 1st Sess., July 30, 1945.

—— Basic Facts on Employment and Production. S. Committee Print No. 4. 79th Cong., 1st Sess., Sept. 1, 1945.

Special Committee on Post-War Economic Policy and Planning. A Sound Plan for Post-War Roads and Jobs. S. Committee Print. 78th Cong., 2d Sess., 1944.

—— Cancellation of War Contracts. S. Report No. 539, Part 3. 78th Cong., 2d Sess., May 3, 1944.

—— Report of Hon. Joseph C. O'Mahoney. S. Doc. No. 106. 78th Cong., 1st Sess., Oct. 14, 1943.

—— The Problem of Post-War Employment and the Role of Congress in Solving It. S. Report No. 539, Part 4. 78th Cong., 2d Sess., June 12, 1944.

Special Joint Committee on the Organization of Congress. Organization of Congress. S. Report No. 1011. 79th Cong., 2d Sess., March 4, 1946.

Temporary National Economic Committee. Economic Power and Political Pressures (by Donald C. Blaisdell). Monograph No. 26, S. Committee Print. 76th Cong., 3d Sess., 1941.

—— Competition and Monopoly in American Industry (by Clair Wilcox). Monograph No. 21. S. Committee Print. 76th Cong., 3d Sess., 1940.

—— Recovery Plans (by Arthur Dahlberg *et al*). Monograph No. 25. S. Committee Print. 76th Cong., 3d Sess., 1940.

War Contracts Subcommittee to the Committee on Military Affairs. Legislation for Reconversion and Full Employment. S. Subcommittee Print No. 12. 78th Cong., 2d Sess., Dec. 18, 1944.

GENERAL SOURCES

Aberman, Sidney. "Towards Full Employment." *The Commonweal,* XLIII (Nov. 9, 1945), p. 91.

Abramovitz, Moses. "Savings and Investment: Profits vs. Prosperity?" *American Economic Review,* XXXII, No. 2, Part 2 (Supplement; June, 1942), 53–58.

"After the Emergency—What Then?" *American Federationist,* March, 1941.

Allen, Frederick Lewis. Only Yesterday. 2 vols. London and New York, 1938. Vol. II.

Allen, Frederick Lewis. Since Yesterday. New York, 1940.

American Federation of Labor. Postwar Program. Washington, 1944.

Anderson, Dewey. "Statement . . . before the Committee on Governmental Efficiency and Economy of the California Legislature Urging Passage of Assembly Bill 2136, Introduced March 7, 1945, by Mr. McMillan at the Request of the Entire Delegation of Democratic Assemblymen." Mimeograph, Committee on Banking and Currency, U.S. Senate. 1945.

Angley, Edward, ed. Oh Yeah? New York, 1931.

Ayres, Leonard P. American Business Activity since 1790. 18th ed. Cleveland Trust Company, March, 1945.

Baerwald, Friedrich. "Implications of Full Employment." *America,* Sept. 8, 1945, pp. 448–449.

Bailey, Stephen K. Roosevelt and His New Deal. London, 1938.

Barnes, Leo. "The Anatomy of Full Employment." *Nation,* May 25, 1945, pp. 593–597.

Baruch, Bernard, and John M. Hancock. War and Postwar Adjustment Policies. Washington, 1944.

Beard, Charles A. The Economic Basis of Politics. 3d ed. New York. 1945. First published, 1922.

Beard, Charles A., and Mary R. Beard. America in Midpassage. New York, 1939.

—— The Rise of American Civilization. New York, 1930.

Becker, Carl L. Freedom and Responsibility in the American Way of Life. New York, 1945.

Bender, George. The Challenge of 1940. New York, 1940.

Beveridge, Sir William H. Full Employment in a Free Society. New York, 1945.

—— The Pillars of Security. New York, 1943.

Binkley, Wilfred E. President and Congress. New York, 1947.

Blaisdell, Donald C. Government under Pressure. Public Affairs Pamphlet No. 67. New York, 1946.

Blakey, Roy G., and Gladys C. Blakey. The Federal Income Tax. New York, 1940.

Block, Maxim, ed. Current Biography. New York, 1940.

Brady, Robert A. Business as a System of Power. New York, 1943.

Brookings Institution, The. A Brookings Bulletin. Washington, March, 1945.

—— The Recovery Problem in America. Washington, 1937.

Burr, Walter. Small Towns. New York, 1929.

Burton, John E., and William R. McWilliams. "Notes on Unemployment and Recovery." Transcontinental Research Inc., Report 20 (revised), March 12, 1940.

Cantwell, Frank V. "Public Opinion and the Legislative Process." *American Political Science Review,* XL, No. 5 (October, 1946), 924–935.

Chamber of Commerce of the United States of America. American Economic Security, Vol. III, No. 1. Washington, 1946.

—— "Governmental Affairs." *Legislative Daily,* Vol. II, No. 255, Dec. 7, 1945.

—— A Program for Sustaining Employment. Report of the Committee on Economic Policy. Washington, 1945.

Chamberlain, John. The American Stakes. New York, 1940.

Chamberlain, Joseph P. Legislative Processes. New York, 1936.

"Charter for America." *New Republic,* Part II, April 19, 1943, pp. 523–542.

Chase, Stuart. Democracy under Pressure. New York, 1945.

Cherne, Leo. The Rest of Your Life. New York, 1944.

Citizens National Committee, Inc. Full Employment and the National Budget. Research Report No. 2-417. Washington, 1945.

Citizens Research Bureau. What the People Think about Full Employment. Chicago, 1945.

Coffin, Tris. Missouri Compromise. Boston, 1947.

Committee for Constitutional Government, Inc. Needed Now—Capacity for Leadership, Courage to Lead. New York, 1944.

Committee for Economic Development. Meeting the Special Problems of Small Business. New York, 1947.

Congress of Industrial Organizations, Political Action Committee. Proceedings of the Conference on Full Employment, Jan. 15, 1944. New York, 1944.

*Congressional Quarterly,* Vol. I. Washington, 1945.

Copeland, Douglas B. The Road to High Employment. Cambridge, Mass., 1945.

Corwin, E. S. The President, Office and Powers. New York, 1941.

Coyle, David Cushman. "Planning Is a Fighting Word." *Harper's Magazine,* June, 1946, pp. 552–560.

Crawford, Kenneth. The Pressure Boys. New York, 1939.

Daniels, Jonathan. Frontier on the Potomac. New York, 1946.

Davidson, Bill. "He Knew Him When." *Collier's,* Dec. 7, 1946, pp. 16 ff.

Davis, Forest. "Millionaire Moses." *Saturday Evening Post,* Dec. 8, 1945, pp. 9 ff.

Donnelly, T. C., ed. Rocky Mountain Politics. Albuquerque, N. Mex., 1940.

Dorfman, Joseph. The Economic Mind in American Civilization. 2 vols. New York, 1946.

Economic Program for American Democracy, An. By seven Harvard and Tufts economists. New York, 1938.

"Elections: 1946." *New Republic,* Part II, Feb. 11, 1946.

Fainsod, Merle, and Lincoln Gordon. Government and the American Economy. New York, 1941.

Finletter, Thomas K. Can Representative Government Do the Job? New York, 1945.

Fitch, Lyle, and Horace Taylor. Planning for Jobs. Philadelphia, 1946.

Gaer, Joseph. The First Round. New York, 1944.

—— Let Our People Live. C.I.O. Political Action Committee, Pamphlet of the Month, No. 3. New York, 1945.

—— The People's Plan for Reconversion. C.I.O. Political Action Committee, Pamphlet of the Month, No. 2. New York, n.d.

—— The Road to Freedom. C.I.O. Political Action Committee, Pamphlet of the Month, No. 5. New York, 1945.

Gaer, Joseph, and Robert K. Lamb. The Answer Is Full Employment. C.I.O. Political Action Committee, Pamphlet of the Month, No. 4. New York, 1945.

Galloway, George B. Congress at the Crossroads. New York, 1946.

Galloway, George B., and Associates. Planning for America. New York, 1941.

Galloway, George B., and Others. The Reorganization of Congress, a Report of the Committee on Congress of the American Political Science Association. Washington, 1945.

Gayer, Arthur D. Public Works in Prosperity and Depression. New York, 1935.

Ginsberg, Eli, and Others. The Unemployed. New York, 1943.

Goldenweiser, E. A. "Federal Reserve Objectives and Policies, Retrospect and Prospect." *American Economic Review,* XXXVII, No. 3 (June, 1947), 320–338.

Gottschalk, Louis, Clyde Kluckholm, and Robert Angell. The Use of Personal Documents in History, Anthropology, and Sociology. Social Science Research Council Bulletin 53. New York, 1945.

Gragg, Charles I., and Stanley F. Teele. "The Proposed Full Employment Act." *Harvard Business Review,* Spring, 1945, pp. 323–337.

Green, William. The American Federation of Labor and Reconversion. Washington, 1944.

Gunther, John. Inside U.S.A. New York, 1947.

Hacker, Louis M., and Benjamin B. Kendrick. The United States since 1865. New York, 1932.

Hankin, E. H. The Mental Limitations of the Expert. India, Butterworth & Co., Ltd., 1921.

Hansen, Alvin. Economic Policy and Full Employment. New York, 1947.

—— Fiscal Policy and Business Cycles. New York, 1941.

Hayek, Friedrich A. The Road to Serfdom. Chicago, 1944.

Harris, Seymour E. "The Way to Full Employment." *New Republic,* June 4, 1945, pp. 783–786.

Herring, Pendleton. The Politics of Democracy. New York, 1944.

—— Presidential Leadership. New York, 1940.

Holcombe, Arthur N. The Middle Classes in American Politics. Cambridge, Mass., 1940.

Hollingshead, August B. "Selected Characteristics of Classes in a Middle

Western Community." *American Sociological Review,* XII, No. 4 (August, 1947), 385–395.

Homan, Paul T., and Fritz Machlup, eds. Financing American Prosperity. New York, 1945.

Hopkins, Harry. Spending to Save. New York, 1936.

Howenstine, E. Jay, Jr. The Economics of Demobilization. Washington, 1944.

Hugh-Jones, E. M., and E. A. Radice. An American Experiment. London, 1936.

Hutchison, Keith. "Beyond the New Deal." *New Republic,* Feb. 10, 1940, p. 168.

Jordon, Virgil. Full Employment and Freedom in America. New York, 1945.

Kefauver, Estes, and Jack Levin. Twentieth Century Congress. New York, 1947.

Key, V. O. Politics, Parties, and Pressure Groups. New York, 1946.

Keynes, John Maynard. The General Theory of Employment, Interest, and Money. London, 1936.

Keyserling, Leon H. "From Patchwork to Purpose." *Survey Graphic,* March, 1945, pp. 95–98.

Kirkland, Edward C. A History of American Economic Life. New York, 1936.

Klein, L. R. "A Post Mortem on Transition Predictions of National Product." *Journal of Political Economy,* August, 1946, pp. 289–308.

Kramer, Dale. The Truth about the Farm Bureau. Denver, Colo., n.d.

Lane, Marie Dresden, and Francis Steegmuller. America on Relief. New York, 1938.

Lebergott, Stanley. "Shall We Guarantee Full Employment?" *Harper's Magazine,* February, 1945, pp. 132–202.

Lerner, Abba B. The Economics of Control. New York, 1944.

Lerner, Max. It Is Later Than You Think. New York, 1939.

Lippmann, Walter. The Good Society. London, 1937.

Los Angeles Chamber of Commerce. "The Full Employment Act of 1945." *Economic Sentinel,* Vol. III, No. 3, October, 1945.

Lynd, Robert, and Helen M. Lynd. Middletown in Transition. New York, 1937.

Lyon, Leverett S., Myron W. Watkins, and Victor Abramson. Government and Economic Life. 2 vols. Washington, 1939. Vol. I.

McCrane, R. C. The Panic of 1837. Chicago, 1924.

McCune, Wesley. The Farm Bloc. New York, 1943.

Marx, Fritz Morstein. "The Bureau of the Budget: Its Evolution and Present Role, I." *American Political Science Review,* XXXIX, No. 4 (August, 1945), 653–684.

Mason, Edward S., and C. J. Friedrich, eds. Public Policy. 2 vols. Cambridge, Mass., 1941–1942.

Mellet, Lowell. Handbook of Politics. New York, 1946.

Men without Work. Report to the Pilgrim Trust. London, 1938.

Moley, Raymond. After Seven Years. New York, 1939.

—— "A Fool Employment Bill." *Newsweek,* June 18, 1945, p. 112.

—— "The Job Budget." *Newsweek,* Feb. 19, 1945, p. 108.

Morgenthau, Henry, Jr. "The Morgenthau Diaries." *Collier's,* Sept. 27–Nov. 1, 1947.

Moulton, Harold G. The New Philosophy of the Public Debt. Washington, 1943.

Murray, James E. "Economic Security and Justice." Radio address, March 18, 1938.

—— "Jobs for Everybody." *Collier's,* Oct. 6, 1945, pp. 33–34.

—— "A Plan for America." *New Republic,* Jan. 21, 1946, pp. 75–79.

Murray, Philip. Re-employment. C.I.O. Department of Research and Education, Publication No. 116. Washington, 1944.

"Murray of Montana." *Nation,* Oct. 10, 1942, pp. 332–333.

"Murray's Megaphones." *Newsweek,* Feb. 26, 1940, p. 62.

National Association of Manufacturers. Can We Avoid a Post-Armament Depression. A Survey of Opinions Submitted by Members of the American Economics Association to the National Association of Manufacturers. New York, 1941.

—— Can We Avoid a Post-Armament Depression. New York, 1943.

—— Fallacies about Our Private Enterprise System. New York, 1940.

—— Five Publications on Corporation Postwar Planning. New York, 1944.

—— Jobs—Freedom—Opportunity. Preliminary Views of the Postwar Problems Committee of the National Association of Manufacturers. New York, 1943.

—— The Public Be Served. New York, n.d.

—— Second Report of the Postwar Committee of the National Association of Manufacturers. New York, 1943.

—— A Study of Depressions. Report of the National Association of Manufacturers' Committee on the Study of Depressions. New York, 1938.

—— The Study of Depressions. Report of the Committee on the Study of Depressions of the National Association of Manufacturers. New York, 1940.

—— Testimony to the Future. New York, 1943.

—— What About the 1937–1938 Depression. New York, n.d.

National Bureau of Economic Research. Business Cycles and Unemployment. New York, 1923.

National Economic Council. Economic Council Papers, Vol. III, No. 12A, September, 1945.

National Farmers Union. "Reports of Executive Agencies on the Full Employment Proposal of the National Farmers Union." Press release. Washington, Sept. 18, 1944.

National Planning Association. *National Budgets for Full Employment.* Planning Pamphlets Nos. 43 and 44. Washington, 1945.

Outland, George. Press release, Washington, June 11, 1945.

Patton, James G., and James Loeb, Jr. "Challenge to Progressives." *New Republic,* Part II, Feb. 5, 1945.

Perkins, Frances. The Roosevelt I Knew. New York, 1946.

Pettengill, Samuel B., and Paul C. Bartholomew. For Americans Only. New York, 1944.

Pierson, John H. G. Fiscal Policy for Full Employment. National Planning Association, Planning Pamphlet No. 45. Washington, 1945.

—— Full Employment. New Haven, Conn., 1941.

—— Full Employment in Practice. New York University Institute on Post-War Reconstruction, 1946.

—— "National Budget as an Aid in Reducing Deficits under Assured Full Employment." *Monthly Labor Review,* August, 1945, pp. 210–214.

Prentiss, H. W. Competitive Enterprise versus Planned Economy. New York, National Association of Manufacturers, August, 1945.

Press Research, Inc. Post-War Jobs, Parts I, II. Washington, 1945.

Progressive Businessmen, Inc. A Job to Do. Washington, 1945.

Pusey, Merlo J. Big Government, Can We Control It? New York, 1945.

Research Institute of America. How Your Congressman Voted. New York, 1946.

Riddick, Floyd M. Congressional Procedure. Boston, 1941.

—— "The First Session of the Seventy-Ninth Congress." *American Political Science Review,* XL, No. 2 (April, 1946), 256–271.

Riesel, Victor. "Labor Is Big Business." *Readers Digest,* January, 1946, pp. 118–120.

Robey, Ralph. "A Clever Trick Designed Just to Fool You." *Newsweek,* July 23, 1945, p. 66.

—— "Lets Hurry, But in the Right Direction." *Newsweek,* Sept. 10, 1945, p. 71.

—— "Mr. Roosevelt Shoots the Works." *Newsweek,* Jan. 22, 1945, p. 71.

—— "More on the 'Fool' Employment Bill." *Newsweek,* June 25, 1945, p. 76; July 9, 1945, p. 72.

—— "One Who Is an Expert Does Some Talking." *Newsweek,* Oct. 15, 1945, p. 78.

—— "Significant Changes in the Full Employment Bill." *Newsweek,* Oct. 8, 1945, p. 78.

—— "The Sixty-Million Job Fantasy." *Newsweek,* Feb. 19, 1945, p. 70.

Roosevelt, Franklin D. Public Papers and Addresses. Vols. I–V. New York, 1938.

Salter, J. T. ed. Public Men in and Out of Office. Chapel Hill, N.C., 1946.

Schattschneider, E. E. Party Government. New York, 1942.

Schmidt, Emerson P. Absorbing the Total Labor Supply. U.S. Chamber of Commerce, Postwar Readjustments Bulletin No. 5. Washington, 1943.

—— Can Government Guarantee Full Employment. U.S. Chamber of Commerce, Postwar Readjustments Bulletin No. 13. Washington, 1945.

—— Full Employment, Its Politics and Economics. U.S. Chamber of Commerce, Postwar Readjustments Bulletin No. 9. Washington, 1944.

—— Maintaining Purchasing Power in the Transition. U.S. Chamber of Commerce, Postwar Readjustments Bulletin No. 14. Washington, 1945.

—— The Problems of Business Incentives. U.S. Chamber of Commerce, Postwar Readjustments Bulletin No. 6. Washington, 1943.

Sims, Newell LeRoy. Elements of Rural Sociology. New York, 1944.

Smith, Russell. "Big Business and the Farm Bloc." Reprint. *Antioch Review,* Summer, 1944.

Snyder, Carl. Capitalism the Creator. An abridgment issued by the Committee for Constitutional Government. New York, 1943.

S.380. Press clippings (7 vols.). Office of Senator James E. Murray. Senate Office Building, Washington.

Terborgh, George. The Bogey of Economic Maturity. Chicago, 1945.

Thayer, Dorothy M. "New Faces in the Senate." Washington *Post,* Nov. 23, 1934.

Twentieth Century Fund. Postwar Planning in the United States, an Organization Directory. New York, 1944.

Union for Democratic Action. Full Employment File, 1945. Washington.

—— "News Flash on Full Employment, No. 7." Washington, Jan. 8, 1946.

—— U.D.A. Congressional Newsletter, Washington, Dec. 15, 1945.

Wallace, Henry A. The Century of the Common Man. New York, 1943.

—— Democracy Reborn. New York, 1944.

—— Sixty Million Jobs. New York, 1945.

Wallas, Graham. Human Nature in Politics. 3d ed. London, 1938. First published, 1908.

Wasserman, William Stix (affirmative), and Lutz, Harley L. (negative), "Should Government Guarantee Employment?" *Modern Industry,* June 15, 1945, pp. 117, 124.

Wernette, John Philip. Financing Full Employment. Cambridge, Mass., 1945.

Whittaker, Edmund. A History of Economic Ideas. New York, 1946.

Wilson, Woodrow. Congressional Government. 13th ed. Boston, 1898. First published, 1885.

Woll, Matthew. Machinery for Reconversion. Washington, 1944.

Wootton, Barbara. Freedom under Planning. Chapel Hill, N.C., 1945.

Wright, Philip G. Outcasts of Efficiency. Washington, 1931.

Wriston, Henry M. Challenge to Freedom. New York, 1943.

# Index

National Resources . . . Board (*Cont.*)
tations on effectiveness of, 52
"Nation's Budget," conception of, 25; *see
also* Budget
*Nation's Business,* 139
Neely, Matthew, 154, 176
Negroes, support of the bill, 87
New Council for American Business, 76
New Deal, 7, 194, 216, 218; federally
sponsored economic policies, 8; influ-
ence of Keynesian analysis, 18 f.; Mur-
ray's support, 39; liberal organizations
grouped politically under banner of,
80; effect of business hostility, 185;
Barkley a "New Dealer," 208; *see also*
Roosevelt, Franklin D.
New England, culture, philosophy, 212
*New Republic,* 96, 103; voting tallies,
151; excerpt 152
Newspapers, *see* Press
New York State, Chamber of Commerce,
117
Niebuhr, Reinhold, 81
Norton, Mary, 154
Nourse, Edwin G., 66, 235*n*

O'Daniel, W. Lee, 125*n*
Office for Emergency Management, 11
Office of Demobilization, 32
Office of War Mobilization, 30
Office of War Mobilization and Adjust-
ment, 32, 33
Office of War Mobilization and Recon-
version, 11, 22, 162; the bill, 35, 66;
blueprints for a permanent coordi-
nating and planning staff, 170
Ogg, W. R., 147
O'Grady, John, 114
Ohio, Hamilton County Republican ma-
chine, 197
Ohio Chamber of Commerce, bulletin,
excerpts, 141
O'Mahoney, Joseph C., 73, 86, 104, 122,
159, 243; why chosen as co-sponsor, 55;
speech during floor debate: effect on
final vote, 119, 125
O'Neal, Ed., 147
"Opposition to the Full Employment
Bill, The—and the Answers," 116
Outland, George, 89, 91, 98, 105, 150, 154,
183, 211; chairman of co-sponsors' com-
mittee, 154; failure of efforts to force
through a generous version of S.380 in
House, 154 f., 175, 176
Oxnam, G. Bromley, 114

Pabst Brewing Company, 9, 46
Panics, 4 ff.; *see also* Depressions
Parel, James D., 147*n*
Patman, Wright, 73, 105, 175, 176, 233;
why chosen to introduce bill in House,
150; problem of securing co-sponsors,
153; pep talk, 154; quoted, 172*n*
Patrick, Luther, 154, 202
Patterson, Ernest Minor, 114
Patton, James G., 21, 22, 23; testimony on
Kilgore bill, 22 f.; amendment to bill,
24, 37, 38, 43 ff.; *see also* National
Farmers Union
Pauley, Edwin, 226
Pearson, Drew, quoted, 102
People, the: efforts to mobilize public
opinion, 74 (*see also entries under*
Mail; Public opinion); Sifton's methods
of reaching, 83 ff.; attempts of Contin-
uations Group to educate, 85 ff.; re-
sponsible political system must reflect
will of, and give power to, 239
*People's Corporation, The* (Gillette), 206
Pepper, George Wharton, 6, 29*n*
Perkins, Frances, quoted, 8
Pettergill, Samuel, 143; quoted, 144
Pew family, rural newspapers, 135*n*
Phippen, Doris, 66
Pierson, John, 21, 45, 47*n*
Planning, for postwar world, 9 ff.; diverse
concepts, 10; attempts to centralize
long-range, 11, 12; function in Executive branch, 26, 51, 167 ff.; Congressional postwar planning committees,
28 ff.; fate of planning measures during struggle over reconversion, 35;
sponsors' major interest in a mechanism for, 123; a first experiment in
economic planning and coordination,
236; *see also* National Planning Association; National Resources Planning Board
Policy, Declaration of: in Act of 1946,
struggle over, 223 ff.; *text,* 228; in first
Senate bill, *text,* 243
Policy formulation, examples of impact
of political mind on, 57 ff.; increasing
importance of staff assistants, 64
Policy-making, Congressional, vii ff.,
236 ff.; defined, x; questions necessary
to understanding of, 189; influence of
external factors, 219
Political Action Committee, C.I.O., 80,
81, 94, 141, 145; pamphlet on full employment, 93

*Index*                                                                              279

Republican Party (*Continued*)
port of, for bill, 103; co-sponsors'
amendments, 103, 121 ff.; uniformity
found impossible, 124 f.; vote on
House bill, 177*n*; interparty align-
ments, 238
Resa, Alexander, 172
Revercomb, Chapman, 34
Rice, Millard, 78
Rich, Robert, 156, 172, 176
"Right to work" principle, 13, 160
"Rights, Human, Statement of Essen-
tial," 115
*Road to Serfdom* (Hayek), 55
Robertson, Edward V., 125*n*
Robertson, Nathan, 74*n*, 97*n*
Robey, Ralph, 187
Robinson, J. W., 210
Rogers, Lindsay, 64; quoted, 62
Roosevelt, Franklin D., 11, 19*n*, 30, 37,
47, 81, 92, 126, 210, 212, 213, 225; rela-
tion of public's broadening conception
of economic rights, to New Deal, 7;
budget messages, 25; National Resources Planning Board a reflection of
liberal social thinking of, 25, 26; election year, 1944; postwar employment
in speeches, 41 ff.; almost universal
faith in, 80; plans opposed by Committee for Constitutional Government:
campaign against Court "packing" by,
143; policy re full employment, 160 f.;
Radcliffe's attitude toward, 194 f.;
Barkley's loyalty to New Deal and, 208;
*see also* New Deal
Roosevelt, Theodore, 217
Rules Committee of the House, methods
of control: powerful influence on substantive policy, 174
Ruml, Beardsley, 21, 76
Rural and small-town areas: press, 135,
186; Congressional districts, 152, 183;
conservatism, 184-87; business-class control system, 184; *see also* Farm organizations
Russell, Scott, 30, 32

Sabath, Adolph J., 174
Sadowski, George, 154
Salant, Walter, 45
Savage, Charles, 154
Saving and interest, Keynesian theory, 16,
19
Schimmel, Herbert, 31, 64
Schmidt, Emerson P., of U.S. Chamber of

Commerce, 105*n*, 139, 140; bulletin by,
83
Schramm, James S., 156*n*
Schwellenbach, Lewis, 162, 163
Scitovsky, Anne A., 45*n*
*Security, Work, and Relief Policies*, 26 f.
Senate: Senators, *see* Congress: Congress-
men
Senate committees, *see* their titles, *e.g.*,
Banking and Currency Committee
Shepard, Geoffrey, 24
Sifton, Paul, 22, 78, 101*n*; organizations
with which associated, 75; activities in
behalf of U.D.A. campaign for the bill,
75, 82 ff., 86, 88, 92
*Sixty Million Jobs* (Wallace), 160*n*
Small Business Committee, Senate, 56,
64
Small-town areas and conservatism,
184 ff.; *see also* Rural
Smith, George, 117*n*
Smith, Harold, 12, 114, 163; leadership
of Budget Bureau, 25
Smith, Russell, 22, 45, 87, 103; back-
ground, 23; plan for a broad employment program, 23 f.
Smithies, Arthur, 25
Snyder, John, 222; responsibility for lining up Cabinet committee, 162; testimony: hostility to principles of a liberal bill, 163
Social legislation, *see* Legislation
Source material, x; interviews, 191-217
*passim*, 257-58; government publications, 259-61; general publications, 261-
68
Southern Conference for Human Welfare, 88
Spahr, Walter E., 142, 158
Sparkman, Representative, 177
Spending, federal: drafting committee's
debate over, 47; Presidential discretion
in adjusting rate, 51; policy of bill declared theory advanced by Keynes,
118; claim that business confidence
undermined by, 130
Spend-Lend Bill of 1939, 19*n*
Stacking, Collis, 45*n*
Staffs, Congressional, 61-78; Murray's committee staffs, 40; need for adequate,
61; growth, 62; functions: increasing
importance, 64; the Full Employment
staff: personnel and functions, 64-78
Stalin, Joseph, 118
Stettinius, Edward R., Jr., 114